Sociology

Sociology

Jack Nobbs JP BSc (Econ)
Senior Tutor and Head of Economics and Sociology Department,
Hewett Comprehensive School, Norwich

Robert Hine BA M Phil
Head of Humanities Department, Stanmore Junior College, Middlesex

Margaret E. Flemming BA
Special Consultant, Office of Research,
New Jersey Department of Higher Education, U.S.A.
formerly Lecturer in Sociology, Harlow Technical College

Macmillan Education

First published 1975
Reprinted 1976 (twice)

Published by
MACMILLAN EDUCATION LTD
Houndmills, Basingstoke, Hampshire RG21 2XS
and London
Associated companies in New York, Dublin,
Melbourne, Johannesburg and Delhi

Filmset by BAS Printers Limited, Wallop, Hampshire
Printed by Bright Sun Printing Press Co., Ltd.

Preface

The last five years has seen a prolific growth of interest at secondary education level in the social sciences generally and in sociology in particular. This has been accompanied by considerable debate as to whether the ideas, concepts, and approaches of sociology are appropriate educational experiences for students at Ordinary Level GCE.

A major problem facing the teacher at this level has been the lack of suitable texts and material with which to work: the choice being between simplified material suitable for less mature students and the sophisticated academic texts with which the university undergraduate wrestles.

This book meets the needs of students and teachers of sociology at 'sixteen-plus' level in so far as it not only provides a digest of appropriate material in the relevant areas, but also attempts to convey the ideas and skills which are required of examination candidates in this subject. It is impressively supported by fitting illustrations which clarify and enliven the text and provide stimulation for further discussion. The work-exercises effectively take the student beyond the book into further reading and research skills which are increasingly becoming important in external examinations.

I am reassured to find textbooks being produced at this level for students and teachers by those with appropriate experience necessary to appreciate and help in the task of presenting ideas and material which are of fundamental importance to the various external examination courses in sociology. I also feel that both students and teacher will find the book extremely interesting and stimulating as well as valuable to their courses.

T Schofield
Chief Examiner
GCE 'O' Level Sociology
Associated Examining Board

30 April 1974

Editor's note

A great advantage of this book is that it combines the expertise of three experienced teachers. There has been a continuous cross-fertilisation of ideas about the approach, methods and content. Apart from writing those chapters related to economics, it has been my privilege to collate the contributions of my two sociologist colleagues. The aim has been to bring together the experience of two men and a woman who have taught sociology in both schools and colleges. The general format followed has been that of units, topics, stimulus work and questions from recent GCE 'O' Level papers. I should like to express my gratitude to Margaret Flemming and Bob Hine for co-operating to produce a book which teachers will find both academically sound and practical.

Jack Nobbs
General Editor

Other titles by Jack Nobbs:
Social Economics, McGraw-Hill, 1969
Social Economics, Decimalised edition, McGraw-Hill, 1971
Economic Problems of the 1970s, Pergamon Press, 1971
Handbook on Objective Testing—Civics (with Marion Walton), Methuen, 1971
Objective Questions in Social Economics, Methuen, 1972
Economics for Advanced Level, McGraw-Hill, 1973
Economics—Exam Guide for 'A' Level, McGraw-Hill, 1973
Daily Economics (with Paul Ames), McGraw-Hill, 1975

Acknowledgements

The authors and publishers acknowledge, with thanks, the following photograph sources:
Barclays Bank Ltd p. 39; Brighton Polytechnic—Faculty of Applied Sciences p. 104; Birmingham City—Public Works Dept p. 131; British Insurance Association (C. C. Ashton) p. 232; Camera Press Ltd pp. 284, 310; Central Office of Information, Crown Copyright p. 177; Brian Chaplin p. 15; Community Service Volunteers p. 217; *Daily Mirror* p. 299; Department of Health & Social Security, Crown Copyright p. 214; East Kilbride (Town Planning Office) p. 133; Electricity Council p. 251; Flamborough C.E. School p. 95 (bottom); Fontarel Ltd p. 165; Friends Service Council p. 224; Granada Television p. 56 (*World in Action*) p. 143 (*All Our Yesterdays*) p. 163 (*The Messengers*); Greater London Council p. 204; Harlow Development Corp. p. 267; Frances Hodges p. 322; India Government Tourist Office p. 51; Industrial & Commercial Finance Corp. p. 150; Keystone Press pp. 185, 186, 190, 281; Lanchester Polytechnic p. 102; London Express News and Feature Service pp. 148, 278, 285; Norwich City Corporation p. 221 (top); Oxfam p. 136; Pace Group p. 240; Paul Popper Ltd p. 25; Post Office p. 257; Radio Times Hulton Picture Library pp. 9, 202, 205; Rowntree Mackintosh Ltd pp. 248, 254; Shelter (Nick Hedges) p. 225; *The Sun* pp. 62, 298; Thames Television p. 95 (top) (*Seeing and Doing*); Topix p. 308; UNESCO p. 309.

The publishers have made every effort to trace copyright holders, but if they have inadvertently overlooked any they will be pleased to make the necessary arrangement at the first opportunity.

The author and publishers wish to thank the following, who have kindly given permission for the use of copyright material:
Associated Examining Board for use of *AEB G.C.E. Questions*; B. T. Batsford Ltd for table from *The Wealth of Britain* by S. Pollard and D. W. Crossley; Blackie & Son Ltd for table from *This Age of Communication* by Roger Manvell; Bedford Square Press for table from *Socially Deprived Families in Britain* by Dr Holman; Central Office of Information for two maps from *Density of Population 1961* and *Percentage Change in Population 1951–61*, and two diagrams from *Britain 1972, An Official Handbook*; Chatto & Windus Ltd for table from *Communications* by Raymond Williams; *Daily Express* for permission to use collage from *The Guardian* 19th November 1973; *Daily Mail* for

permission to use collage published in *The Guardian* 19th November 1973; Granada Publication Ltd for a table from *The Home and The School* by J. W. B. Douglas (MacGibbon & Kee 1964), Figure I and titles from *The Effects of Television* by J. D. Halloran; *The Guardian* for collage from *The Guardian* 19th November 1973, and article dated 26th January 1973; Controller of Her Majesty's Stationery Office for Table 28, Television Viewing from *Social Trends No. 3*, one table each from *Registrar General U.K.*, *Registrar General Statistical Review*, *Dept of the Environment Housing Statistics*, *Dept of Employment Gazette July 1972*, *Monthly Digest Statistics July 1972*, *Inland Revenue Survey of Personal Incomes 1969–70*, and *Classification of Occupations 1970*; Independent Broadcasting Authority for two illustrations from *I.T.V. 1973*; JICNARS for Table 66 from *National Readership Survey July 1971–June 1972*; Lloyds Bank Limited, for chart from *Lloyds Bank Review July 1969*; New Science Publications for six tables and one graph from *New Society* (the weekly review of the Social Sciences); Oxford Delegacy of Local Examinations for use of *Oxford G.C.E. Questions*; Penguin Books Ltd for tables from *Voters, Parties and Leaders*, by Jean Blondel, *Sense and Nonsense in Psychology* by H. J. Eysenck, and *Must Labour Lose?* by Abrams and Rose; Routledge & Kegan Paul Ltd for tables from *Social Mobility in Britain* by D. V. Glass, *Family and Kinship in East London* by Wilmott and Young, *The Experience of Higher Education* by Peter Marris, *The Changing Social Structure of England and Wales 1871–1961* by D. Marsh; *The Sunday Times* for headlines used in various editions of *The Sunday Times*, and two maps from 'The Reluctant Fifth' in *Sunday Times Colour Supplement* 2nd September 1972; 'Reproduced from *The Times* by permission' article from *The Times* 8th December 1972 also *The Times* Masthead in a collage from *The Guardian*; United Nations copyright © for one table each from *Infant Mortality in the United Kingdom per 1000 Live births 1851–1971*, *UN Demographic Yearbook*, *United Nations Statistical Yearbook*, and a chart from *Monthly Bulletin of Statistics*; University of Cambridge for a table from *University Reporter*.

The publishers have made every effort to trace the copyright-holders but if they have inadvertently overlooked any, they will be pleased to make the necessary arrangement at the first opportunity.

Contents

8   The Welfare Society

9   The Economy and Employment

12   The Individual and Society

1 Approaches to the Study of Society
Unit 1 What is Sociology?

Over the past thirty years sociology has grown in popularity and developed considerably, so we would expect people to know more about the subject than they generally do. Many have a notion that sociology is about people: but some think that sociology is all about helping the unfortunate and doing welfare work, while others think that sociology is the same as socialism and is a means of bringing revolution to our schools and colleges. Certainly sociology is about people. But understanding some of the problems of people is only a part of sociology. It is true that sociology does lead the student to look very closely at the society in which he lives. But for many years sociology was banned in the Soviet Union as a bourgeois ideology, so the leading European Communist country did not think of sociology as being particularly revolutionary.

Looking in the *Oxford English Dictionary* we read that sociology is 'the study of the history and nature of human society'. But we all have different ideas about what is meant by human society. So perhaps the best way to discover the meaning of the word 'sociology' is to find out what the study of sociology involves.

The word 'sociology' was first used by the French philosopher Auguste Comte in the late 1830s. Since then other writers have placed their own interpretation upon its meaning and have arrived at a definition which is generally acceptable:

Sociology is the scientific and systematic study of people in groups. It usually means looking for patterns of behaviour amongst people living in organised communities.

Later on we shall see exactly what is meant by 'scientific' and 'systematic', but for the moment let us assume that these words refer to the thorough and organised way in which we, as sociologists, study how people live.

Throughout the world people live in groups: the smallest grouping is usually the family, and the largest group is a nation or possibly a federation of nations; in between are a host of different groups such as a school, workplace, neighbourhood, village or town, and we refer to these as *communities.* It is easy for us to think of the family as a group, but it is harder to work out precisely who belongs to a particular community. As sociologists we must always define the limits of any community which is to be studied. For example, if we are making a study of a school we must say from the outset whether or not we will be considering the caretaker as part of our study.

All groups have some kind of organisation and purpose to them, and the way in which people of the group behave towards one another tells us something about the nature of the group. Sociologists look for these patterns of behaviour, and try to understand the causes which shape them.

Is sociology just common sense?

What makes sociology an exciting subject is that it tells us more about ourselves and the way in which we live. There are those who regard the findings of sociologists as just common sense which any good observer of society would have realised. What such people fail to appreciate is that although the sociologist often starts his studies with a sensible idea, for example, that people who receive less education do not get as good jobs as those who have had more education, he then sets about finding out, with a degree of academically acceptable precision, whether this is really the case, and what proportion of poorly educated people in fact have been able to get good jobs. Even more important, sociologists often are able to disprove widely-held wrong ideas that people have had about the society in which we live.

1.1   What is meant by society and social system?

Society may be regarded as a living organism whose structure is being constantly renewed. (Radcliffe-Brown)

The word 'society' is one of the least precise sociological terms: it can be used to describe a modern industrial state or a dozen bushmen wandering in the Kalahari desert. These days 'society' is usually employed to mean a country or a nation. Once again we have the problem of setting the limits of our definition. Societies are usually found in one place; their people have common patterns of behaviour; they have rules which are usually observed by the majority of their members, but which may be changing constantly, although they are always identifiable. Four factors usually characterise a society:

1 geographical location
2 common habits and customs
3 the maintenance of order
4 self-perpetuation.

These days if a sociologist is dealing with a specific society he looks at the formation of its *social system*. The social system is formed by the way in which individuals in a society behave and interact. Studying this interaction between two or more individuals gives us an understanding of *social relationships*. Every member of society has some form of social relationship with everyone whom he may come into contact with or deal with in some way. The family as a group has certain patterns of behaviour within that group: children may treat their parents with respect; a man may expect his wife to do the cooking while she may expect him to do the decorating. These social relationships within the family constitute part of its *social structure*. On a larger scale, for example, in a school or factory, the patterns of behaviour found between various members of the group are also social relationships, and this whole network of different relationships creates another kind of structure. Taken altogether, the various structures (family, school, factory, neighbourhood, town, etc.) form the social system.

All groups involve social relationships, but the existence of a social relationship does not necessarily mean the existence of a group. An example of a social relationship that does not entail a group would be that of two Englishmen staying at the same hotel in a foreign country, having never been properly introduced, yet acknowledging each other's presence by saying 'good morning' at breakfast; this simple greeting creates a social relationship of a temporary kind and no more.

Groups, as opposed to mere social relationships, usually involve some kind of co-operation to achieve a particular end. The common goal of a school is to educate its pupils, therefore there is co-operation between pupils and teachers to achieve this aim. Every member of the school has certain rights, obligations, and duties to perform: the pupil has the right to attend lessons; the teacher is obliged to teach; and the head has a duty to run the school. These rights and obligations are essentially rules of behaviour. Quite obviously not all members of the group have the same rights and obligations. The two most basic characteristics of a group are:

1 co-operation
2 a sense of belonging.

Societies are made up of people: people are born, age and eventually die. For this simple reason societies are constantly changing with time. Social relationships change and so too do social structures and the social system they form. It is one of the tasks of the sociologist to look at the changes that are occurring in society. Later we shall examine more closely the factors which make for social change, but we should also realise that there are factors which renew the structure of society as well as changing it. Many of the institutions of society such as the educational system, the economic system, the religious system, and the legal system, may provide the basis for some social change but in other ways they are responsible for passing on traditions and practices that will help maintain the fabric of society.

1.2   Sociology and social science

The term *social science* is a general one meaning the study of human relationships in society; for this reason some people equate social science with sociology; however, this will not help us in a definition of either. Instead let us say that sociology may be regarded as a branch or *discipline* of social science. Elements or parts of the other disciplines of social science such as economics, politics, anthropology, psychology, demography, history and even philosophy, are contained within sociology; but elements of sociology are likewise found in the other social science disciplines. All the social science disciplines examine human relationships from a particular viewpoint, but sociology may perhaps claim a broader perspective of society (see Figure 1.1). For when a sociological study focuses upon a particular group within society it will inevitably consider the forces which may affect that group and which are dealt with by other disciplines, such as economics or psychology before reaching conclusions from a sociological viewpoint.

How is sociology related to the other disciplines of social science?

Sociology may be regarded as being to social science what mathematics is to the natural sciences of, say, physics or chemistry: a vital component which cements the discipline together. A student of politics or economics cannot afford to neglect sociology in his studies, just as it would be impossible to study physics without some knowledge of mathematics.

The Social Sciences

History is the study of events which were created by people (geology is

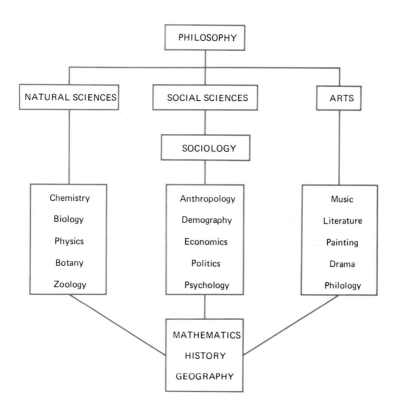

Figure 1.1 *The relationship between sociology and other studies*

history without people). Historians this century have been increasingly aware of the need to understand events in the light of social factors such as increases in population, the psychology of individuals, or the importance of social classes. There are specialised branches of history—economic history, social history, political history—but all involve human activity and human relationships in the study of the past.

Economics is concerned with getting and spending: the study of the spending and financial habits of people. The economist is concerned with the use that people make of money and capital resources. Sociologists try to establish the economic patterns of different groupings and the economic forces which affect people's lives.

Politics is the study of governments and power. The sociologist studies the nature and composition of groups who seek or who have attained power. Voting behaviour interests political sociologists and psephologists.

Demography is the study of population. Perhaps it may be regarded as sociology on a large scale. Demographers look at changes in the population and sociologists relate these changes to society.

Psychology is a discipline of social science concerned with the experience and behaviour of people, how they react to certain conditions. Sociologists are usually more concerned with psychology applied to groups. (Psychology is often confused with psychiatry which is a discipline of medical science.)

Anthropology (the science of man) is the closest discipline to sociology. The anthropologist used to be concerned primarily with the biological changes in human development, but social anthropology today may be regarded as sociology.

All the disciplines of social science are concerned with human behaviour patterns. Each has developed its own specialisations, but has found a common link in sociology through human relationships. (See Figure 1.2.)

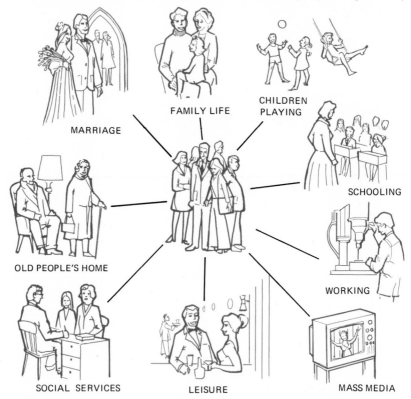

Figure 1.2   *All aspects of life find a common link in sociology through human relationships*

Unit 2 Sociology as a Science

2.1 How scientific is social science?

It is accepted that the natural sciences are 'scientific', yet some people doubt whether the social sciences can be regarded as being scientific in the same way. Of course, it really depends upon what is meant by 'science': the original Latin word, *scientia*, means knowledge, but the modern word 'science' has come to have a more specialised meaning. The careful, systematic way in which the natural scientist conducts his experiments and possibly makes predictions from the results of his work, causes his work to be regarded as 'scientific'.

One of the arguments against the social sciences being scientific is that they concern people in their human relationships, and as people vary as individuals there is no consistency of behaviour. An experiment connected with the natural sciences can be repeated anywhere in the world by another natural scientist and the same results will be obtained: this is because the natural scientist conducts his experiments on *matter*. But even if it were possible to set up experimental conditions with human beings, without putting them at physiological or psychological risk, it is argued that the variations between individuals (let alone societies) would be so great as to make any results meaningless. People who argue in this way add that even members of the same family vary, so that it would be of little use to compare findings made in a study of a British community to those of, say, an Arab community. But this argument reveals a lack of understanding of both the sociologist's aims and *sociological evidence*. An individual's behaviour may be of interest to a psychiatrist or social psychologist, but usually sociologists are looking for *common patterns of behaviour* found in groups, and comparisons with other groups can be sociologically significant. The surprising thing is that although we may have individual personalities and different genetic constructions, we do tend to have fairly regular behaviour patterns, and the sociologist is able to obtain a considerable amount of information about societies and communities by observing and comparing these patterns.

The sociologist or social scientist sets about gathering information in a systematic and thorough way which can be quite scientific. The techniques of gathering evidence (known as *data*) for a sociological investigation may include the use of statistics, and statistics as a branch of mathematics is scientifically acceptable.

One of the tests applied to a scientific subject is whether predictions can be made about it, given that certain conditions prevail. For example, when a chemist pours the right proportions of hydrochloric acid and sodium hydroxide together he can predict that the result will be salt and water, but as sociologists we cannot really predict with the same degree of accuracy how people will behave. In fact the social scientist is not concerned with a one hundred per cent degree of accuracy about people, and totally accurate predictions about human behaviour are not necessary in social science. The natural sciences do not always stand up to the same tests of one hundred per cent accuracy. Meteorology is a branch of natural science, but is the weather forecaster always right? All disciplines of natural science and social science have their particular techniques of investigation; each is as accurate as its limitations of investigation will allow. If projections are made in the social sciences they are used only as guides towards the ways in which people *might* behave in the future, not as pointers to how they *will* behave.

2.2   Some theories of social science

Do sociologists always agree with each other about their subject?

Just as doctors conduct a diagnosis of their patients, so too sociologists make a diagnosis of society. Not all doctors agree on their findings or the ways of approaching particular illnesses, and neither do all sociologists agree on their findings. There are many theories of social science and ideas about the nature of society. Anyone may claim to know what is wrong with society and what ought to be done to remedy its problems. Anyone may have distinct views about such matters as politics, economics and race relations. The difference between a qualified sociologist and the ordinary man in the street is that the sociologist will accumulate data in a systematic way about some of the problems of society, instead of pronouncing what should be done purely from his own personal observations. Sociology and most other social science disciplines have the following four characteristics, which are similar to those of many natural science disciplines.

1   Sociology is *empirical*. This means that it is based upon things observed and intelligent reasoning about them, and not upon supernatural phenomena.

2   Sociology is *theoretical*. The observations made are summarised in a logical way as part of a theory about the nature of society.

3   Sociology is *non-ethical*. Sociologists do not question whether their observations of society are necessarily good or bad for society (although very

often this rule is bent somewhat in writing up observations). The observations are conducted without bias one way or another.

4   Sociology is *cumulative*. Different sociological theories are constructed out of other theories which have been modified or corrected in the light of fresh evidence.

Although there are many different theories of sociology, most sociologists construct their own theories out of the many, choosing those parts of the different theories that seem best and most accurate. For example, two important groups of theories have been *historical* and *functionalist* yet few sociologists would rely completely on either as a means of analysis or explanation of social theory.

Historical theories have fallen into two groups: one which sought to look at society as a whole and saw society undergoing an evolutionary process; the other which does not seek to explain everything about society in terms of history but rather looks for changes that are occurring. The first group was originally characterised by Auguste Comte (1798–1857) and Karl Marx (1818–83). Marx's influence upon social theory has

Auguste Comte is usually regarded as the father of modern sociology

been considerable. He developed his theory after he had amassed a great deal of historical and economic data, and this theory sought to explain mainly in terms of economics everything about what had happened in history, what was happening, and what would happen to society. The all-embracing theory of Marx was first seriously challenged by Max Weber (1864–1920). Weber held that Marx's theories were too economically biased, and because no social scientist is able to look at the whole of society in depth a complete explanation of society was not possible.

Functionalist theories were largely developed by social anthropologists during this century. A number of leading academics still subscribe to functionalist views, but most modern sociologists reject the main conclusions of these theories. The functionalist view is that everyone has a set position and task in society (function) and that we are all interdependent upon one another in the successful running of society. Because functionalism is unable to explain adequately the changes that take place in society the term *dysfunction* was invented to explain how revolutions and dissatisfaction occurred to produce social change.

Of course, we cannot elaborate upon all the theories of sociology as they are too numerous to mention. Nevertheless it would be useful if students of sociology looked up something about the contributors to the development of this subject.

Unit 3   The Tools of the Sociologist

A study of the way in which sociologists make their observations and gather data will give us a clearer idea about the nature of the subject. Once we have found out *how* sociologists work we are able to see the kinds of problems and questions that are dealt with in this subject.

Today what is known as the *quantitative approach* is used by most sociologists. It involves four principles of investigation based upon the empirical method:

1   the observation of some aspect of society
2   the accumulation of data about this aspect
3   the putting together (correlation) of this data
4   the reporting of these findings.

Before a sociologist investigates an aspect of society he usually has some idea or theory, known as an *hypothesis* about what he may find when his investigation is concluded. The sociologist must take care not to let his hypothesis affect his conclusions by only looking for evidence which will support his original idea and disregarding any evidence which may disprove his hypothesis. A sociologist must be completely unbiased when conducting investigations and writing up his conclusions. Indeed, he must expose his findings to the most rigorous testing to see whether his hypothesis is valid. If a sociologist allows his personal feelings and possible prejudices to shape his investigation and conclusion, then his findings will not have a scientific validity. Let us consider an extreme example. A sociologist holds the view that poor children who come from broken homes will become juvenile delinquents. In order to prove his hypothesis he investigates the cases of several hundred juvenile delinquents who came from poor homes and whose parents were divorced or separated. Because all the cases meet his requirements of a poor background and a broken home, his response rate is one hundred per cent correct, owing to his selection of just those juvenile delinquents. What the sociologist failed to do was to consider the many more (the majority perhaps) of children who were poor and who came from broken homes, but who did not become delinquents; nor did the sociologist look for other causes of delinquency which may have caused children from wealthy and stable homes to become juvenile delinquents. Employing the four principles of investigation, this so-called sociologist was wrong because:

1   His observation was prejudiced.

2   The data, ie information, that he accumulated on juvenile delinquency, was chosen to prove his hypothesis.

3   His correlation of data did not consider the possibility of other causes of delinquency.

4   No doubt such a bad sociologist reported his findings in a biased manner.

Fortunately there are few sociologists of the type just described. When mistakes are made in sociological investigation it is usually due to the investigator's failure to see or consider one or two vital factors. W. G. Runciman in his *Social Science and Political Theory* (Cambridge University Press, 1963) tells of one, now famous, example of error when political sociologists and opinion pollsters made a tremendous mistake in predicting the outcome of the American presidential election of 1948. Almost all commentators and a famous opinion poll forecast the defeat of the presidential challenger, Harry S. Truman, by a wide margin. Truman won the election handsomely. The opinion poll had sought to find out how people would vote by telephoning them. The mistake was that most people who had a telephone (the financially better-off) were Republicans

and not likely to vote for Truman, the Democratic party candidate. This
mistake is not likely to be repeated in future by organisers of opinion polls.

3.1 Sampling

The lesson of the Presidential election of 1948 is that sociologists must
take the greatest of care when deciding which people will be part of the
sample investigated. Ideally a sociological investigation should include
everyone under investigation, but just as it would have been impossible
to find out the opinions of every single American voter in 1948 over a
short period of time, so too it is often impossible for a sociologist to consider everybody in his investigation. For this reason samples are taken of
the population: population in this sense means everyone under consideration when data is being gathered.

What is a representative sample?

In general, the larger the sample taken the more representative of the
population it will be—provided that bias is avoided. For a survey, no
matter how large, would be biased if only motorists were asked whether
the tax on petrol should be lowered, or only families with two children
were investigated as to the adequacy of the family allowance. Bias could
occur in many ways if the sample is not carefully thought out, therefore
sociologists try to make their sample as representative of the population
as possible.

Two factors usually limit a sample, just as they limit any investigation:

1   time
2   money.

The more time and money a sociologist has at his disposal, the more
thorough his investigation can be; more time and money could mean a
larger sample, and perhaps a more accurate conclusion. If we wished to
investigate the problem of homelessness in Britain and had several years
and plenty of money we could employ many investigators. Because
resources of both time and money are usually limited, we should use
them to the best advantage. A wise way of using our resources would be
to concentrate them in those towns and cities where most homelessness is
found, rather than to seek out cases in places where it is not so great a
problem.

Most sampling will involve the use of *statistics*. There are ways of
checking whether statistical figures can be relied upon as being accurate.

This involves the use of mathematical techniques. Most statistics have a validity if the sample exceeds three hundred. Statistical methods exist whereby degrees of error in the sample and findings can even be tested, and very accurate results obtained. When Disraeli said, 'Statistics is the art of lying with precision,' he was speaking as a politician, not as a social scientist. Because the use of statistics is so important in all fields of social science, not least in sociology, it is usually taught as part of most sociology courses in universities, polytechnics and institutions of higher education, and the importance of statistics continues to grow. Statistics are the basis of good judgement in sociology as they enable us to allow for bias in our investigation and thereby make for precision in our findings.

3.2   Social surveys

Sociologists usually gather data and other information by carrying out a *social survey*. A social survey involves systematically gathering facts about people. C. A. Moser, describing social surveys in his book *Survey Methods in Social Investigation* (Heinemann Educational Books, 1971) states, 'When it comes to the subject matter the only common factor is that they are concerned with demographic characteristics, the social environment, the activities or opinions or attitudes of some group of people.' There have been some famous exceptions, mainly in the last century, but almost all modern social surveys keep to the rules of being unbiased and systematic. Equally, although there are many ways of conducting social surveys, the two limitations which apply to sampling, time and money, restrict the depths to which any survey may go. There are, nevertheless, three steps which should be followed before undertaking a social survey:

1   gather as much existing information as possible about the subject of the survey
2   decide how far the survey will go
3   whenever possible carry out a *pre-test* or *pilot survey* before commencing the main survey.

Existing information can take many different forms: usually it is published material such as books, newspapers, or government reports. It may involve asking advice from experts in the subject that is to be surveyed. The reason existing information ought to be considered is that it would be pointless to repeat a survey which had already adequately covered the subject. Even more important, consideration of other works will provide pointers to what is likely to be found in the survey, together with some of the problems that may be encountered. If the problems of a previous survey can be planned for, or, better still, avoided, time and effort can be concentrated elsewhere. The original hypothesis of the investigators may well be amended after information has been gained from this preliminary study. Existing information often provides interesting material for comparison once the survey has been conducted. It might, for example, be interesting to compare the spending habits of young people in a survey conducted today with the results of a similar study conducted ten years ago, and see what changes, if any, have taken place.

The aim of a survey should be defined at the outset, taking into consideration the limits imposed by time and money and the amount of information already available. A poorly organised survey could result in the gathering of a mass of pointless and irrelevant information, and the omission of much important material. Once the resources for conducting the social survey have been established the searching out of information can be organised systematically within the bounds of those resources.

Pre-testing or pilot surveys are often valuable because they may show up faults in the design of the survey. For example, questions may be included which people do not understand, or which might lead them to give wrong answers. A pilot survey of, say, five per cent of the population that is to be surveyed may give an indication of the likely *response rate*: it will show how many people would be prepared to answer questions. If a pilot survey showed that only half of the people surveyed (known as *respondents*) were prepared to answer questions and the population of the survey was to be 500, then 1000 respondents would need to be found to achieve the target of 500. Pre-testing and pilot surveys may reveal how long it takes on average to answer the questions. If it were found that a survey planned to take five minutes for each respondent took ten minutes in pre-testing, then it would be necessary to double the time allowed in order to get adequate replies, and time might not be inexhaustible.

3.3   Questionnaires

In the last century, social surveys were often carried out by one investigator who recorded his observations after living among and talking to people who interested him. One of the most famous nineteenth-century works of sociological interest is Henry Mayhew's *London Labour and the London Poor*, which was first published in 1851. With two collaborators Mayhew interviewed thousands of Londoners and wrote a fascinating account of their ways of life and the many trades that flourished in the

Completing a questionnaire

capital more than a century ago. Another survey was B. Seebohm Rowntree's *Poverty: A Study of Town Life*, which was carried out in York in 1899.

These days more than ninety per cent of social surveys involve the use of a *questionnaire* of some kind. This can take a number of forms. Either the respondent is asked a series of questions, the answers to which are filled in on a form by an interviewer, or else the respondents complete the forms themselves. Depending on the kind of information sought, both methods have their advantages and disadvantages.

The questions that are asked in questionnaires can be of the type where the respondent is asked a set question and marks off an appropriate or limited reply. For example, to the question 'How much money do you earn?' the respondent may be asked to reply by ticking one of a number of boxes, labelled perhaps:

under £20 per week	£35–£40 per week
£20–£25 per week	£40–£45 per week
£25–£30 per week	£45–£50 per week
£30–£35 per week	over £50 per week

This type of question is known as the *pre-coded* variety (see Figure 1.3).

1.3   *Part of a pre-coded questionnaire*

LEISURE ACTIVITIES

Questionnaire for Young People

Since it is hoped to find factual evidence from these questions about local needs of young people, please answer them as honestly as you can, and add any ideas or suggestions for improvements. The answers are strictly confidential for the purpose of a computerised survey and it will be impossible to identify any individual filling in one of these forms. Please answer in appropriate boxes.

SEX   Male = 1; Female = 2 ☐   AGE ☐

1. How do you spend your leisure   (a) Weekday evenings ☐
   (Mostly at home = 1. Mostly out = 2)   (b) Week-ends ☐

2. If the answer to 1a and/or 1b is 2, Where do you go:
   (please tick)

	Dance	Youth club	Coffee bar	Public house	Friend's home	Football	Tennis	Athletics	Other
Weekday evenings									
Week-ends									

3. Have you any hobbies or special interests   Yes = 1 No = 2 ☐

   If yes please list them:

4. Do you spend any leisure time with your family at:
   (please tick)

| Concerts Theatre ☐ | Picnics Football ☐ | Cinema Watching TV ☐ |

5. Are you encouraged to bring your friends home?   ☐
   (Girls=1. Boys=2. Both Sexes=3.)

6. Do you think your parents are   ☐
   (too strict=1; not too strict=2; or are you undecided=3)

7. Where were you last Saturday at:
   At home with family=1; At home by yourself=2;
   Out alone=3; Out with friends=4.

   7 a.m.   ☐   12 noon   ☐   5 p.m.   ☐
   7 p.m.   10 p.m.   12 midnight

8. How much spending money do you have?

   £   p

   a) Pocket money
   b) Wages
   c) Part-time job

9. What do you spend it on?   £   p
   If you cannot define the   Clothes
   amount but spend some money   Food
   on these items put a tick   Make-up
   in the '£' column.   Cigarettes
                                  Drink
                                  Sport
                                  Hobbies
                                  Magazines
                                  Savings

10. To whom would you go if you had a problem?   ☐☐☐

    3 answers from:
    Parent=1; Friend=2; Teacher=3; Family doctor=4; Police=5;
    Citizen's Advice Bureau=6; Youth employment=7; Samaritans=8;
    Young people's advisory service=9; Others=0.

    Figure 1.3   Part of a pre-coded questionnaire

When the respondent is asked to answer a general question, such as
'What do you think of the Government's economic policy?' in his own
words, either writing down his reply or dictating it to the interviewer,
this is known as an *open-ended* question. For obvious reasons pre-coded
questions are easier to analyse, but often they cannot be used to guage
accurately such things as the strength of a respondent's feelings on certain
matters.

The usual method of using questionnaires is to have a trained interviewer. When the interviewer, who may be a comparative, and often a complete, stranger to the respondent conducts a face-to-face interview, we call this a *formal interview*. Formal interviewing requires special skills on the part of the interviewer. In the first instance the interviewer often has to find the respondents and encourage them to answer the questions. The only compulsory questionnaire is the census form which is discussed in Chapter 5, so to get replies from reluctant respondents to other questions may be quite difficult. During a formal interview the interviewer must try to give an impression of 'neutrality', firstly so that the respondent does not give replies which he thinks the interviewer would like to hear, and secondly so that the respondent is not embarrassed to answer any of the questions on the questionnaire. Middle-aged women have been found to be the best kind of interviewers as they seem to get on well with people of all ages and social backgrounds. *Informal interviewing* is more difficult than formal interviewing: this is when the interviewer tries to get a more relaxed atmosphere in order to draw out the respondent's feelings, opinions and confidences, and yet subsequently reports his findings in an objective, ie non-biased, way. Very often informal interviewing is a *follow-up* to formal interviews after a respondent has shown some interesting characteristics which the investigators wish to look at in greater depth. Considerable skill on the part of the interviewers is required for this kind of work, as they must build up a relationship with the respondent, be objective, and yet not destroy the respondent's trust or divulge publicly what they have been told in confidence.

The commonest form of investigation without an interviewer is the use of *mail questionnaires*, when a respondent is sent the questionnaire through the post accompanied by a pre-paid envelope for the reply. The two main advantages of the mail questionnaire are that it is cheap and results can be obtained rapidly. If costs are limited, then the difference between paying a day's wage to a trained interviewer who may be able to see a dozen respondents, and posting out several hundred questionnaires for the same price, may be a deciding factor. It has been the experience of investigators using the mail questionnaire that they receive between two-thirds and three-quarters of the replies within the first week (this does *not* mean a response rate of 66–75 per cent); after three weeks there are hardly any replies at all. Sometimes questionnaires ask a question which would be best answered by a family discussing the reply: for example, a question on family expenditure. Sociologists call this *intra-household consultation*. If people can reply to the questionnaire at their leisure, or at least when they are all together and not just when the interviewer calls, then a more precise reply may be obtained, especially if they have to look up documents to give a reply. Questions of an intimate personal nature often receive a better response with the anonymity of a mail questionnaire than if they are asked by a strange interviewer. Some people say that if the interviewer is not properly trained, such things as his speech, dress and manner may put off the respondent, and that this does not happen with a mail ques- · tionnaire. Quite often interviewers have difficulty in making contact with selected respondents from a carefully chosen representative sample, and time may be lost before the meeting is arranged. This too will not happen with mail questionnaires.

The main disadvantage of mail questionnaires, and therefore an advantage of having trained interviewers, is that there is always a chance of the wording being confusing and the questions being misunderstood: for this reason the choice of words in all types of questionnaire is of the greatest importance. The answers given to a mail questionnaire must be taken as final, and no allowance is made for the possibility of people misunderstanding questions and being inaccurate in their replies. Sometimes questions require a spontaneous response, before the respondent has the chance to think up a reply and obviously this is not possible with a mail questionnaire. Other questions may be of a 'follow-up' type depending upon the answer to one particular question, eg 'Do you take part in an active sport? If "Yes" which one, and for how long each week?' If the respondent has had the chance to read through all the questions before answering, he may frame his replies to match all the questions. On occasions the truthful answer can only be obtained when a husband or wife is not present: a husband may not like to fill out the real answer to a question on how much he spends on beer each week in an intra-household consultation.

Sometimes interviewers add extra information about respondents after an interview, perhaps giving an assessment of the character, environment and even honesty of the respondent. This cannot be done with a mail questionnaire. Such factors as the type of question to be asked, the time and money available, and perhaps the need for extra information about the respondent, must all be taken into account before deciding the appropriate type of questionnaire and interviewing techniques to be used.

3.4 Methods of observation

As has been said, most surveys involve a questionnaire of some kind, but important sociological research has been conducted using other kinds of social survey. Instead of seeking a mass of information that questionnaires might provide, some investigators prefer to gain an impression of many aspects of their subjects' behaviour which could not be contained in a series of questions no matter how well devised. The general name for this kind of investigation is the *observational approach*. Television documentaries, often about social problems, use this technique by filming the conditions under which people live, the way in which they speak and what their attitudes to things are—a *qualitative* rather than a *quantitative* approach is used.

There are some kinds of social activity and situations where it is best for the investigator to live among the subjects of his research. This is known as *participant observation*. Usually this method is employed when dealing with small communities, such as villages, or primitive tribes. The insight gained by living and working among small communities can be far greater than it would have been if the observer were an outsider and not accepted by the community. Provided the participant observer is constantly aware of the need to be objective in his study (and this could prove difficult as he is bound to develop friendships, or his very presence might cause his subjects to act unnaturally) a deep understanding of the community is possible.

In contrast to observation there are techniques of surveying which use only existing data and archive material such as government documents or similar published information. These techniques are usually employed in large-scale research projects where demographic material is the source of the sociologists' work. Quite often different sets of data are compared over a period of time, and changes or differences are recorded. Case studies of individuals are used by social psychologists, but by their nature they can only be on a small scale.

How do sociologists decide which approach to use?

The nature of the subject to be studied largely determines the method of approach. The resources available determine the depth to which investigations can be carried out. The rest of this book examines various aspects of society, or the different groups into which people form themselves. If we investigate the way in which people behave towards one another, and the structure of different institutions, we shall gradually build up a picture of the society in which we live. Before we could begin to study society we have had to learn the ways in which sociological investigation is conducted and some of the theories on which sociology is based.

Terms used in this chapter

community	anthropology	pilot survey
social relationship	behaviour patterns	pre-coded questionnaire
social system	empirical	
social structure	hypothesis	

Further examples of terms will be given at the end of each chapter. You will find it useful to enter them in a book with a short explanation next to each one.

Questions

1 Give the best definition of sociology that you can, and then indicate what are the strengths and weaknesses of your definition.

2 Give four examples of groups in society and some of the social relationships which help form the structure of the groups.

3 Why is it that psychology has been described as sociology on a small scale, and demography as sociology on a large scale?

4 How does the sociologist differ from the man in the street in forming his opinions about society?

5 Given a population sample of five hundred, how would you make it representative of Britain?

6 Michael Young and Peter Willmott's survey *Family and Kinship in East London* (Routledge and Kegan Paul, 1957) was intended to assess the impact of a new housing estate upon life in Bethnal Green. Secure a copy and find out:

a What was the fictitious name of the new housing estate?
b What was the population of Bethnal Green in 1955?
c What was the social class of most of the people?
d How did one of the researchers get to know the people so very well?
e How many people did they use in their large General Sample?
f How did they pick this random sample?
g How many people refused to co-operate?
h What criteria were used to find the people for the Marriage Sample?
i How long did the researchers take over each interview?
j How many pilot interviews were carried out?

7 Compile a questionnaire to be used with your group or class members in an attempt to determine their:

a reading habits
b attitude to religion
c views about a topical problem, eg population control or pollution.

8 In 1970, fifty-four per cent of sociology graduates were women. Are there reasons why sociology should be more a woman's subject than a man's? (A view was expressed by D. R. Webb in *Sociology* Vol. 6 No. 3, January 1973.)

9 Greater use should be made of the social sciences to determine legal reforms, according to *The Law Commissioner's Annual Report 1971–72*. How could sociology be used to help decide upon necessary reforms in the law?

10 If the sociologist says something that turns out to be true, it is thought to be obvious, but if it is found to be untrue he is regarded as a fool. Can you think of ways by which the sociologist might earn more respect?

Questions from GCE 'O' Level Sociology Examination Papers

1 Sociology is not a collection of facts but a different way of seeing the world. Illustrate. (AEB, November 1972)

2 It has been suggested that a scientific method includes the following six processes:
i   identifying a specific problem
ii   selecting appropriate methods to study the problem
iii collecting relevant data
iv   analysing the data
v   interpreting the data
vi   reporting findings and conclusions.
Take any sociological study that you are familiar with and show how it fits in (or does not fit in) with the six stages quoted above. Make sure that you refer clearly to *one* particular piece of research. (AEB, June 1973)

3 Describe and explain some of the methods used by sociologists in their studies. Give examples from *one* piece of relevant research. (AEB, November 1972)

4 Explain clearly but briefly what you understand by *three* of the following terms:

experiment	group
questionnaire	hypothesis

(AEB, November 1970)

5 Take any *one* sociological study with which you are familiar, describe briefly its aims and comment on the methods used and the results achieved. (AEB, June 1974)

6 What do you understand by scientific method? To what extent are sociologists scientific? (AEB, November 1974)

7 Explain what is meant by *one* of the following kinds of sociological research methods and describe its use in *one* sociological study with which you are familiar: random sampling, participant observation, or a longitudinal study. (AEB, November 1974)

2 Social Differences
Unit 4 What is Stratification?

A characteristic common to almost all societies is the way in which they may divide up into different layers or *strata*. In industrial societies such as Britain today we may think of a simple division into two *classes*, a working class and a middle class (leaving for the moment the tricky definition of class). Earlier this century there was also a recognisable upper class, but this group is now identified by most sociologists as having merged with the middle class. Some other terms of stratification employed are *estate*, *status*, and in Indian society, *caste*. All these terms imply some kind of ranking or hierarchy. Throughout history strata have been recognisable: in ancient times there were slaves and freemen, in medieval society there were lords and villeins. As time passes different divisions have emerged, reflecting the changes that have taken place in society, yet hierarchies have continued to exist. Many philosophers have sought to understand the reasons for these divisions, and some have advanced theories as to how the differences between them could be eliminated. Even in countries where revolutions have occurred and ideals such as those of the French Revolution—Liberty, Equality and Fraternity—have provided the inspiration for change, eventually some new hierarchy has asserted itself.

Stratification provides sociologists with a convenient means of distinguishing between different groups, and even of distinguishing divisions within groups themselves; yet too often the terms of stratification appear rather loose and care must be taken in their definition.

4.1 Estate

Estate systems existed in Europe from late Roman times even into the last century in some countries. The hierarchy in medieval England consisted of:

Royalty	Free tenants	Cottars
Nobility	Villeins	Serfs
Lesser gentry		

Essentially the system was based upon the ownership of land, and in the higher ranks, upon the numbers of fighting men that could be provided in times of war. Since power rests ultimately upon military force, those who possessed arms and controlled numbers of fighting men were unwilling to allow their authority to be weakened by any change in the system. The Church reinforced this rigid hierarchy: the medieval Church too had its upper and lower ranks, which ranged from powerful archbishops to poor village priests, and it regarded with suspicion any ideas which might appear to threaten its own position in the social order. Anyone who challenged the feudal order or the teachings of the Church might be regarded as a heretic and liable to the most extreme penalties. Thus we have two estates, the nobility and the Church. Later a third estate developed: the townspeople increased their power from about the twelfth century onwards until they were able to dominate society in the late eighteenth and nineteenth century with the coming of industrialisation. The summoning of the 'Estates General' in Paris in May 1789 was the prelude to the French Revolution, since it was the Third Estate or *bourgeoisie* who demonstrated their newfound power in the famous 'Tennis Court Oath', by demanding a National Assembly in France.

The rise of the Third Estate has been attributed to a number of factors, ranging from the Black Death to the establishment of the Protestant religion. One theory is that the Black Death, the plague that swept Europe between 1347 and 1350, killing a third or more of the population, caused the depleted agricultural population to demand higher farm wages and this in turn encouraged the land owners to turn to wool production on a larger scale in England. Land owners were no longer dependent upon subsistence farming, and merchants and townspeople grew prosperous on the new trade. Trading is linked to the growth of towns and industrialisation; Max Weber, and R. H. Tawney (in his book *Religion and the Rise of Capitalism*), maintained that industrialisation occurred in Europe because of the Protestants' freedom to lend money and indulge in commerce. The Catholic Church had forbidden the lending of money at high interest rates as the sin of usury, thereby stifling commerce, while to Protestants such as the Calvinists success in business was held to be a sign of God's favour. Whatever theory is advanced for the development of commerce, and we have given just two examples from many, it is a fact that the growth of towns and cities meant that power passed from the landowning aristocracy to the merchant classes in the eighteenth and nineteenth centuries.

Karl Marx was one of the first to analyse class differences

4.2   Social class

Of all the different terms of stratification the word class is perhaps the most confusing and even social scientists interpret the term differently. If we talk about the working class or middle class, certain images come to mind, yet we may all have different conceptions of class. Karl Marx was one of the first writers to analyse class differences, in the middle of the

last century. He saw class as being a phenomenon of any society where ownership of wealth and the means of production, factories or land, gave an economic basis for stratification.

In *The Communist Manifesto* (1847), written in collaboration with Friedrich Engels, Marx outlined different stages in history in which the ownership of property gave one group control over others. From ancient society based on slavery to feudal society resting upon the labour of villeins and serfs, the group which controlled and owned the means of producing food and goods was the dominant class. Marx argued that there was a constant struggle, a class struggle, and this conflict between the different classes brought about changes in society. He believed that in the nineteenth century the bourgeoisie, who owned and controlled the means of production in the capitalist system, dominated the wage-earners or *proletariat*. Everything, Marx said, depended upon the ownership of capital (wealth)—it shaped religion, government, and even the family. The class struggle between the proletariat and bourgeoisie would eventually end in a victory for the working class if they were to unite and overthrow the owners of capital. Of course, many of Marx's observations were based upon the appalling conditions that were the results of industrialisation in the nineteenth century where little was done to alleviate the distress of the poor. Nevertheless, he made the essential point that class was primarily based upon economic circumstances.

Separated from Marx by half a century, Max Weber (1864–1920) had seen a further development of capitalist society. Instead of the small middle class (shopkeepers and small farmers) being drawn down into the working class as Marx had predicted, the middle classes had grown in importance and number. The main reasons for this were the development of education and literacy, and the increase in working-class participation in government and politics through an extension of the franchise (see Chapter 7). This new middle class, consisting of such people as clerks and skilled workers, had no wish to overthrow the existing social system. For their part, the working classes were organising themselves into trade unions and gaining increased benefits from raised standards of living.

Both Marx and Weber saw class as being related to the economic conditions of an industrialised society. If we were asked what it was that constituted class, we would usually reply that it was income, or education, or the kind of job that someone has. Usually sociologists base definitions of class upon occupation, because the kind of occupation that someone has is to some extent dependent upon their education and it will give us an idea of the income that they have. Obviously class cannot be based upon income alone. Would an unskilled labourer who won thousands of pounds on the football pools automatically join the middle classes? Is a newly qualified teacher, who earns less than a docker, a member of the working class? The type of occupation that someone has would seem to be the best guide to the classification of classes. This use of occupation to give a rough guide to class is found in newspaper reports, for example 'Mr Bloggs a thirty-two year old bank clerk', and in court, where together with an accused person's full name, age and address, their occupation is also requested.

The Registrar General, who is in charge of the government's statistical department, divides the population into five classes based upon occupation (see Table 2.1).

		1961
Class 1	capitalists, managers, scientists, professionals, etc.	4%
Class 2	small shopkeepers, lower professionals, farmers, etc.	15%
Class 3	skilled workers, clerical workers, etc.	51%
Class 4	semi-skilled workers	21%
Class 5	unskilled manual workers	9%

Table 2.1   The five-point occupational scale

The Registrar General's five-point scale was originally drawn up in 1911, since when many changes have taken place in the kinds of occupations that people have (*occupational structure*) with the result that the scale has become somewhat vague and rather limited in its scope. In 1950 John Hall and D. Caradog Jones developed a seven-point scale also based upon occupations (Table 2.2). Many sociologists recognise that the Hall–Jones scale has its limitations, for example some believe that it is too biased in favour of *white-collar* (non-manual) workers, yet compared with the Registrar General's scale which placed graduate teachers in Class 2 and non-graduate teachers in Class 3 it is more sophisticated. Usually sociologists use adaptations of the Hall–Jones scale in their work.

Class 1	professional and high administrative
Class 2	managerial and executive
Class 3	inspectional, supervisory and other non-manual, higher grade
Class 4	inspectional, supervisory and other non-manual, lower grade
Class 5	skilled manual and routine grades of non-manual
Class 6	semi-skilled manual
Class 7	unskilled manual

Table 2.2   The Hall-Jones Scale

So far we have talked of the working class and the middle class, and said that the upper class has merged with the middle class during this century. Many people still presume that there is an upper class, but although they were recognisable as landed gentry in the eighteenth and nineteenth centuries, they are not recognised as such today by most sociologists (unless we mean the three or four thousand members of the aristocracy who constitute less than a ten-thousandth part of the population, which is far too few to constitute a distinct social class). On the continent a fourth class is made up of the peasantry, who are small farmers of their own land, which usually does not exceed forty acres. Because of the enclosure of the land in Britain which began in Elizabethan times and reached a peak during the industrial revolution, a peasant class is not found in Britain today—with possible exceptions in the highland areas of Scotland and Wales. In Britain only three per cent of the population is engaged in farming, but in France almost a third of the population is connected in some way with agriculture; the peasant class is thus of importance to Continental sociologists.

4.3   Caste

The Indian caste system has interested sociologists for many years. Some 3500 years ago invaders from the north, known as *Aryans* imposed the caste system; there is no conclusive evidence that they originated the idea of caste in India, but it seems to be the most likely explanation. The Hindu religion divides the population into five basic groups. The four highest groups are known as *Varnas* (colours) and beneath them come a group without caste, the *Untouchables*. The four Varnas consist of:

1   *Brahmans*   a priest caste
2   *Kshatriyas*   a military caste
3   *Vaishyas*   a merchant or agricultural caste
4   *Sudras*   a labouring caste.

Within these groups there are thousands of subdivisions; among the *Brahmans* there are more than 500 subdivisions and there are over 200 divisions of people without caste. Caste affects the whole way of Indian life despite laws against discrimination such as the Indian Constitution's law of 1950 which officially abolished 'untouchability'. To a large extent skin colour differentiated caste (the lighter the colouring the higher the caste) but the occupational structure of India does not truly reflect caste —for example not all *Kshatriyas* are soldiers, and many *Sudras* have made money in business. Even so, caste is still important in Indian society and attitudes have changed little since India's independence in 1947.

It is clear that any understanding of caste must be accompanied by a knowledge of Hinduism. The doctrine of *karma* maintains that anyone who behaves well on earth will enter a higher caste after rebirth, in other words Hindus believe in reincarnation, and it is this that keeps people within their alloted caste without too much resentment. In recent times, nevertheless, many untouchables have turned to Bhuddism (which does not recognise caste differences and is a separate religion) as a means of obtaining self-respect. There are strict laws on what food may be eaten by Hindus; one authority (J. H. Hutton, *Caste in India: Its Nature, Function and Origins*, Oxford University Press, 1963) considers that these rules on food maintain the system more than anything else. Marriage is not permitted between different castes, so membership of one caste is hereditary and permanent. The religious restrictions (known as *taboos*) ensure that very little contact occurs on a social level between castes. The caste system is, as a consequence, very rigid and unlikely to change. As we have seen with the estate system in Europe, change occurs with commercialisation and industrialisation. India is still largely a rural society, and this has helped to maintain the caste system. The vast geographical distances of India have also meant that there are considerable regional differences in the position of various castes—some have prospered despite a low caste, usually through the purchase of land after success in commerce, while others have remained poor in isolated villages. Professor F. G. Bailey (*Tribe, Caste and Nation*, Manchester University Press, 1960) believes that the caste system has profoundly altered since India's independence, but the roots of the system based upon tradition and ritual are still strong.

Unit 5 Social Mobility

As we have seen, estate and caste systems are rather rigid, making it difficult for anyone to get out of the position in society into which he is born. In the early development of industrialisation during the nineteenth century, people were no longer tied to the land and were free to seek jobs in the towns, but the harsh conditions of employment with low wages and slum conditions (Marx referred to the industrial proletariat as 'wage slaves') did not really entail much more freedom for most of the population. By the end of the century, however, conditions were improving and new kinds of jobs were created. Increasing educational opportunities and some political power did allow certain groups to better themselves: to give just one example, the founding of the Amalgamated Society of Engineers in 1851 marked the beginning of a new craftsman's union whose members' services were clearly needed by the manufacturing employers, and so engineers were able to improve their economic and social position. The growth of the new middle classes at the end of the century came only from the newly-educated working class. Improved economic status meant an improved social status; the possibility of changing position in the hierarchy is termed *social mobility*. When someone improves his or her position in society, this is known as *upward mobility*. A much rarer occurrence is when someone falls to a lower position in the social hierarchy and this is termed *downward mobility*. Sociologists usually measure social mobility by comparing occupations over a generation: if the son of an unskilled labourer becomes the director of a merchant bank then upward mobility has taken place (such a rise would indeed be rare).

5.1   Factors affecting social mobility

The case of the engineers in the nineteenth century is an example of one of the causes of mobility: the development of a new kind of skill or type of job, especially when the numbers of people who have that particular skill are limited, means that upward mobility can take place because of a change in occupational structure. Another, more recent, change in the occupational structure has been the development of electronics and technology. Computer programmers are an example of a new occupation which has grown out of a change in the occupational structure. Generally the advance of technology and economic growth mean the creation of more jobs higher up the social scale: instead of the muscle power of six unskilled labourers digging a trench, one skilled machine operator driving an excavator can do the job, and do it more efficiently. Economic growth has meant that there are more people in middle-class occupations year by year.

Education too is an important factor in upward mobility, because the better an education one has, and the higher the qualifications that are gained, the more likely it will be that an occupation higher up the social scale can be obtained. A labourer's son who gets a university place is not likely to become a labourer himself. Education is a fairly clear means to upward mobility.

In Britain there are regional differences in the kinds of jobs open to school-leavers. In a remote valley where coal is mined, employment available to the school-leaver who is not prepared, or is even unable, to move, may be restricted to mining. In a small town where there are a few little factories the choice is also very restricted.

Motivation is an important factor affecting mobility. There may be restrictions of an economic kind on the type of job open to someone, but if there is a motivation or determination strong enough either to move somewhere where the opportunities for advancement are greater, or to go on to further study and gain higher qualifications, then upward mobility may be achieved.

The number of children in a family will also play its part in social mobility. Over a generation the larger families of manual workers may mean that some of the children of the manual worker will enter occupations of a non-manual kind through the changes that occur in the occupational structure.

Factors which affect social mobility are:

1 occupational structure
2 education
3 distribution of opportunity
4 motivation
5 family size.

One of the difficulties of calculating social mobility, when measured over a generation, is to establish a constant point on the social scale: what was regarded as low social status thirty years ago may be more highly regarded today, or the reverse may have happened. During the years between the wars a secure clerical job held high status at a time of high unemployment. Are such jobs so well regarded today? At what point on the scale do we place, or how much prestige are we to attach to, new types of job that have been created over a generation? The variables, such as income, education, or life styles, that constitute class make it difficult to establish the relevant point on the ever-moving social scale or *index of occupation*. The social mobility between father and son, termed *inter-generational mobility*, is dependent upon the numbers of occupations of one kind within the population. If the number of bricklayers, in proportion to the total population, were to remain constant over a generation, and a bricklayer's son became a solicitor, then (given that the number of solicitors in relation to the total population had also remained constant) we would have an example of *perfect mobility*. Such conditions of constant occupational structure are few. If we take a point on a scale today and contrast the different positions of, say, father and son we can only make general comparisons from it, yet these can be interesting, as Table 2.3 reveals.

Father's occupation	Professional and high administrative	Managerial and executive	Higher inspectional and supervisory	Lower inspectional and supervisory	Skilled	Semi-skilled	Unskilled
	1 %	2 %	3 %	4 %	5 %	6 %	7 %
Prof and high admin	38.8	14.6	20.2	6.2	14.0	4.7	1.5
Managerial and executive	10.7	26.7	22.7	12.0	20.6	5.3	2.0
Higher insp and supervisory	3.5	10.1	18.8	19.1	35.7	6.7	6.1
Lower insp and supervisory	2.1	3.9	11.2	21.2	43.0	12.4	6.2
Skilled manual	0.9	2.4	7.5	12.3	47.3	17.1	12.5
Semi-skilled manual	0.0	1.3	4.1	8.8	39.1	31.2	15.5
Unskilled manual	0.0	0.8	3.6	8.3	36.3	23.5	27.4

Table 2.3 Sons' occupations in relation to fathers' occupations (men aged 21 and over, England and Wales—sons' present occupation)

Source: *Social Mobility in Britain*, ed. D. V. Glass, Routledge & Kegan Paul, 1963.

International comparison of social mobility would provide an even more complex task.

5.2 Self-assigned class

Marx considered that when the working-class fully understood their position in society, that is to say the way in which they were exploited by the factory owners or landowners, they would rise in a revolution; this awareness he called *class-consciousness*. More than a century ago there were clear divisions in society between the worker and wealthy capitalist, but today the divisions of class may not be so readily apparent. We may have many different views about what is meant by class and the extent to which divisions exist. Some people maintain that we are moving towards a *classless society*, whilst others feel that there are still marked class differences. Some of the criteria that sociologists use to define class are:

occupation, education, income, power, prestige, life style, speech patterns, and possibly appearance; yet attitudes towards class are also of importance. Some of the differences between working-class and middle-class groups are revealed in their overall view of society known as *social perspectives*.

What are the different social perspectives?

The middle class tend to regard society as a kind of ladder where it is possible to move up the hierarchy rung by rung (see Figure 2.1). Through such things as ability, initiative or hard work it is possible to 'get on', even though this may mean sacrifices at some stage of an individual's life. This perspective is one of *individualism*. A working-class perspective is to

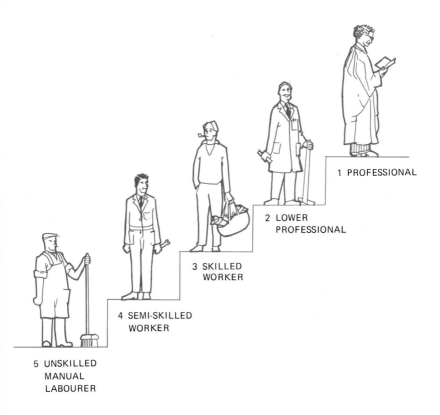

Figure 2 1   Registrar General's five-point scale of occupational structure

divide society up into *us* and *them* (the latter may refer to governments, landlords, bosses or virtually any official who has some kind of authority). The division is more or less permanent, unless one is lucky, so for the most part you must put up with your lot and try to make the best of things as they are now rather than worrying too much about the future. This perspective is termed *collectivist* as it is a view of society as being the two groups *us* and *them*.

Sociologists are interested in the way in which people regard their own position in society, and the position of others. When asked about class most people would say that there are three classes in society, an upper class, a middle class, and a working class. We have already said that there is no such thing as an upper class in sociological terms because class involves so many factors and it is impossible to differentiate between the upper and middle classes (using whichever scale we choose) in many of the factors other than occupation that constitute class. We shall, however, see that there are many differences between the broad classifications of working class and middle class. No social survey these days will include the category upper class. If asked which class they belonged to themselves, a large number of people would place themselves in a category higher than that assigned to them by the Registrar General, or indeed any other sociologist's scale. A survey by F. M. Martin in Greenwich and Hertford in the 1950s found that a quarter of the manual (working class) respondents thought of themselves as being middle-class (*Social Mobility in Britain*, ed. D. V. Glass, Routledge & Kegan Paul, 1954). In a later survey (1961) Mark Abrams and R. Rose found that the percentage of working-class people who thought of themselves as being middle-class was even higher. Although their book *Must Labour Lose?* was mainly concerned with political attitudes, these figures confirm the tendency to think of oneself as being in a higher social class than one really is.

It is clear from this kind of survey that most people recognise that there are class differences. In order to make themselves seem more important, perhaps for reasons of snobbery, a fair percentage will place themselves on a scale higher than their true position.

The value that is placed upon the different jobs held by people is related to an overall view of society. It is surprising perhaps that there is often a considerable agreement when people are asked to rank types of employment in order of importance. In 1956 Michael Young and Peter Willmott gave a list of thirty occupations (graded by the Hall-Jones scale) to a number of East End of London manual workers (remembering that the Hall-Jones scale is biased in favour of middle-class occupations). The East Enders were asked to grade the occupations according to their

	Labour voters %	Other voters %
Upper middle class	0	3
Middle class	14	31
Lower middle class	16	16
Total who thought themselves to be middle-class	30	50
Skilled working class	27	28
Labouring working class	40	18
Total who thought themselves to be working-class	67	46
Don't know	3	4
	100	100

Table 2.4 Self-assigned class of manual workers
(Source: Abrams and Rose, *Must Labour Lose?*)

ideas of importance; what emerged was a high degree of similarity between Hall-Jones's ranking and the East Enders' ranking at the top and to some extent the bottom ends of the list. In the middle and towards the lower end of the list the East Enders gave more importance to skilled manual occupations and less importance to the less skilled non-manual jobs. The criteria upon which the East Enders based their choices included ability, education, income, social standing, and how much the occupation contributed towards the good of society. A small group of the sample were found to have very different views from their fellow respondents; these tended to place more emphasis on the social contribution of the occupation, ie the benefit to society of the occupation. Doctors of medicine always head the list when the criterion of benefit to society is applied, though this is not really surprising as similar surveys conducted in other countries have also found that doctors invariably headed the list.

Unit 6 Social Structure and Social Change

In Chapter 1 it was noted briefly that there is interaction between individuals and between groups in the form of social relationships. The network or patterns of these social relationships create a social structure;

as the relationships change, the structures of society change. Here is one example which may help in understanding this idea: 150 years ago a workman was economically weak, others were ready to do his job for the same low wages, conditions of employment were poor, and the workman was humble before his employer and would address him in a subservient manner; workmen are in a stronger economic position today, particularly when labour is scarce, and this being the case the employer will address the workman with some respect; a change in the social relationship between employer and employee has taken place.

Patterns of social behaviour (usually in groups) = social structure

Most of this book is an examination of different aspects of behaviour: behaviour in the family, behaviour in the educational system, behaviour of people who act differently from most others, and so forth. Taken as a whole this builds up a picture of the social structure of contemporary Britain. We cannot freeze society at a given moment in time in our examination of society today, but we can examine the general trends, as well as the changes that have already taken place, against a background of life in contemporary Britain.

6.1   The social structure of Britain

It would be wrong to assume that sociology consists of a series of separate studies of aspects of society such as the family, the educational system or the economic system. The way in which we are brought up in the family, the way in which we learn at school, the way in which people behave towards us at work are all part of a process of experience that affects our attitudes and makes us what we are as individuals. However, we are not examining individuals, but society as a whole. If we study how the family is related to the educational system, how the educational system is related to the economic system, etc., we shall see the structure of our social system. Attitudes are important because different attitudes produce different forms of behaviour; and the most basic difference of attitude found in society as a whole is that which exists between different classes. There are a host of other differences, differences by age, sex, religion, race, and many more, but for simplicity most sociologists use class differences as a starting point since they underlie many of the major differences in society.

How do class differences affect the social structure?

The constant changing or *dynamism* of society means that sociologists need frequently to change their theories in the light of fresh evidence of social change. One theory is that class differences are disappearing in Britain as the better-off members of the working class are beginning to adopt middle-class life styles and values. This is known as the process of *embourgeoisement*, and is the view of F. Zweig founded upon his study of highly paid workers in four industries (*The Worker in an Affluent Society*, Heinemann Educational Books, 1961). Some of the middle-class patterns adopted took the form of a change in family relationships and the purchase of material possessions formerly enjoyed only by the middle classes. An opposite view is taken by J. H. Goldthorpe and others in their book *The Affluent Worker in the Class Structure* (Cambridge University Press, 1969). Deliberately looking for evidence of embourgeoisement, they did find a resemblance in life styles to those of the middle class among some of the better-off working class, but in the important question of attitudes and values fundamental differences still existed between the classes. The former working-class *us* and *them* perspective had been replaced by the view that social status (standing) depended upon income and spending habits.

Class, although not entirely resting upon economic circumstances, is, as we have seen, tied largely to the economic factor of occupation. Certainly the number of manual occupations decreases in Britain year by year and changes in the occupational structure contribute towards upward mobility. Economic change certainly causes social change, but the important element of *behaviour* is largely shaped by the attitudes and values found in the family, amongst friends, and the experience of school and work. It is here that the working class and middle class divide in their experience of life, and these divisions remain through life.

6.2 How class affects our lives

Quite naturally we associate a person's life style with his class. A manual labourer from the East End of London will have a different way of life from a stockbroker living in a Sussex village. We would expect different patterns of behaviour from a vicar's wife and a trawlerman's wife. Although we are conscious of some of the differences of class, it may be difficult to pinpoint exactly what makes those subtle differences. Before we hear someone speak we may try to sum people up by their age and the clothes they are wearing; hearing them speak may provide a pointer towards their social class because of accent and choice of words. If they tell us their occupation we have an even clearer picture of their social class. Why should these things be meaningful, and of how much importance is class in our lives?

We shall see later how the upbringing of a child and the kind of education received, together with the experience of work, more or less condition us in advance to our place in society. If the embourgeoisement thesis is carried to its logical conclusion class differences will become so minimal that eventually we shall be living in a classless society. Unfortunately conditions such as family environment, schooling and occupation that create and reinforce social class differences are still strong, and although there are many changes in class behaviour, there are equally powerful forces which maintain a division between the working class and the middle class.

Members of the working class enjoy a greater material prosperity than ever before, but the middle classes have enjoyed increased benefits too. The Welfare State was instituted during and immediately after World War II to create equality of opportunity in education for all, and to provide security for the aged, sick and unemployed (see Chapter 8). Professor R. M. Titmuss in his *Essays on the Welfare State* (Allen & Unwin, 1963) argues that in reality the middle classes have gained far more from the provisions of the Welfare State than have the working class. Several examples may provide some illustration:

1   The cost of education beyond the school-leaving age is high, but this is a privilege enjoyed proportionately far more by the middle class than the working class.

2   House purchase provides income tax relief greater than any subsidies received by rent-paying tenants of council or private accommodation. A house will rise in value and, with inflation, the mortgage repayments become less in real terms. A far greater percentage of the middle class than the working class purchase their own house, and find it easier to obtain mortgages.

3   Because the middle class are more familiar with their rights and speak with greater authority to such people as doctors or officials they are likely to receive more considerate treatment.

4   Credit and more favourable repayment terms are more likely to be made available to people in middle-class occupations which are considered secure and carry pensions.

Problems of homelessness and poverty are still found in Britain and, with rare exceptions, these are working-class problems. If we lived in a classless society with full equality of opportunity for all in education, adequate sickness and unemployment benefits and pensions not geared

People in middle-class occupations enjoy better credit facilities from banks

to previous earnings, we might be nearer the ideals of the creators of the Welfare State. Unfortunately the machinery that provides the benefits cannot help being biased towards the middle class, while the working class are often unaware of some of the benefits that they might enjoy through such things as further education and investment for the future.

Unit 7 Status and Power

7.1 Status

We have already come across the word 'status' when considering the ranking given to various occupations. Status may be defined as the social honour or prestige that is given to certain positions in society. It is the position occupied by a person or group relative to others in the same social system. To begin with, this position is determined by the family circumstances into which a child is born, the kind of education received and the occupation that is followed. The hierarchy that seems inevitably to be found in almost all societies means that there will be different status groups. Through life it is possible to change one's status by achievement comparable to others—in the case of occupational status either through upward or downward mobility. The status held by an individual or group will determine their rights, duties and behaviour towards others.

What is the difference between class and status?

Max Weber, in his book *Class, Status and Power*, distinguished between class and status in advanced industrial societies. Weber was interested in the way in which the new middle classes had gained so much political power; he felt that this was not only due to their class position. The prestige and success of the middle classes he considered due to their status in society. Social classes were stratified by Marx according to their relationship with the means of production (as wage-earning employees or as a professional class) and their wealth. Status groups were stratified by Weber according to such things as education, occupation and what he termed 'styles of life', making finer distinctions between groups than Marx's economic definition. Changes in status are more rapid than changes in class over any given period of time, for example the status accorded to a First Division professional footballer or to a pop star is greater now than it was twenty years ago, but there has been little fundamental change in class over the same period. Not so long ago air hostesses were accorded considerable status, but today the job does not seem as glamorous as it did, being regarded by some people as simply that of a flying waitress.

Because status provides more subtle gradings than class differences sociologists these days have tended to look more towards status differences in their analysis of society. This means that less importance is given to economic interests and emphasis is given to the status or prestige which various groups enjoy within the community. Such studies occur at times when there is least class conflict, but when strikes and economic crises occur (to give but two examples) attention is directed towards power.

7.2 Power

In the last century the problems of social class could be clearly associated with political power, but when the threat of revolution subsided as the working class gained the vote (if not political power) attention was turned towards the problems of democracy. In recent times the action of some trade unionists is seen as a challenge to our democratic system, and the question is raised whether the Government should govern or give way to the demands of powerful trade unionists who hold key jobs in the economic system.

In Britain our political parties obtain their unity through their representation of class interests. In other countries religious groupings may provide the basis of political parties. Identification with a status group, rather than identification with a class interest, may cause some to support a particular party.

In the last resort all power rests on force, but because more than ninety-nine per cent of the population recognise the right of the Government to govern by passing laws, the Government does not require force of arms to gain acceptance of its authority. This situation exists largely owing to the fact that people feel that they are being represented in Parliament, or that they are able to change the Government in a peaceful way at election times. There are some theories of power, such as those of Vilfredo Pareto (1848–1923) or Gaetano Mosca (1848–1941) who maintain that the small group at the top of the social hierarchy, the élite, are always in real control of society, no matter which political party may run the Government. Other theorists, such as C. Wright Mills in his book *The Power Elite* (Oxford University Press, 1956), consider that power circulates between different status groups, one being at the top for a while and eventually being replaced by another. A third theory, as advanced by James Burnham in *The Managerial Revolution*, is that society is moving towards a situation where political control is moving out of the hands of the traditional top status groups and passing to a new class of managers and experts who may not own the enterprises in which they work but are vital to the direction of big business and the economy and therefore in reality have overall political control (see Topic 29.2).

Most of the chapters which follow this one are at least in part an examination of the ways in which class and status affect society.

Terms used in this chapter

hierarchy	dynamism	embourgeoisement
manual worker	social perspective	styles of life
varna	classification	
social mobility	ranking	

Questions

1   In Disraeli's *The Two Nations* Egremont said, 'I was told that an impassable gulf divided the Rich from the Poor'. What almost impassable gulfs still exist between those in social class 1 and those in social class 5 of the five-point occupational scale?

2   D. Lockwood (*The Blackcoated Worker*, Allen and Unwin, 1958) showed that although a clerk is regarded by sociologists as proletarian in terms of social class, he tends to identify himself with the middle class. Give reasons for this attitude.

3   What measures are used by a small group of high-class white people in Rhodesia to prevent the upward class-mobility of the Africans, although the white population is outnumbered by the Africans by twenty to one?

4   J.F. 'Coming in on Saturday?'
    A.S. 'No. Five days is enough for anybody.'
    J.F. 'Oh, so you're not bothered about getting some extra coal out for the country?'
    A.S. 'I suppose that's why you come in on Saturdays?'
    J.S. 'Is it . . .! We come in for some extra brass and that's that.'
(Source: Dennis, Henriques and Slaughter, *Coal is our Life*)
Why is it that working-class men may have sound reasons for being apparently less patriotic than middle-class men?

5   Look up the consideration that led to sixteen socio-economic groups being identified in the 1961 Census. See D. C. Marsh's *The Changing Social Structure of England and Wales 1871–1961* (Routledge and Kegan Paul, 1965).

6   On 12 March 1973, *The Guardian* reported that the majority of British companies operating in South Africa were paying substantial numbers of workers below subsistence wages. What prevents these workers from waging a Marxist-type class war against their capitalist employers?

7   What factors do you think will prevent a classless society existing in Britain in AD 2000?

8   Find examples from your own experience of people who have undergone:
a upward social mobility
b downward social mobility.

9   What prevents the USSR from being a classless society?

10   Comment upon the following extract from a letter to *The Times* (25 August 1972): 'You can't help being born in a slum but you certainly don't have to stay in one and that is what the British way of life is all about.'

Questions from GCE 'O' Level Sociology Examination Papers

1 Distinguish between middle and working class, and discuss the major differences between the two. (Oxford Local Examinations, Summer 1970)

2 What do you understand by 'the working class'? How is it changing? (Oxford Local Examinations, Summer 1971)

3 'When people's behaviour takes account of the existence of others, and is affected by expectations about others, we call it social.' Give three examples of different kinds of social behaviour and describe the roles and norms associated with each of your examples. (AEB, November 1972)

4 In what ways has the economic and social situation of the middle class changed since 1945? (Oxford Local Examinations, 1974)

5 What do sociologists mean by 'social mobility'? What are the problems involved in measuring social mobility? (Oxford Local Examinations, 1974)

6 Discuss the suggestion that Britain has become a 'classless' society. (Oxford Local Examinations, 1975)

7 What are the arguments surrounding the suggestion that we are all becoming 'middle class'? (AEB, November 1974)

8 The coalminer and the assembly-line worker might both be described as 'working class'. Explain the differences in life style, general values and behaviour which exist between them despite the fact that they are members of the same 'social class'. (AEB, November 1974)

3 The Family
Unit 8 The Family in Society

There are three people in the photograph: a woman, a man and an infant. We usually describe people grouped together in this way as a *family*. Most of us have had some experience of being a member of a family group in the course of our lives. For example, we may have grown up in a group which included people we called *father*, *mother*, *brother* and *sister*. These are all terms which are primarily confined to people who are part of a family group. Also, books, magazines, films and television programmes

A modern family

have shown us the lives of other family groups, real or imaginary, so that we have all formed ideas about the family. However, we must remember that sociologists are interested in the general characteristics of human behaviour rather than the lives of individual human beings. Personal experience is a good place to start from, but it cannot give us the whole picture. In looking at the family, it is useful to draw on personal experiences when, for example, these can shed light on the more widespread patterns of human behaviour, but on the whole we shall be concentrating on the most general characteristics of the family in society.

In its widest sense 'family' refers to a group of people who think of themselves as belonging to a separate group in society and who are related to one another by ties of either blood or marriage. This group is also recognised by other members of society who see these individuals as tied to one another by certain relationships.

8.1 Type of families

The terms, father, mother, brother, sister, refer to certain positions in the family group. These positions are made obvious by the way the people who occupy them behave. For example, a mother looks after her baby, and a husband and wife show affection towards one another. These positions are called *social roles* by the sociologist and are the patterns of behaviour which we expect from a person occupying a particular social position. The sexual and social roles of husband and wife are often described as *conjugal roles*. The family takes many forms in society, the most fundamental of which is the *nuclear family* (sometimes also called the *conjugal family*).

The Nuclear Family

For a group to be called a nuclear family there must at some time be a father, mother and at least one child. The family in the photograph at the beginning of the chapter is an example of a nuclear family. This type of family structure is found in almost all societies, although the length of time in which the family remains in this form varies even within the same society. The physical fact of a man and a woman producing (or adopting) a child lies at the heart of this pattern of family structure.

When the nuclear family is viewed from the point of view of the children's position in the group, then it is called the *family of origin*. By contrast, when the children grow up and have children of their own they will be looking at the family group from the social status of parents.

Looked at from this point of view, the nuclear family is called the *family of procreation.*

Statuses and roles together make up the organisation of the family, and this is called its *structure.* There is a way of showing the structure of a family group by using symbols. In Figure 3.1 the symbol △ is used to denote a male, the symbol O to denote a female and = to denote their sexual union. How would you describe the social structure of this family group?

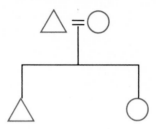

Figure 3.1 . An example of a nuclear family

This family group has one father, one mother, and two children. Each child has either a brother or a sister. Brothers and sisters are called *siblings* so we can say that each child has one sibling. We can describe the pattern of the social structure of the family by using diagrams and by referring to the statuses and roles within it, but it is important to remember that the family is not really a concrete object in society that is always the same; it is part of society and is influenced by changes in that society. At any time a single family will be changing if only because the people who occupy the positions of father, mother, and children will be growing older and the children will soon start to fill positions of father and mother in a new family which they have made for themselves. Families therefore have *life-cycles.*

The Extended Family

The *extended family* (sometimes also called the *consanguine family*) is a common family structure and includes within it the nuclear family pattern. It has been suggested by C. Rosser and C. Harris in *The Family and Social Change* (Routledge and Kegan Paul, 1965) that the extended family is 'any persistent kinship-grouping of persons related by descent, marriage or adoption, which is wider than the (nuclear) family, in that it characteristically spans three generations from grandparents to grandchildren'. All the members of the group do not need to live under one roof for a family group to be an extended family. The structure of one such extended family is shown in Figure 3.2. Where are the nuclear families in the diagram? The extended family may be *patrilineal* or *matrilineal*. A

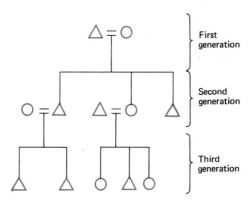

Figure 3.2   An example of an extended family

patrilineal extended family reckons descent through the male line, a matrilineal extended family reckons descent through the female line. Figure 3.3 illustrates the social structure of an example of a patrilineal extended family.

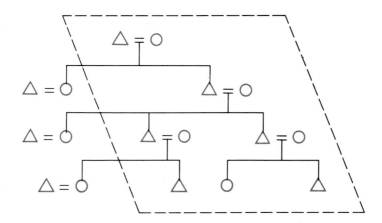

Figure 3.3   A patrilineal extended family: broken lines indicate the boundaries of this patrilineal extended family

8.2   What are the social functions of the family?

A child born into society must be fed and looked after. In many societies, the parents of the child are responsible for his welfare and, in this way, perform a function for society in general by looking after the next generation and ensuring that it will survive. As the child grows up, surrounded by brothers and sisters, his parents and, sometimes, by members of the extended family group, he will gradually learn things about the society in which he lives. For example, he will learn its language, its ideas about right and wrong, its ideas about what is funny and what is serious and so forth. In other words, the child will learn the *culture* of his society through his contact with, at first, the members of his family. The sociologist calls the way in which an individual acquires the culture of his society *socialisation*. Socialisation is not confined to interaction between parents and their children, nor does it finish in childhood but goes on through life. At the present time, research by social scientists indicates that the early years of socialisation are important in the development of the individual because they have enduring effects on his ideas and attitudes.

The behaviour that is considered naturally masculine or feminine is, in large part, the product of the culture of the society. Through socialisation, the individual learns the appropriate *sex roles* of society. For example, in our society, we consider anything involving hard manual work to be man's work. However, it is not unusual in African societies, such as the Arusha, for women to toil in the fields and carry the heavy loads. Children explore the roles they will play as father or mother in adult life in their games and, in our society, when parents give children toys, girls are usually given dolls and boys motor-cars, and these have the effect of preserving the traditional differences in the sex roles. At the present time, many people are concerned about the way in which our culture limits the choice of behaviour open to the sexes. The general movement which has come to be called Women's Liberation (Women's Lib) reflects the concern for women to have opportunities and recognition on an equal footing with men.

In some societies, where there are no modern industrial methods of factory production, the extended family is the most important unit in society. As a member of the extended family an individual is able to eat, have somewhere to sleep, and also is able to count on someone looking after him if he is ill. In such traditional societies, the extended family is the unit around which all other activities are built. For example, the Masai are a people who live in the areas that we know as the countries of Kenya and Tanzania. Their main activity is looking after their herds of cattle, sheep and goats which supply them with a staple diet of meat, milk and blood. Each extended family has its own herd, and men, women and children all have separate parts to play in looking after and tending these animals. The children of the Masai are socialised into the Masai language which has words for every tiny aspect of the condition of the cattle. In contrast, children growing up in our culture are socialised into a language which does not have the same vocabulary in defining the condition of cattle.

In such a traditional society a person's work and responsibilities are decided not by passing examinations, as in our own society, but by factors such as his age and whether or not he is married. The traditional society is therefore based on *ascribed* rather than *achieved* status. For example, in Masai society, a man who is becoming old will go through a ceremony which establishes him as an old man in society. After the ceremony, his role has changed and he will not join in cattle-raiding expeditions with the younger men.

8.3 Can we do without the family?

Although the family performs numerous functions in society, this does not necessarily mean that there is no possibility of anything else taking its place. There have been many planned experiments which have tried to find other ways by which, for example, children can be brought up in society. Examples of experiments in communal living, where children are the concern of the society as a whole, are groups such as the Israeli kibbutzim and the communes of the People's Republic of China. However it would be misleading to think of these experiments as providing complete alternatives to the family in society. For example, the allocation of social functions, such as child-rearing, to other groups does not mean that the family has no significance in society, rather that it is freed from that particular activity in the context of the different demands of a communal society.

The Israeli kibbutz has been watched with interest by many societies. In the early kibbutzim, infants were taken to Children's Houses after only a short time with their parents. The physical separation from their family continued into adult life, the children growing up together and being looked after by specially trained nurses (called *metapelets*) and teachers, only being at their parents' home or seeing their parents for a few hours each day. Women therefore were free to take on any work on the same terms as men. Today, these patterns are changing and the separation between parents and children is less complete; in many kibbutzim, children return to spend the night at their parents' flat, and women are involved in the traditionally feminine types of work such as working in the communal kitchen or laundry.

In the communes of the People's Republic of China, the family is supported in its social role by the presence of communal services, such as free crèches, nurseries and canteens. The provision of these services in the commune releases members of the family for participation in the work of the commune.

8.4 Marriage

A wedding is a ceremony at which a marriage is recognised. What, then, is marriage? Again, we are looking at patterns of relationships between people. The wedding service is an official way in which new relationships between a man and a woman, as husband and wife, are recognised by the couple themselves and established in the eyes of the society to which they belong.

Marriage does not necessarily always take place between one man and one woman (see Figure 3.4). For example, the Masai practise a form of

Type	Description		Examples
MONOGAMY	One man + One woman	Husband + Wife	Great Britain; Europe; U. S. A; most 'western' societies.
POLYGYNY	One man + Several wives (simultaneously)	Husband + Wives	The Masai of East Africa; Moslem societies e.g. Egypt allow a man four wives
POLYANDRY	One woman + Several husbands This is less usual than POLYGYNY	Wife + Husbands	The Sinhalese of Ceylon
POLYGAMY	This is a category which embraces POLYGYNY and POLYANDRY. It is sometimes used as a general term to replace these.		As above (2 & 3)

Figure 3.4   *Forms of marriage*

polygamy, called polygyny; that is, Masai men take more than one woman as their wife. This has many social and economic advantages for the group. For example, when a man has more than one wife they may combine their herds and place them under the care of one or two of their children. Polygyny also creates a hierarchy of social statuses and roles within the family. For example, in the Masai family, the first wife always has more authority and the right to wield this over the wives who follow. Her son has all the rights of an heir, inheriting the herds and ultimately becoming the male head of the family. Tensions and conflicts do arise between the different wives, but there are strong loyalties towards female relatives in Masai families and this often helps to resolve conflicts. For example, by custom, a man is expected to please his mother, therefore the eldest son will take note first of his mother's wishes. If this gives rise to complaint amongst the other wives, their fathers and brothers will be willing to take up the complaints with the head of the family.

In our society, romantic ideas about marriage abound. It is generally thought that people fall in love and that this is the basis for their decision to marry. All this would sound very strange to many people, for instance in Afghanistan or other Moslem societies, where marriage is customarily arranged by the respective parents of the couple.

An Indian woman waits for her selected husband

The social recognition given to marriage makes it more likely that the parents of children born into society will continue to remain together while they care for their offspring. In many societies, children are an economic asset. For example, in the Masai, fathers want many children, particularly boys, as they can help in looking after the herd and later go on raids to bring back more cattle to the group. In our society, children are not so economically important to the family and many married couples decide to have only one or two children. In this way marriage has become separated from the idea of having children and the happiness of husband and wife is often looked on as being just as important as raising children.

Unit 9 The Family in Britain Today

In advertising family holidays by the sea, British Rail sometimes makes use of posters showing a mother, a father and two or three children playing in the sunshine at the seaside. Pictures like this show us how we have come to think of the family in our society as typically being the nuclear family.

9.1 The family in industrialised societies

Today families made up of two generations, parents and children, are usually found living together under one roof. The widespread presence of the nuclear family has led some sociologists to suggest that there is a 'fit' between the demands of living in industrialised society and the nuclear family. For example, in an industrialised society men are required to fill jobs as industry expands. This demand for working men, and men skilled in certain occupations, means that there must be a labour force which is prepared to move to places where the jobs arise. It is argued that a person who is a member of the nuclear family is more free to do this than a person bound by many close ties with his relatives.

In industrial societies a decline has taken place in the range of activities which are performed by the family. For example, in terms of economic functions, the members of the extended family in an industrial society, such as Britain, are not so closely dependent on one another for support as in traditional societies. In our society there are organisations outside the family group, such as the factory or the office, where we can be employed and earn money by which to support ourselves. Also, the workplace is separated from our home and it may be some distance away from where we live; we may have to travel to work each day for a regular forty hour week. We can see that, in these ways, economic functions are the concern of other, specialised groups in society. For example, a man goes to his work at the local branch of Barclays Bank, in return for which he receives a salary. He will spend this on the things he needs, such as food sold in multiple food stores such as Sainsbury's, clothes sold by such stores as Marks and Spencers, and light and heating supplied by the Electricity Board. The family today, therefore, is a unit which uses up goods in society rather than being a unit which spends its time producing goods, for the benefit of family members.

There are other ways in which the functions performed by the family in traditional societies have come to be the concern of specialised groups in modern industrialised society. For example, in Britain today, the knowledge and skills which are needed by people living in society change very quickly. No one family can ever hope to pass on to its children a wide enough variety of new knowledge and skills. There are instead schools and colleges which, to some extent, supplement the social function of the family in socialising children into the culture of society.

Most schools and colleges in Britain today are provided by the State. Government departments and local authorities are responsible also for the provision of other services such as the National Health Service, social security benefits, child allowances, pensions, low rental housing, homes for the care of old people. The services of the Welfare State then, contribute to the economic security and well-being of the members of the society. In this way, the Welfare State modifies and supports many of the social functions which, in non-industrialised societies are largely the concern of the extended family unit (see Topic 27.5).

However, particular social functions remain confined to the nuclear family in modern industrialised societies. For example, R. M. McIver and Charles Page in their book *Society* (Macmillan, 1950) suggest these essential social functions are: having children, looking after them and socialising them into the culture of the society. The reproductive function of the family is limited to sexual relations between certain adults. For example in our society it is usually held that sexual relations ought to be confined to husband and wife. In this way the children born in society are the responsibility of particular adults and are cared for by them.

9.2 The traditional working-class extended family

In some localities the extended family remains a vigorous part of the individual's experience of growing up in a family. These are traditional working-class areas which have a history of employment in difficult and strenuous manual occupations such as coal-mining, working on the docks, shipbuilding and deep-sea fishing. In these traditional working-class areas, families have lived and worked for generations, members of the extended family living close to one another, often next door or on the same street. This makes it possible for relatives to see a lot of one another, and to be at hand whenever help is needed. This pattern is called a *mutual support system* and, whether by habit or from choice, this pattern of relationships is characteristic of traditional working-class communities. The sociologist calls such areas *close-knit communities*.

'Mum' and her Married Daughter

In a traditional working-class community, a woman usually expects to keep up a close relationship with her mother after marriage. This is not difficult as 'mum' usually lives close by. Family life often centres on the close relationship which exists between 'mum' and her married daughters. Michael Young and Peter Willmott in *Family and Kinship in East London* (Routledge and Kegan Paul) found that in Bethnal Green there was a considerable degree of contact between married daughters and their mothers (see Table 3.1).

(General sample—133 married women with mothers alive and not in the same dwelling)

Residence of mother	Number of married women	Women who saw their mother in previous 24 hours
Same street or block of flats	23	23
Elsewhere in Bethnal Green	49	33
Adjacent borough	25	4
Elsewhere	36	3

Table 3.1 Contacts of women according to distance of mothers. (Source: Michael Young and Peter Willmott: *Family and Kinship in East London*, Routledge and Kegan Paul, 1957.)

Willmott and Young found that 'mum' helped her married daughter in many ways: for example she might 'speak for' a house for her daughter by explaining the daughter's position to the rent collector and asking him to reserve a house when one became available. In traditional working-class communities 'mum' is also at hand to help her daughter by looking after the children while their mother goes out to a job during the day.

Husband and Wife

In looking at the relationship between husband and wife in traditional working-class families we must remember that this relationship usually takes in the relationship between the wife and her mother. The lives of husband and wife are closely bound up with what is going on round at 'mum's place'.

The wife's role is usually thought of as being properly concerned with looking after the children and the home. The husband is the breadwinner but domestic chores or helping with the children are not seen as being appropriate to the masculine role. Leisure-time activities are also often carried on separately, husbands spending time with their workmates and women with their female relatives and friends. The separation between husband and wife often extends to the point where the wife does not know, or think it any of her business to know, how much money her husband earns. This type of conjugal role relationship is termed *segregated conjugal role*.

The way of life of younger married couples appears to be changing so that now husbands do not think it unmanly to give their wife a little help with some domestic chores. The different patterns of family life which are shown in the course of plays, advertisements or shows on television may be one of the reasons underlying these changes.

Parents and Children

Relationships between parents and children are also changing. For example, Michael Young and Peter Willmott in *Family and Kinship in East London* noticed how young fathers were spending time at the weekend playing with their children, taking them for a row on the lake in a nearby park. Aside from gradual social change, changes in personal circumstances may alter parents' roles.

Old People

The close contact between members of the extended family in traditional

A husband parted from his wife has five children to bring up

working-class communities is an important source of support for old people.

9.3   The privatised working-class family

Many recent changes in the wider social structure have affected the old, traditional, working-class communities. For example, rehousing schemes have drawn families away from close-knit communities and this has affected relationships between members of the extended family. The effects of this change on the organisation of the family is noted by Willmott and Young in their study of Bethnal Green families living on a new housing estate on the outskirts of London. The separation of the nuclear family from the extended family group encourages the family to spend more time with each other and to spend money on their home, their children and *home-centred activities*. The life of the nuclear family is more private and self-contained, carried on free of close contact with everyone else in the neighbourhood. This *privatisation* is described by Willmott and Young as a change from face-to-face relationships to window-to-window relationships.

Husband and Wife

Conjugal role relationships have also changed, husband and wife increasingly acting as partners and sharing activities to do with the home and the children. In other words, segregated conjugal roles are changing to become *joint conjugal roles*. For example, in her study of housebound mothers, Hannah Gavron (*The Captive Wife*, Routledge and Kegan Paul, 1966) notes a young working-class wife who recalls: 'My father was never at home, not so's you'd notice, while my husband, well he's at home all the time and that makes for sharing.' In this study, Hannah Gavron describes how many of the working-class mothers, at home with young children and living away from the friends and family that they had known when they were growing up in a traditional working-class area, were very miserable and looked to their husbands as the only relief which they had from isolation and loneliness. Hannah Gavron suggests that, in these circumstances, joint conjugal roles are an expression of a desire for emotional closeness on the part of working-class couples.

Parents and Children

We have seen that with privatisation, parents turn their attention to their own immediate family of procreation, spending time and money on the home and on their children.

The family structure and life-styles of the more prosperous working class today might lead us to think that this group has really now become part of the middle class. However, Peter Willmott and Michael Young, in their study in which they considered the social organisation of the East London suburb of Woodford (*Family and Class in a London Suburb*, Routledge and Kegan Paul, 1960), found that despite outward appearances: 'Inside people's minds . . . the boundaries of class are still closely drawn.' In suburban Woodford, families of middle- and working-class background remained socially separate groups in the community.

9.4   The middle-class family

The social structure of the middle-class family today is typically the nuclear family pattern. The middle-class family is generally interested in 'getting on'. This desire for upward social mobility is reflected in a willingness to move to new areas if this means a better job or promotion. This results in the nuclear family often living many miles from members of the extended family group. Middle-class residential districts are areas where there is shifting population, few people being either related to one another or knowing one another closely. This type of community is called a *loose-knit community*.

Husband and Wife

In middle-class families the geographical separation of men and women from their parents frequently begins when the individual takes some form of training or extended education at a college or a university. This separation from kinsfolk and the experience of leading independent lives affect the way in which husbands and wives get along together. In middle-class families it is often thought appropriate that husband and wife share the responsibilities of looking after the home and the children. Also the couple is likely to have mutual friends of both sexes, and leisure time is frequently spent by husband and wife together. In *The Captive Wife*, Hannah Gavron suggests that middle-class joint conjugal roles, in contrast to the privatised, working-class conjugal roles, are a way in which husband and wife show that they expect the individual to be able to carry on and enjoy a high level of independence within marriage.

Parents and Children

In middle-class families, parents tend to raise their children according to current ideas of experts about how children should be brought up. Usually, this means parents attach importance to such things as taking the children on visits to plays, concerts, exhibitions, museums and historic places, giving them books to read, arranging music lessons, and encouraging the children to express their ideas and opinions. Parents also encourage their children to spend time on school work, rather than, for example, sitting watching television. Middle-class parents, by encouraging their children to sacrifice present pleasures, often hope that their children will secure future goals and rewards such as having interesting and rewarding jobs.

The Middle-class Extended Family

In middle-class families the distance which separates parents and married children reduces the amount of personal contact possible between members of the extended family. However, most middle-class families have telephones and are able to keep in touch by frequent telephone calls. In addition to telephone calls, letters and visits by car help to keep members of the middle-class family in contact with one another.

In middle-class families parents of married children often discreetly provide financial support for the young couple particularly at times such as the birth of their first grandchild. In the interests of a career, many middle-class people postpone taking a paid job in order to take courses at colleges and universities. Young married couples therefore have a low income at the outset of their married life and financial help from parents and in-laws helps them over this period in the economic life cycle of the family.

Conclusion

Although the nuclear family is the group which is usually found living together under one roof in Britain today, the extended family still plays an important part in the way people of all social classes live. The Welfare State has helped to free the family from many of its immediate anxieties in caring for members. In these circumstances, the nuclear family is more free to develop closer emotional ties. This development is important if we consider how much anonymity an individual may experience in society today. For example, at work many people are involved in dull, repetitive activities and they can easily be replaced by someone else. At home, with his family, the individual may be able to compensate a little for the frustrations and anonymity which he experiences at work.

Unit 10 The Family and Social Change

Introduction

The family is part of society and therefore it influences, and is itself influenced by, changes in the wider social structure. The family today is part of a society where mass-produced goods, such as foodstuffs, cars, televisions, electric irons and vacuum cleaners, are everyday things. In the nineteenth century only a limited range of goods were mass-produced and domestic life was very different.

The circumstances of the family have been affected by other changes: for example, the work of trade unions and the services of the Welfare State have helped to guarantee the family some income even in times of unemployment or ill health. Children are able to receive free education at state schools until they are sixteen. More people can read and write, and ideas are passed on more rapidly because of the circulation of newspapers and magazines and the effect of radio and television.

How has the family responded to these changes in British society and in what ways has it helped to influence some of the changes that have taken place since the nineteenth century?

10.1   Family life in nineteenth-century Britain

In Victorian times it was a popular idea that family life was the backbone of the life of the country and therefore the family was looked upon as a very important part of society.

By the middle of the nineteenth century, manufacturing industries were expanding and the factory owners and businessmen who had prospered from the rise of industry had emerged as a new social class, the middle class. The middle class, with their newly-acquired wealth, lacked the social recognition that was given the aristocracy and the old-established upper-class families. In an attempt to gain this recognition, wealthier middle-class families often imitated the way of life of upper-class families. The importance and solidarity of family life in the middle classes became an influential model for the rest of society.

In working-class families, the ideas of respectability and solid family life were usually held in high regard, but the reality of hard, manual work for long hours, under poor conditions and with low wages, often made such a way of life impossible. There are many descriptions by nineteenth-century writers of the very poorest urban population whose conditions of life were so wretched that family life, as understood by the prosperous middle classes, was virtually impossible. Many individuals lived as vagrants with no permanent experience of being a member of a family group.

We will concentrate on some of the more conspicuous changes which have taken place in the course of the last hundred years.

10.2 Changes in family size

The nineteenth-century family was larger than the family today. Amongst the middle classes, the average family size was five or six children for couples who were married in the 1870s, while amongst the working classes, families were usually even larger. The number of children living, however, did not always reflect the number of pregnancies that had taken place. This was because, due to factors such as poor health, bad housing, deficient nutrition, costs of medical services and poorer knowledge and education about caring for mothers and their babies, more children died in infancy than today.

The average family size today is a little over two children for couples marrying in recent years. The reason for the decline in family size lies with the decision of couples to plan the number of children that they want, and the availability of reliable forms of contraception. The move to adopt family planning began in the middle classes in the 1870s when they were experiencing a threat to their newly-acquired wealth and social status by the rise of competition from foreign industry and a decline in business profits. Faced with the problem of maintaining the traditionally large family on a declining income, the middle classes made the decision to limit family size.

Gradually the idea of smaller families came to be accepted also amongst working-class families. This was not widespread until the beginning of the twentieth century when the crushing poverty experienced by the working classes was beginning to recede and the possibility of an improvement in living conditions encouraged families to adopt family planning. By this time also the move for compulsory elementary education, first introduced in 1870, had become effective and children were no longer an economic asset to their parents. The use of contraception amongst working-class couples grew during the unemployment of the 1930s. However, after this time the use of birth control methods declined and the average size of working-class families has continued to be a little greater than those of middle-class families.

10.3 Parents and children

To the Victorians, 'father' enjoyed a very special position in the family. He was head of the household and, as such, he commanded a great deal of respect. Of course, the image and the reality were often very different things and it was only possible for this role to be played out to the full in wealthy middle-class households. The working-class father, however, was still head of his own particular family and he was expected also to have authority over the other members of his family.

In wealthier middle-class homes children might not see much of their parents, spending most of their time with nannies or governesses. It was usual for parents to send their sons to private boarding schools. In this way, middle-class families hoped to secure entrance for their sons into the professional occupations which had traditionally been confined to the sons of upper-class families.

In working-class families children were an economic asset to the family as they were able to work in the factories and bring home money. These advantages began to disappear with the passing of the Factory Acts of 1833 and 1847. The Acts gradually became effective in limiting the employment of young children and the Education Act of 1870, by requiring children to attend elementary schools, also gradually had the effect of reducing the numbers of children employed.

Today relationships between parents and children have changed. In particular, 'father' is no longer a stern and forbidding figure. Two psychologists, John and Elizabeth Newson, in *Four Years Old In An Urban Community* (Allen & Unwin, 1968) summarise some of their research into the relationships between parents and children in a sample of families living in Nottingham. In this, they describe the way in which fathers today help in caring for their children and how many of them join in playing with their children.

" Got those boys to bed yet, Harry ? "

How have these changes come about? In the twentieth century young people cannot go out to work full-time until they are sixteen. Under these circumstances children are an economic liability. Also smaller, planned families allow parents the opportunity to give each child individual love and affection. The amount of time which parents can give their children has been affected by changes such as the shortening of the working week. In the nineteenth century this was between seventy and eighty hours for many members of the working-class; today the forty-hour week is widespread. Also, we have seen already how social changes have brought about the privatisation of some families, so that more time and money is spent on the children and the home. Today there is a more equal relationship between husband and wife, parents and children.

10.4 The woman's role

In the nineteenth century marriage was considered to be the right goal for every woman. Middle-class girls were brought up with this objective in mind and, once married, they passed from being under the authority of their father to being under the authority of their husband. In middle-class families it was thought to be a mark of refinement and wealth if a wife remained at home and did not involve herself in any kind of paid employment. Most married women therefore spent their time at home, either pregnant or recovering from pregnancy and supervising the running of the household with the aid of domestic servants, nannies and governesses. A middle-class woman who was not married would very often live with the family of a married relative. Many lower middle-class, unmarried women held positions as governesses.

In the working classes, wages were so low that every available member of the family had to work. Despite many pregnancies, married women worked as often as possible.

The dependent role of women in society was reflected in their lack of legal rights. For example, before the Married Women's Property Act of 1882 the wife's possessions became her husband's property when she married. Divorce was virtually impossible for a woman because of the legally complicated grounds that had to be established, the cost and the scandal. J. S. Mill, in his book *The Subjection of Women* (1869), summarised the married woman's position in the nineteenth century: 'There remain no legal slaves except the mistress of every house.'

Today over eight million women are in some form of full-time employment and over half of these are married. More women, and particularly married women, are employed today. However, there is still some preference for women to be employed in occupations which seem closest to their traditional roles as wives and mothers. For example, women out-number men in schoolteaching and occupations such as nursing are traditionally associated with women employees.

How have these changes come about?

In the 1870s, as we have seen, middle-class married women began to have smaller families. This allowed them, for the first time, the opportunity to take an active role in society and return to a job after raising a family. At that time, however, there were restraints on women taking a job and having a career, as many employers and husbands believed the woman's place to be in the home. The waning of this attitude was accelerated when, under the emergency conditions of World War I, women took on jobs which had previously been filled by men.

The extension of equal legal rights and the franchise to women in the course of the last hundred years has also contributed to the change in the woman's role. The gradual development of women's education in the twentieth century has improved the possibilities of women entering almost all types of work on an equal level with men. However, this equality is not always reflected in the wages women receive, although the Equal Pay Act of 1970 has made it necessary for employers to pay women equal wages where they are doing the same as, or broadly similar work to men.

The growth in women's employment has helped to allow a married woman today to be economically independent of her husband.

10.5   Marriage and divorce

Marriage has also changed since the nineteenth century. Developments such as the improvement of birth-control techniques with 'the pill' have made it possible for marriage to be separated from parenthood. Today we do not think it is unreasonable for a man and his wife to wish to divorce if their marriage is causing them unhappiness, and the social stigma once attached to divorce has now largely disappeared.

The increase in the number of divorce petitions has gone up from an annual average of 460 in the five-year period between 1876–80, to 110 895 petitions for dissolution and annulment of marriage in 1971. This looks like a startling increase until we remember that, as with any statistics, they must be looked at with great care and interpreted in the light of other factors, such as changes in the population, the law, and our attitudes to divorce, that have affected the figures. For example, in the nineteenth century it was hardly possible for anyone, particularly a woman, to obtain a divorce. Divorce was expensive and therefore confined to the rich. It was only in 1923 that changes in the law made it possible, for the first time, for wives to secure a divorce on the same grounds as their husbands. The grounds for divorce were extended by the Matrimonial Causes Act of 1937 and this change in the law brought an increase in the numbers of people petitioning for a divorce. The numbers increased again after the Legal Aid and Advice Act of 1949, when people could apply for legal aid if they were not able to afford the costs of a divorce suit.

The latest change in the law is the Divorce Reform Act, 1969, which became effective in 1971. The Act is different from earlier divorce laws because it involves a new way of looking at divorce. Rather than trying to find out who is the guilty party in the breakdown of a marriage, the new Act provides for divorce being granted on the grounds of the 'irretrievable breakdown' of a marriage. In 1971 there was a fifty-five per cent increase in petitions for dissolution and annulment over the number in 1970.

The Future

What will the family be like in the future? Will it continue to be a pattern of human association in society?

These are interesting questions to consider even though the answers will be speculative. The family is part of society and is therefore affected by, and itself effects, changes in society. Recent developments in medical technology, such as improved methods of contraception and new methods for encouraging conception, have extended the range of choices open to members of the family. In the future it is likely that other scientific and technological developments will affect the family, possibly contributing to profound changes, such as a move to adopt alternative forms of human association. For example, we may find ourselves in the situation where people no longer associate with one another in terms of family groups but instead relate to some new and, as yet, un-named principle of human association.

Terms used in this chapter

the nuclear (or conjugal) family	conjugal role	socialisation
the extended (or consanguine) family	sex roles	home-centred
status	marriage	activities
role	working wives	

Questions

1   Make a diagram using appropriate symbols to show the groups of people whom you would consider as your family. Is this basically a nuclear or an extended family?

2   Suppose that mothers instead of fathers were the ones who generally went out to work to support the family, what differences would this make in family life? What changes would have to take place in the wider social structure?

3   Parents and children

a   Find out how many magazines are entirely given over to discussing matters which concern parents and the way they bring their children up.

b   When were they first published? In the nineteenth or twentieth century?

c   What is their circulation?

d   Are magazines of this sort growing or declining in number?

e   Find out how many families that you know take these magazines.

f   Do they find that the magazines influence them in any way?

g   If you are able, find copies of any family magazines that were published ten, twenty and fifty years ago. In what ways have ideas about family life changed in that time?

4   Family life

a   In the course of one week, how many radio or TV programmes concentrate on events in the life of an imaginary or real family? Why do you think there are such programmes?

b   Which of these programmes do you listen to or watch regularly?

c   What do you enjoy about these programmes?

d   How realistic would you say they are?

5   The following graphs represent the results of surveys carried out by children in two schools. Draw up a questionnaire that will give you information on the same topics but give this questionnaire to members of your class. How do your results compare with those of schools A and B? Why do you think your results are the same as or different from those of school A or B shown in the graphs?

SCHOOL A in a large Northern city

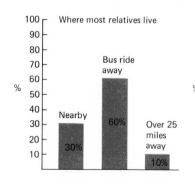
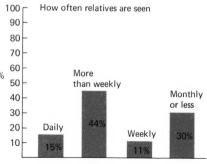

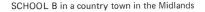

SCHOOL B in a country town in the Midlands

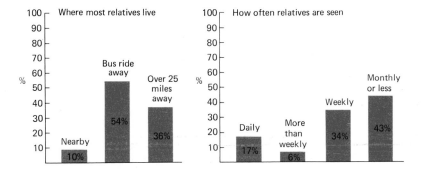

6   If there were no family system would it be necessary to invent one? Can you think of alternatives to the family? If so, how would these be organised and what difference would it make to society?

7   Is the woman's place in the home? Is the man's place in the home?

8   Sex stereotyping

a   Take a woman's magazine and put into categories the types of articles that appear in the magazine, for example, 'cooking', 'children', 'housework'. See how many articles appear in each category. From looking at the numbers in each category what aspects of the woman's role, would you say, are most emphasised by this magazine?

b   Plan the contents of a family magazine of your own.

9   The Welfare State

Find out which Welfare State services have helped members of your own family at some time or are helping them at the present time.

10   'Civilisation confronts us with difficulties of our own making and sets new conditions on motherhood.' Margaret Mead, *Family*, Macmillan, N.Y. 1965.

What, in your opinion, are the problems which confront a woman who is a wife and a mother and who also goes out to work?

a   Consider this particularly in terms of the provisions which are available in your area for looking after young children, while a mother is at work. For example:

i   How many private nursery schools are there in the area? How much does it cost to send a child there? How large are the classes and what are the schools' facilities? What hours are the schools open?

ii   How many state nursery schools are there in the area? What is the average class size? What facilities are there for the children? What hours are the schools open?

b   How many factories or offices in the area have crèches or nurseries for the children of employees? Do employees have to pay to leave their children at these? What are the facilities?

c   Are there any supervised playgrounds in your area? What hours are they open?

d   Are there any playgroups in your area? Who runs them and how much does it cost for parents to leave their children at these groups?

Questions from GCE 'O' Level Sociology Examination Papers

1   What is a family? Describe some of the different kinds of family organisation you have read about and explain why they are all families. (AEB, June 1972)

2   To what extent is it true to say that the extended family no longer exists in Britain? On what evidence is your opinion based? (AEB, November 1971)

3   'Far from being the basis of the good society, the family is the source of all our discontents.' Discuss. (AEB, November 1970)

4   Imagine a country in which living in families was officially prohibited. Describe the difference this might make to that society. (AEB, Specimen Paper for New Syllabus, 1972)

5   Distinguish between an extended and a nuclear family. Is the latter more important than the former in contemporary Britain? (Oxford Local Examinations, 1970)

6   Account for some of the changes which have taken place in the pattern of family life in recent years. (AEB, June 1968)

7   In what ways have relationships within the family changed during the last 100 years? What kind of evidence is there to support your views? (AEB, June 1973)

8   What does the table below tell us about family size in Great Britain since 1870? How would you explain this change?

Great Britain

Number of live births	Proportion of women (per 1000) with specified number of births, who were first married in:		
	1870–9	1900–9	1925
0	83	113	161
1–2	125	335	506
3–4	181	277	221
5–9	434	246	106
10 or more	177	29	6
all	1000	1000	1000

(AEB, June 1970)

9 What are the major social factors affecting family size in contemporary Britain? (Oxford Local Examinations, 1973)

10 A hundred years ago the average number of children in a family was about six; what is the corresponding average now? Explain this change. (AEB, November 1972)

11 Newspapers often refer to the generation gap. How acceptable or useful do you find this phrase? (AEB, June 1972)

12 On the basis of what you know of research findings what advice would you give to a mother who wanted to return to work but was worried about the effect this might have on her children? (AEB, November 1971)

13 Monogamy without divorce, monogamy with easy divorce, polygamy. Describe how each of these three kinds of marriages would be likely to affect relationships within the family. (AEB, November 1972)

14 *a* What factors have caused the changes in the divorce rate since 1900?

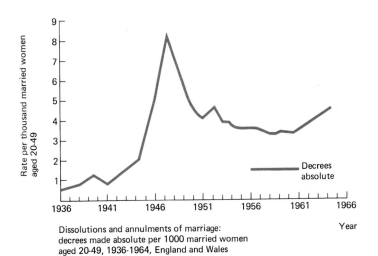

Dissolutions and annulments of marriage: decrees made absolute per 1000 married women aged 20-49, 1936-1964, England and Wales

b What effects, if any, have these changes had on family life? (You may find the above graph useful.) (AEB, June 1972)

15 Describe and account for changes in the divorce rate in Britain during this century. (Oxford Local Examinations, 1975)

16 What are the essential functions of the family? How does the State assist the family in fulfilling these functions? (AEB, June 1973)

17 Discuss the suggestion that the most important cause of the decline of the 'extended family' is geographical mobility. (Oxford Local Examinations, 1975)

4 Education
Unit 11 The Development of Education

11.1 Education and the economy

The public education system in Britain dates from the nineteenth century, when it became clear that an industrial society necessitated an efficient labour force. The governing classes realised that it was in their own interests to have a better-educated working class.

In 1837, Lord Brougham criticised the British government for 'having done less for the Education of the People than any one of the more civilised nations of the world.' At this time only about one-tenth of the population of this country had any schooling, whereas in Germany about one-sixth went to school. Brougham went on to add that in Britain, 'the kind of education afforded was far more lamentably defective than its amount'. In 1833 the government initiated an annual £20 000 educational grant which went mainly to the National Society for the education of Anglicans, and to the British and Foreign Society for the education of non-conformists. These two voluntary societies were providing most of the schools. When this paltry grant is compared with the £3500 million spent on education in the mid-1970s, then (even allowing for the depreciation in the value of money) one can begin to appreciate the great importance placed upon education in a modern economy.

The main economic function of education today is to ensure that there is a labour force educated in accordance with the needs of a technological society. In pre-industrial societies it was customary for sons to follow their father in the family profession, trade or business. Figure 4.1 depicts the family tree of the Butlers; observe how the family passed on their learning and skills in the occupational spheres of the church, education, diplomacy and politics.

In modern society much vocational training is undertaken at the place of work. However, schools encourage career incentives, and the establishment of training in job-skills at technical colleges and polytechnics has brought changes in the structure of education. It is still the main task of the schools to supply a good general all-round education. The Central

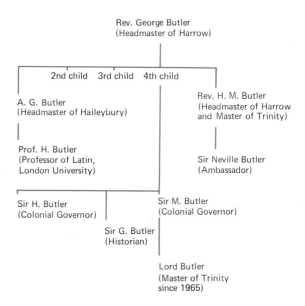

Figure 4.1   *Lord Butler's family tree*

Advisory Committee on Education's report *School and Life* argued that 'the principle of basing school-education primarily on the needs of industry is bad', while Professor S. T. Cotgrove ('Education and Opportunity', *British Journal of Sociology*, Vol. 13, No. 1, 1962) contended that 'Any discussion of the relations between education and occupation will quickly bring to light the existence of a constellation of ideas and values which are strongly opposed to any vocational element in secondary and university education.'

Most British schools aim to educate their pupils in basic subjects until the age of at least thirteen and then structure a curriculum which encourages a limited amount of specialisation so that likely vocational urges may be tapped. This may be accomplished by arranging special courses, eg courses that cater for those who are contemplating commerce or engineering as a career. A progressive practice is for an insistence to be placed upon all pupils studying basic subjects such as English and mathematics, and then allowing students to choose from an option system. The following option scheme was offered to fourth-year pupils at the Hewett Comprehensive School in Norwich for the years 1973–5 (see Table 4.1).

Option 1	*Option 2*	*Option 3*
Physics (O)	Chemistry (O)	Biology (O)
Physics (CSE)	Chemistry (CSE)	Biology (CSE)
History (O)	Biology (O)	General Science (CSE)
History (CSE)	Biology (CSE)	+Social Economics (O)
+Social Economics (O)	+Human Biology	+Social Studies
+Engineering	(CSE)	(CSE)
Drawing (O)	Geography (O)	Geography (O)
+Engineering	Geography (CSE)	+Latin/Classical
Drawing (CSE)	History (O)	Studies (O/CSE)
+Typing (CSE)	Religious Education	(see note)
Dress and Fashion	(O/CSE)	+Office Practice
(O/CSE)	+Typing (CSE)	(CSE)
Art and Craft (CSE)		Art and Craft (O)
+*Link courses:—*	+*Link courses:—*	Art and Craft (CSE)
a Motor Mechanics	*a* Motor Mechanics	+Engineering (O)
(CSE)	(CSE)	+Social Studies
b Child Care/Home	*b* Child Care/Home	(CSE) (Link course)
Management (CSE)	Management (CSE)	
c Design for Living	*c* Design for Living	
(CSE)	(CSE)	

Option 4		*Option 5*
+Social Economics	Dress and Fashion (O)	+Social Studies
(CSE)	Dress and Fashion	+Child Studies
Religious Education	(CSE)	+Office Practice
German/French/	Cookery and Nutrition	+Typing
Spanish (O/CSE)	(O)	Art
(see note)	Domestic Science	Woodwork
+Child Study (CSE)	(CSE)	Metal work
Music (O/CSE)	+Pre-Catering (Boys)	+Engineering
(see note)	(CSE)	Science
+Engineering Drawing	Metal work (O)	(Link course)
(O)	Metal work (CSE)	
+Engineering Drawing	Woodwork (O)	
(CSE)	Woodwork (CSE)	
+Building Drawing		
(O)		
Art and Craft (O)		
Art and Craft (CSE)		

Table 4.1   Fourth Year Options, Hewett Comprehensive School, Norwich, 1973–1975

Notes

1 +New subjects offered.
2 Pupils taking *one* foreign language cannot take a subject from option 5 which is for non-linguists only.
3 Pupils taking *two* foreign languages—Some may be able to fit in a subject from option 4, others may not be in a position to do this. Advice will be given by year tutors.
4 *Latin and Classical Studies*
   Pupils wishing to commence Latin and recommended to do so, will normally be expected to do a 3-year course to 'O' level, terminating at the end of the first year in the Sixth Form (Lower Sixth).
   Classical studies is a two year course.
5 *Music*
   Pupils wishing to offer music, but unable to fit this into option 4, should nevertheless opt for this subject, and advice will be given by year tutors.
6 Link courses in motor mechanics/child study and home management/ design for living.
   Pupils offering these courses take the link subjects social studies in option 3, and science in option 5. They may then select their remaining subject from option 4.

Link courses provide very useful studies especially where it is possible to correlate subjects. Traditional school subjects have been retained in watertight compartments for far too long. One subject is not more noble than another and the linking of varied subjects makes for a more all-round education. For example it is useful for a teacher of economics to:

a discuss motor insurance and road traffic problems with a motor mechanics group
b instruct a home management group in domestic budgetary problems.

At the end of the third year pupils continued to study basic subjects, but in addition selected one subject from each of the five options. Thus a student who hoped to be a scientist might well choose:

physics from option 1
chemistry from option 2
biology from option 3
German from option 4
metalwork from option 5

If he did not wish to become one-sided he might well choose a subject such as art in option 5.

Vocational education extends beyond the schools into the field of further education. Some of the types of courses which link the educational system closely with the economy are listed below:

1   evening classes
2   day release (usually one day a week, during working hours)
3   block release (study at college for short periods and then returning to work for longer periods)
4   sandwich courses (eg alternate six-monthly periods of full-time study in a college and supervised experience in industry)
5   full-time courses
6   industrial rehabilitation courses and vocational training at a government training centre.

There is a wide variety of full-time vocational and technical courses for people in various occupations, leading to appropriate qualifications at the end of a course of up to five years. Some of these qualifications include:

1   Ordinary National Certificate (ONC) following two years' part-time education usually between the ages of sixteen and nineteen.
2   Ordinary National Diploma (OND) following two years' full-time study. (In 1973 about 4000 ONDs were awarded, over three times the number granted in 1963.)
3   Higher National Diploma (HND) requiring two years' full-time or three years' sandwich study. HND standard approaches degree level except that it is more narrowly and vocationally based.

The Raising of the School-Leaving Age (RoSLA) in 1972/3 has had far-reaching effects upon the educational system and upon the economy. Although boys and girls of less than average ability might prefer work to school at the age of fifteen, and many employers who are not looking for high academic qualifications would be glad to have them, some sociologists have long doubted the logic of letting slow learners leave school early. In a technological society slow learners may need more time for study. Great efforts have been made so that another year at school will be of value to the 285 000 extra pupils. Some of the aims of RoSLA courses have been:

1   to ensure that the pupils do not regard the raising of the school-leaving age as a wasted year
2   to provide lively teaching situations and experiences appropriate to young school leavers
3   to ease the transition from the world of school to the world of work

4   to tap vocational incentives without lessening the general educational
value of another year's schooling
5   to engender a sense of community and social service.

Special courses filled a gap and had the advantage of encouraging
teachers to rethink and restructure syllabuses more suitable for young
school leavers. But these courses could only fill a temporary gap because
the extra number of young people staying on until sixteen (who would
have left but for statutory measures) has merged into the normal pattern
of school life. It would have been undesirable for them to have remained
a separate group especially as some are as gifted as those who previously
remained in voluntary attendance. Before 1973 some young people who
would have liked to have stayed on, left school for the world of work
because of poor economic circumstances and other family pressures.
Whether or not children stayed at school until they were sixteen depended
a lot on where they lived (see Figure 4.2).

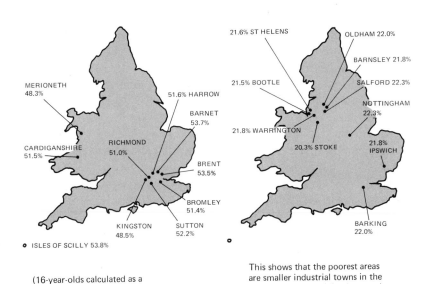

MERIONETH 48.3%
51.6% HARROW
BARNET 53.7%
CARDIGANSHIRE 51.5%
RICHMOND 51.0%
BRENT 53.5%
BROMLEY 51.4%
KINGSTON 48.5%
SUTTON 52.2%
ISLES OF SCILLY 53.8%

21.6% ST HELENS
OLDHAM 22.0%
BARNSLEY 21.8%
21.5% BOOTLE
SALFORD 22.3%
NOTTINGHAM 22.3%
21.8% WARRINGTON
20.3% STOKE
21.8% IPSWICH
BARKING 22.0%

(16-year-olds calculated as a
percentage of those aged 13 three
years before)

This shows that the poorest areas
are smaller industrial towns in the
North and north Midlands - together
with the tip of the same environment
in East Anglia and London

Figure 4.2a   *Top ten areas for children staying on at school*
Figure 4.2b   *Bottom ten areas for children staying on at school*
(Source: Government Social Survey, 1968)

The demands of the economic system upon the educational system have meant that 'formal' or 'classical' educational methods have been largely abandoned. At one time the educational system was divorced from the realities of life and employment. The public schools, such as Harrow and Eton, taught the classics mechanically at the height of the nineteenth-century industrial revolution; boys spent hours composing Greek and Latin verse rather than learning anything related to the real world outside the school. Fortunately in the modern world there is close correlation between the educational system and the economic system. It is generally appreciated that 'what characterises an advanced industrial society is the extent to which skills at all levels of the occupational hierarchy are increasingly acquired within formal educational institutions' (Olive Banks, *The Sociology of Education*, Batsford, 1968).

11.2   Changes in the functions of education

The need to prepare people to fulfil the essential economic tasks required of them as adult members of society seems so obvious that it may come as a surprise to think that the vital importance of education was so long neglected. But education has not merely an economic function.

Today education is often expected to have a stabilising function in society. In spite of the so-called generation gap and student unrest, the educational system tends to work towards the maintenance of existing standards of society. Schools usually endeavour to preserve the existing order of things, although all good schools must be prepared to accept some changes from without and within. For example, the Education Act of 1944 laid down that there should be 'ease of transfer' between secondary schools, but this has for the most part become unnecessary because of the large-scale adoption of comprehensive systems of secondary education. Morning prayers of a very religious nature have been replaced in many schools by assemblies where pupil participation is greater and where the subject matter is often of a wide sociological content rather than of a strict religious nature. The whole atmosphere of a contemporary school is one of far greater freedom and less uniformity. Many schools have replaced school uniform by a less rigid school-attire; the curriculum is far wider and the choices are much greater. You should consider how far changes in educational institutions are a reflection of changes in society as a whole, or how far educational changes have inspired community changes.

In spite of necessary changes without which a society would decay, every society is faced with the desire to preserve and transmit its *culture*.

Culture, in this context, is used in the sense of a way of life that is characterised by generally accepted standards of behaviour, beliefs, conduct and
morals. However, although each country has its own special culture,
within the culture of a nation there are class differences which make for
'middle-class' and 'working-class' cultures. English education has been
largely dominated by middle-class culture because the majority of
teachers are the products of a middle-class upbringing.

Although in this country schools have a very large say in their organisation and curricula, as distinct from the practice in some European
countries where the state exercises rigid controls, most British teachers
are in general agreement concerning the main educational objectives.
There are individualists in the educational world, and few people would
wish this to be otherwise, but there is a consensus of opinion about the
culture that ought to be passed on to pupils. There is undoubtedly less
conformity nowadays about what ideas should be transmitted relating to
some topics such as law and order, marriage, sex and religion. Do you
think that schools tend to be too conservative in the preservation of
culture? So long as the way is left open for flexibility and gradual changes,
several sound arguments can be put forward in support of education
playing a traditional role.

1   The attitudes, beliefs and customs of society have been formulated over a
long period and there must be good reasons why society adopted these ideas
and ideals.

2   Our national heritage is preserved by conserving, to some extent, the
patterns of existing society.

3   Whereas revolutionary attitudes may sweep away much that is out-of-
place and wasteful in a modern society, it is possible that valuable cultural ideals
may be lost at the same time.

4   We have a responsibility to transmit to posterity the best things that have
been handed on by past generations.

5   It would be unfortunate if peculiar national traditions and characteristics
disappeared under a cloak of dull uniformity.

The preservation of our culture may be well served by adopting the
ideas of the Fabian Society which was formed in 1884. These ideas were
founded on the conduct of the Roman General, Fabius, who patiently
awaited the right moment. If we attack those things which we regard as
wrong within our society with the Fabian 'inevitability of gradualness',
we are more likely to ensure that the best aspects of our culture are
retained during the period in which they deserve to be preserved, but
gradually replaced by more relevant ideas and ideals as society itself
changes. In the words of an old prayer:

Give us the strength to accept with serenity the things that cannot be changed. Give us courage to change the things that can and should be changed. And give us the wisdom to distinguish one from the other.

The function of education in relation to law and order has been subject to considerable changes. Attempts have been made to replace the old sergeant-major type of barrack-square order by self-discipline. Clearly schools must be places of order if any learning is to take place, and it is in nursery and infant schools that an individual is first confronted by objective authority in the form of the teaching staff. The head teacher is still regarded as the pinnacle of law and order in the disciplinary framework of the school, but the large size of many secondary schools means that law and order within the school depends upon the authority of form-tutors or year-tutors. If the pupil commits an offence against the accepted standards of the school community (eg in relation to bullying, theft or disobedience) then he must learn that punishment will follow in the same way as society punishes those who break its rules or offend its standards. Contemporary schools often place more importance upon rewards than upon penalties. What reasonable rewards do you think can be offered to young people at school today?

Self-discipline means that an individual conforms to the code of the society without being compelled to do so, but because he accepts the rules of the community be they written or unwritten. This means that the rules should be sensible and that the individual must be rational enough to realise that they are applied for the benefit of the school community in general and will thus benefit him in the long run; presumably he does not want to be treated violently or for his personal belongings to be stolen by other members of society. Some schools have been able to abolish all school rules and rely entirely upon self-discipline or upon school councils and committees to impose law and order. If everybody behaved as they would be expected to behave in a good family then the school might not need written rules. But what is a good family?

As society outside the school walls has abolished the cat-of-nine-tails, the birch and the hangman's noose, so in most schools corporal punishment plays little part nowadays. Often theories and principles lag behind what happens in practice. When the staff of Risinghill School decided that caning was unnecessary they objected when the headmaster, Mr Duane, told the children. The staff said later, 'We didn't mean you to tell the children' and Michael Duane said simply, 'But you are not doing away with corporal punishment unless you tell the children' (Leila Berg, *Risinghill: Death of a Comprehensive School*, Penguin Books, 1969). Although the staff's view in this case may seem unreasonable, nevertheless there is some peculiar logic in the fact that pupils may behave better if they believe that the deterrent of corporal punishment is in existence. What do you think? If the head teacher is to be responsible for character training, do you think that he ought to adopt a policy of absolute honesty in all cases?

The *political functions* of education have undergone radical changes. Plato believed in educating an *élite* who would act as future rulers of society. Our own monarchical system has been modelled somewhat on Platonic principles, except that the hereditary system may not produce people with sufficient latent potential to be capable of being turned into an élite ruling class. However, if the monarch is little more than an ornamental figurehead, the intellectual quality of the élite is of minor significance because real political leadership is held by the prime minister and his cabinet.

Until the Reform Act of 1884 gave universal suffrage to adult males, and the Representation of the People Act of 1928 gave the vote to adult women, political power in Britain was held by the aristocratic class who formed the only *educated class*. The structure of society was based on upper middle-class conservatism with the great distinction between 'Upstairs-Downstairs' symbolised in the couplet:

> God bless the squire and his relations,
> And keep us in our proper stations.

Liberal government replaced Conservative government without there being any real challenge to the class structure of society. Until the origins of the Labour Party, in the early part of the twentieth century, it was generally accepted that political leaders should be drawn from the upper classes. In 1923, when Baldwin was asked to form a government he acted upon the principle that 'it should be a government of which Harrow should not be ashamed'. Even in the second half of the twentieth century the *Times Guide to the House of Commons*, 1966, shows that when the Labour government had a majority of ninety-seven seats, 189 of the Labour MPs had an Oxbridge background. In 1966 forty-three per cent of the Labour cabinet had a public school background, although only a very small percentage of the electorate had attended a public school. But gradually it has been realised that the masses must be educated so that they may at first share, and later take responsibility for, the political leadership of society. After the third Reform Act was passed, Robert Lowe shrewdly reminded Parliament that it was their duty to: 'Educate your masters!' Perhaps you can add to the following reasons why education has such a vital political function in a democratic society.

1   All citizens ought to be educated so that they can play as full a part as possible in the government of the country, either as electors or elected.

2   A liberally educated society is more likely to bring forth a government not dominated by extremists.

3   Education should lead to an air of tolerance and a willingness to protect the position of minority groups.

The educational system should be organised so that the best leaders in society emerge because of good selection, training and opportunities.

11.3   The growth of an educational system in Britain

When we look at the educational system today it is difficult to appreciate that a public education system in Britain has been developed in a little over a century. A national system of education grew gradually from Forster's Education Act of 1870. Although this Act was supposed to provide adequately for elementary education it would be a mistake to believe that Britain had a universal compulsory system from 1870. The new locally-elected school boards set up by the Act had great difficulty in getting the children to the schools and it took two more Acts to make education compulsory:

1   Sandon's Act of 1876 stated that it was the duty of parents of children aged between five and thirteen years, to see that they received elementary instruction.

2   Mundella's Act of 1880 made it the duty of every school board to get to school all its children of school age.

The next vital piece of educational legislation was Balfour's Act of 1902 which set up Local Education Authorities in place of the school boards. The provision of public secondary education was now in the hands of the LEAs: new maintained secondary schools were built and the old endowed grammar schools were also aided from the rates. A proportion of scholarship places were offered to the bright children from elementary schools— the 'educational highway' had not been built, but an 'educational ladder' was in the early stages of construction. The Fisher Act of 1918 abolished fees in elementary schools; it also gave LEAs the power to provide nursery schools and to raise the school leaving age to fifteen. The 1944 Education Act has been the blueprint upon which most educational developments have been based until the comprehensive explosion in secondary education began in the 1960s.

The 1944 Act laid down important principles:

1   There should be free education for all.

2   Regard should be given, as far as possible, to the wishes of the parents.

3 Full-time and part-time education should be provided for those over compulsory school-leaving age.

4 Educational planning should be based upon local experience, interest and knowledge.

5 There should be set up a three-tier educational system consisting of three stages:

a   *Primary* (2 to 11)
     nursery (2-5)
     infant (5-7)
     junior (7-11)—now often called 'middle' (8-12)

b ⁻ *Secondary* (11 to 15-plus)
     modern   ⎫
     grammar   ⎬ now often comprehensive
     technical ⎭

c   *Further*
     technical colleges
     art schools
     agricultural institutes
     teachers' training colleges—now colleges of education
     universities.

6 The school-leaving age should be raised to sixteen.

7 There should be equal opportunity for all.

Although we have gone a long way to ensuring equal opportunity for all (see Topic 12.4), there is still room for far greater achievements in this sphere.

Unit 12 Education and Socialisation

12.1 Socio-linguistics and learning

As we have seen, the family is the first important agency of socialisation. The second agency of socialisation and a no less important one is the school. From the age of five years or earlier we come into contact with many other children and meet different adults who will regulate our daily lives. Because we must attend school for at least eleven years, what happens to us at school will be of considerable importance. Not only will we acquire knowledge of different subjects, but we will also form relationships with our classmates and teachers. Perhaps values and attitudes which differ from those of our family will be shaped whilst we are at school.

Of course the basic values of society are mainly learnt at home, but a school usually considers that one of its functions is to prepare pupils for adult life. In the middle of the last century the function of the school was thought to be only to make a child literate and able to do simple arithmetic, in other words simply to prepare children for work of the most routine and manual kind. Today educationalists recognise that schools have a variety of tasks to perform, particularly as there are many more job opportunities open to school leavers in our advanced technological society. But school is not simply a place of training for future work: schools also help in the development of our personal qualities, teach us how to deal with other people, and perhaps make us aware of some of the problems that need to be faced in society.

The three primary functions of the school are:

1   the development of personal qualities
2   the teaching of the values and norms of society
3   the transmission of knowledge and learning.

In the process of socialisation, relationships with others are important. In school these are twofold:

1   *Pupil-teacher relationships* During the school day the teacher replaces the parent as the main adult influence on a child's life. The younger or more emotionally unstable a child is, the more important this relationship will become. For this reason children in primary schools have a class teacher who is with them most of the day, and remedial classes spend more time with their class teacher. Because a teacher must divide her or his time between the whole class, the role of the parent is never entirely duplicated. A teacher may have different standards from the parents, and because a school is an institution on a larger scale than the home there is a difference in the child's environment. A good teacher, especially of young children, tries to bridge the gap between home and school as much as possible by contact with the parents. As we grow older and enter secondary education the specialist disciplines of the teachers do not always allow for the special relationship with the pupils, and this may be passed on to the form teacher or year tutor. In the secondary school situation the pupil learns to rely less directly upon the teacher and more upon himself to achieve success, thus the secondary school teacher has a different role from that of the primary teacher.

2   *Inter-pupil relationships* The classmates, or *peer group*, usually form the basis of friendships in school. Sometimes groups of special friends develop within the class; this can be seen when sides are picked for a game of football, or by where children choose to sit. Each group has

its own values and means of self-identification, sometimes with a special language or slang, or with the exchange of presents on birthdays or at Christmas. Very young children imitate their parents in games of 'mothers and fathers'; as they grow older boys will start to play tougher games, adopting a tougher masculine role. Because there are so many other children of the same age group around, school is an excellent place for this aspect of the socialisation process. The modern trend of smaller families means that the peer group in school has an increasingly important role to play in a child's socialisation.

12.2 Education and social class

Many studies have shown that children of working-class backgrounds are less successful in school than those from middle-class homes. One important study has been Brian Jackson and Dennis Marsden's *Education and the Working Class* (Penguin), but many other sources also reveal that working-class children start school with a disadvantage which is rarely overcome. This disadvantage has nothing to do with inherited intelligence, as children with working-class parents who have been adopted into middle-class homes at an early enough age achieve the same success as do middle-class children, but has much to do with the home background. This is not to say that there is anything wrong with a working-class background, indeed many working-class children enjoy advantages over middle-class children in other ways, but the values of society are largely middle-class values and success is often measured in terms of achievement at school and the kind of job that one has. Achievement at school we may term *scholastic achievement*. Home background is determined by the many *socio-cultural* factors. Why do middle-class children do so much better at school than working-class children? One explanation is given by Basil Bernstein in an article entitled 'Social Class and Linguistic Development: A Theory of Social Learning' (Chapter 24 of *Education, Economy and Society*, edited by Halsey, Floud and Anderson, Collier-Macmillan, 1961).

Bernstein maintains that it is a lack of ability in language on the part of working-class children that hinders their success. The ability to read and write is slowed down, and because so many intelligence tests are based on skill with words the middle-class children have a considerable advantage. Intelligence tests involving arithmetic do not show such a difference between children of middle- or working-class backgrounds (see Figure 4.3 a & b). Because language is so important in schools (we must be able to read and write as the first essential skill) middle-class children perform

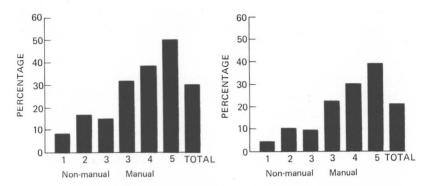

Figure 4.3a   *Children with 'poor' problem arithmetic score*
Figure 4.3b   *Children who have below-average oral ability*
(Source: From Birth to Seven, *a survey made in 1972 by the National Children's Bureau of 17 000 children born in the week 3 to 9 March 1958)*

much better. Bernstein suggests that there are two kinds of language, *public language* and *formal language*. Public language is spoken in the houses of working-class children, and is characterised in a number of ways. Formal language is a middle-class speech pattern (this has nothing to do with accent) which can convey more complicated meanings. Even the thought processes are affected by the use of language, and a child who is able to use formal language may think more clearly and grasp new ideas more readily.

Some examples of public language are:

1   Short and simple, often unfinished, sentences.
2   Repetitive use of conjunctions such as 'so', 'then', 'and', 'because'.
3   Little use of subordinate clauses.
4   Muddled information as there is digression from the subject.
5   Limited use of adverbs such as 'thoroughly', 'impatiently', 'hastily'.
6   Lack of use of impersonal pronouns such as 'one', as subjects of conditional clauses or sentences.
7   Sympathetic circularity: using statements and phrases that signal answers to previous speech sequences, for example 'wouldn't it', 'you see', 'you know', 'just fancy' rather than what is actually said. The meaning is implicit in the speech.

For the most part, teachers are themselves middle-class, or have adopted middle-class life styles, speech patterns and vocabulary. This means that unless they take great care with their speech they may not be readily understood by working-class children. The learning of new things involves a discipline of thought, and middle-class children are more often prepared for such mental discipline at an earlier age.

In Britain a third of all homes have fewer than six books. Middle-class children are more likely to enjoy the benefits of early reading books and hear a wider vocabulary. Often they are taught the advantages of *deferred gratification*: to put off immediate pleasure or satisfaction and to enjoy it more after something has been accomplished, for example not to watch television until the toys have been cleared up, or, when older, not to go out until homework is finished. Middle-class children are more concerned with achievement, as the virtues of education and a good career are emphasised by their parents. The middle-class child is more likely to understand some of the complexities of relationships. The following is an example of the difference between a working-class mother and child and a middle-class mother and child in a relationship which is changing as a child misbehaves:

Working-class mother: 'Don't jump in the puddles!' (Child continues jumping.)
Middle-class mother: 'Please keep out of the puddles or your new shoes will be ruined.' (Child continues jumping.) 'If you don't stop, Mummy will get very cross.'

The working-class child is given a simple direct order; when the order is disobeyed the consequences are immediate and possibly painful. The middle-class child is, by way of contrast, informed why he should not jump in the puddles; when he still disobeys he is given a warning signal 'if' of the possible consequences. Reasons and consequences are given to the middle-class child, while the working-class child is simply given an order. This is a stereotype example, but in school the middle-class child will have been prepared to expect reasons for, and consequences of, learning.

Jackson and Marsden in their study of eighty-eight working-class, grammar school boys in Huddersfield found a conflict between the different values of the home and school. Their achievement at school was seriously affected by such things as lack of homework facilities, and their parents' failure to understand its importance. Parental support was found to be important: only those boys who had some connection with a middle-class situation (such as having a middle-class mother) completed the course. The working-class, grammar school boys who did not have this connection rejected the grammar school values and sought support and identification with their working-class peers. Socio-cultural factors which tend to improve the chances of greater scholastic achievement of middle-class children are:

1 greater parental concern with education
2 books and speech at home designed to help a child's vocabulary
3 middle-class speech patterns and norms of behaviour in school
4 more opportunity for travel and stimulation through educational visits
5 higher levels of parental expectation
6 the deferred gratification of 'study now and get a better job later'
7 economic provision to stay on at school after the age of sixteen
8 homework facilities (and even private tutors).

A middle-class child is six times more likely than a working-class child to gain a university degree in Britain today. Educational psychologists have long recognised the importance of preparation for learning and personality development before a child attends school: it is said that half of what we learn is learnt before the age of four years, and a good infant school teacher can often recognise the potential delinquents at five-and-a-half years. The middle-class children enter school with a considerable advantage, and are able to extend their chances of success inside the school system. In recent years ministers of education and local education authorities have recognised the imbalance between the educational opportunities of working-class and middle-class children, and money is now being provided for better schools and smaller classes in the poorer districts. This will go some way towards providing an equal educational opportunity for all children, but the most important formative influence of the home cannot be legislated or financially provided for by any educationalist.

12.3   Ability and achievement

Some abilities are probably inherent—that is to say, some people are fortunate enough to possess natural ability in certain spheres. An individual may have natural verbal or number ability: he is good with words and subjects that require literacy, or he is good with figures and subjects that require a mathematical approach. This is not to say this ability remains for the whole of his life; a person can allow artistic or musical ability to rust because of lack of usage, but ability may be developed to a very high peak through encouragement, tuition and practice. A resemblance can be seen to Christ's parable of the talents. The more talent or ability possessed in a certain educational or vocational activity the greater the possibility of development, depending to a large extent upon opportunities available. The less ability possessed in any sphere the more an individual is likely to cease to persevere so that innate ability lies dormant.

Success breeds success: failure to achieve anything may well breed failure.

Although the idea that there are individual differences in innate ability is generally accepted in Britain, it should be pointed out that many educationalists, especially in the USSR, largely reject the theory of innate ability and argue that abilities are learned rather than inborn. Many Russian educationalists believe that mental testing is both unsound and misleading (Simon, B. and Joan, ed. *Educational psychology in the USSR*, Routledge & Kegan Paul), and if Russian children are slow to learn it is the teachers who are judged to be inadequate. This approach is a welcome counteraction to those people who condemn apparently backward children with such clichés as, 'You can't make a silk purse out of a sow's ear'. Nowadays it is customary for pupils to be taught not in the light of their *overall ability* but rather according to their *aptitude* in a particular subject. As a result of *streaming*, a pupil may be placed in a top stream for mathematics, but in a low-ability stream for English. One advantage of this system is that a pupil is usually capable of worthwhile achievement in some subject so that he is not dismissed as a complete failure in everything. If a pupil becomes an expert in some activity then he gains confidence to strive for greater achievements even in those subjects where he has less ability.

Some believe that children with greater ability are held back if they are taught with others of lesser ability, and this is the reason why groups of 'high-fliers' are sometimes selected to be groomed for greater achievements. However, there is little sociological evidence to prove that those with greater ability are held back by the others; there is evidence to suggest that the less able are helped by being taught alongside their brighter colleagues in a particular activity so long as the less able are not treated in a condescending way so that they are made to feel inferior. Those with most ability should learn at an early age that they live in a society comprised of people with varying abilities; the able should appreciate that it is to the advantage of society as a whole that they should assist the less able to progress.

It is impossible to measure intelligence quotients exactly:

$$IQ = \frac{\text{mental age}}{\text{chronological age}} \times 100$$

It is often thought that intelligence cannot be increased appreciably although knowledge can. We saw in the last topic that environmental factors have considerable influence over pupils' abilities and achievements. The better the home-background, teachers and schools, the better will be the pupil's response. We have been studying implications of educational ability, but the ability to pay for educational advantages must not be ignored (see Figure 4.4).

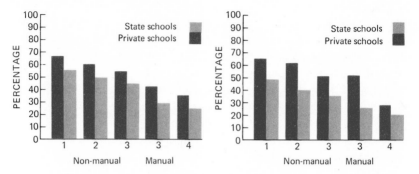

Figure 4.4   *Differences between state and private schools*
   a)   *Percentage of 'good' readers at seven years old who are attending state and private schools*
   b)   *Percentage of children with 'good' arithmetic ability attending state and private schools*
(Source: From Birth to Seven, *a survey made in 1972 by the National Children's Bureau of 17 000 children born in the week 3 to 9 March 1958)*

Ability to pay still plays a part in the educational achievement of those who enter direct-grant grammar schools and public schools. At further education level, students' grants are not of a universal standard and those at universities have better provisions than those at colleges of education, while some parents do not make the full parental contribution to the student's grant. Working-class students find it very difficult to live on the grant, but middle-class students may receive additional financial assistance from their parents. Generally, a person with mediocre innate ability has more chance of improving his position, and moving up the social-mobility class league, if he comes from a middle-class background.

Most infant and junior (or middle) schools are *neighbourhood schools* so that the schools in working-class areas are made up of pupils with a working-class upbringing, whilst those in middle-class areas consist of children with parents of middle-class status. The middle-class parents are frequently more enthusiastic about their children's educational achievements. Some working-class parents mistrust education. 'What good does it do you? Are you any better off (ie happier) as a clerk or as a teacher? . . . at the back is this vaguely formulated but strong doubt of the value of education.' (Richard Hoggart, *The Uses of Literacy*, Chatto &

Windus, 1957) Dr J. W. B. Douglas in *The Home and The School* (MacGibbon and Kee, 1964), found that far more grammar school places were obtained (these were in the days when the eleven-plus examination was the yardstick) by middle-class children whose parents were anxious for them to succeed. (See Table 4.2.)

Social class	Academic record of primary school	Grammar School Places Awarded %	Measured ability at 11 %	Teachers' comments %	Mothers' wishes %
Middle Class	good	53.2	48.0	61.2	57.7
	fair	35.5	34.8	49.2	46.9
	poor	14.6	23.0	39.4	36.1
Manual working class	good	26.8	19.6	32.3	30.6
	fair	13.3	14.0	20.0	26.6
	poor	4.8	7.8	14.8	17.9

Table 4.2 Academic record of primary schools by social class: award of grammar school places, comparison of observed and expected results (Source: J. W. B. Douglas, *The Home and the School*, MacGibbon and Kee, 1964)

Achievement then is closely related to social classes. Bernard Rosen, in *The Achievement Syndrome*, produced startling results, finding that only thirty-two per cent of a group of boys from the three lowest social classes scored high marks on an achievement scale, while eighty-three per cent of boys from the two top social classes scored high marks.

In the field of further education, highest educational achievement is found amongst the socially privileged. Table 4.3 shows a distinct bias in favour of the middle and upper-middle classes.

Similarly, Table 4.4 indicates that students who achieve entry into Cambridge University (usually with high grades at 'A' level) number higher among those from the middle class. A similar pattern is found at a good 'redbrick' university such as Leeds, but not to the same extent.

12.4 Opportunity

The 1944 Act laid down the principle of *equal educational opportunity*. Our examination of the differences in achievement according to various social classes, leads us to the conclusion that considerably more progress

	% (approx.)
Higher professional	19
Other professional and managerial	41 } Non-manual 71%
Clerical	11
Skilled	17
Semi-skilled	5 } Manual 24%
Unskilled	2
Not known	5
Total %	100

Table 4.3   Social class of students' fathers by occupation 1961–2
(Source: *New Society*, 5 November 1964)

	Cambridge %	Leeds %
Group A		
Professional, senior managers, company directors, teachers, writers, etc.	75	45
Group B		
Junior managers, business owners, shopkeepers, salesmen, clerical workers	15	25
Group C		
Foremen and manual workers	8	30
Not known	2	—

Table 4.4   Students' social class according to father's occupation, at selected universities
(Source: Peter Marris, *The Experience of Higher Education*, Routledge and Kegan Paul, 1964)

Age	1970	1980 (projected)
2–4	306 000	359 000
5–10	5 475 000	6 058 000
11–15	3 657 000	4 746 000
16	239 000	546 000
17	131 000	238 000
18	46 000	73 000

Table 4.5   Pupils in all schools, 1970 and 1980 (projected)
(Source: AEB 'O' Level Sociology question, November 1970)

is necessary before equal opportunity for all is obtained. Study Table 4.5 which gives the total number of boys and girls at school in 1970 and an estimate of the numbers in 1980, according to age-groups.

The candidates who were given Table 4.5 in their examination were asked: Why has there been an increasing demand for education among

1 the 2 to 4 age group
2 the 15-plus age group?

This GCE question hints at two important omissions in our present educational system:

1 the lack of provision for nursery education for the under-fives
2 the need for extension of educational opportunities for those contemplating going on to some form of further education.

'Equal opportunity for all' seems an impossible goal while class divisions have so much bearing upon whether or not children can adjust to society (see Figure 4.5). Greater opportunities will be provided by changes in occupational structure; an affluent society employing more skilled and professional workers means that fewer children start school in a state of deprivation. Contemporary research into educational expansion indicates that children from working-class homes are the most likely to take advantage of new opportunities. An upgrading of job-opportunities makes for an increase in the *social mobility* function of education.

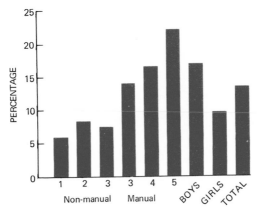

Figure 4.5   *Percentage of 'maladjusted' children in each social class, and the total percentage of boys and girls*
(Source: From Birth to Seven, *a survey made in 1972 by the National Children's Bureau of 17 000 children born in the week 3 to 9 March 1958)*

Nowadays, more skilled workers are required and the education system must be geared to provide highly qualified people. Although it is often feared that educational standards will decline with an extension of opportunities, there is no real proof that this happens, because the nature of educational processes may change. Kingsley Amis has complained about 'tapped untalent', suggesting that students have insufficient talent to take advantage of opportunities currently offered. However, King points out, 'There is an interesting cyclical relationship involved in which an industrialised society needs money to provide education and educated people to make money.' (R. King, *Education*, Longmans, 1969)

Social selection prejudicial to the working class is probably the greatest single factor aggravating attempts to secure equal opportunities throughout society. Table 4.6 shows that only twenty-five per cent of male Oxbridge students had fathers whose occupations were classified as manual and agricultural workers, although sixty-four per cent of all employed males aged forty-five to fifty-nine years fall into these classes —forty-five to fifty-nine years being the likely age of the students' fathers.

Parental occupation	Applications %	Acceptances %	All economically active males aged 45–59 in Great Britain %
Administrators and managers	13	13	6
Professional, technical, etc.	25	27	8
Other non-manual	23	24	22
Manual and agricultural	28	25	64
Unidentified	9	6	—
Total	100	100	100
Number in sample:	7407	3625	

Table 4.6 Percentages of Oxbridge applications and acceptances by occupation of parents. (Percentages may not add up to 100 due to rounding.) (Source: *Cambridge Colleges: Statistics of Admissions for 1972 Entry*)

Great advances have been made, especially in the last 100 years: in 1861, according to the Newcastle Commission, only 5.4 per cent remained at school beyond the age of thirteen. Secondary education in

Britain is now provided for everybody, and there has been a continual and rapid expansion in further education. But if this country is to compete successfully in a technological age, then a tremendous expansion of present opportunities at every stage is essential. The Robbins Report of 1963 stated that 'About everywhere we have travelled we have been impressed by an urge to educational development . . . which has often been translated into plans for expansion far surpassing the scale of British plans.'

Unit 13 Educational Structure in Britain

13.1 Schools

The Education Act of 1944 envisaged two stages of school education:

1 primary
2 secondary.

The primary stage extends from the age of two to eleven years and includes nursery, infant and junior (or middle) schools. Nursery schools have been very few in number until the 1970s; the Government's White Paper of December 1972, *Education: A Framework for Expansion*, promised that in the next ten years nursery education would be made available to the two-to-five year olds whose parents wished them to have it. Apart from the clamour for the extension of nursery education by the mothers of the pre-school age group and by such pressure groups as organisers of play-groups, the Plowden Report of 1967 and the Halsey Educational Priority Report of 1972 both recommended much more nursery education. It is in these formative years that the basis of a good education is laid down. As sociologists we are interested in schemes which attempt to improve the achievement of children whose home circumstances handicap them when they arrive at school. Although the Government White Paper of 1972 pledged an increase of about 300 000 nursery school places, the Plowden target will not be achieved until 1981–2. The White Paper accepted several of the recommendations of Dr Halsey's Report and many of the nursery projects will be directed towards helping educational priority areas. The Government has not set out any hard and fast lines about the way in which nursery education is to develop; it is hoped that local authority plans will reflect local needs and social pressures. The increased scope of nursery education will help towards an earlier identification of children with social, medical and psychological problems. Most nursery expansion will be within the framework of the school structure with classes for the under-fives forming part of primary schools. Although there are many who would have wished to see more money spent upon pre-school playgroups, the National Children's Bureau which investigated twenty playgroups set up in Southwark in the 1970s found that the needs of the most severely deprived children were not best met by playgroups run by mothers. Participation in playgroup activity was often not possible for the most deprived and the mothers were the ones who were the least suitable to help. During 1974–5 £15 million was to be made available for the extension of nursery education. Most of the youngsters attending nursery schools will only be there part-time, but allowance has been made for about fifteen per cent to attend full-time, mainly for social reasons. It is expected that LEAs will take account of other provisions for the two-to-five year old age group, and prepare schemes which incorporate the contributions of voluntary playgroups, day nurseries and all other forms of day care with the school nursery classes. It will be necessary to establish the closest possible link between home and school, so mothers will be encouraged to give practical help in running playgroups and in assisting nursery teachers. There will be a great need to increase the recruitment of nursery assistants and to extend courses for training nursery teachers.

The rest of primary education will continue in much the same way. Compulsory education in Britain legally begins at the age of five years and usually at the age of seven children go on to their junior (or middle) schools. Some of the most exciting developments in educational practice during the last twenty years have taken place in infant and junior schools, where considerable attention has been paid to work of a creative nature and the fullest possible development of the individual child. A child's education is no longer confined to mastering the 'three Rs' (reading, writing and arithmetic) but children are taught to participate in the work of their neighbourhood and in the interests of society as a whole. This is especially true where LEAs have been allowed to abolish the eleven-plus and so have been freed from the demands of competitive examinations. In the past it has been frequently the practice for junior schools to concentrate upon pupils in the 'A' stream with the best teachers allocated for their tuition, while the children in the 'C' stream were left largely to fend for themselves. Although the 1944 Education Act made transfer at the age of eleven compulsory, there has been a growing feeling amongst educationalists that the transfer age of eleven was not necessarily the best, and certainly ought not to be so arbitrary. The Plowden Report recommended

Young children investigating pond life in a classroom situation

Children using a gun clinometer to help them calculate the height of a church tower

the ages of eight and twelve as far more suitable for transfer and many schools have been reorganised into two main age-ranges:

4-plus to 8-plus—first schools
8-plus to 12-plus—middle schools

It is not a good thing for children to experience too many changes in the learning situation during their early life: an extension of the first school period to five years gives them an opportunity to gain confidence in number ability and in reading before being moved to a different environment. The extra year in the first school gives them a continuity and greater social stability when they greatly need it and they are thus more capable of developing their *basic educational skills*. The exciting educational experiments which have been developed in junior schools have given encouragement to the extension of this period of education. It is thought by many educationalists that the children will gain considerably from an extra year in the middle school before being transferred to the secondary stage. It must also be borne in mind that the retention of pupils at the secondary stage from the age of eleven to eighteen or nineteen constituted an extremely long period in one educational institution.

Secondary organisation has undergone great changes since the latter part of the 1960s. The 1944 Act outlined a three-tier system of secondary modern, technical and grammar schools, but left the exact form of secondary education to be worked out. There were also high schools, junior colleges and bilaterals which made for greater variety, but generally the three-tier system prevailed throughout England and Wales. Doubts, however, about the eleven-plus examination, which in many cases appeared to make an irrevocable decision at a very early age, and the 'creaming off' to grammar schools of an élite twenty per cent (average) of pupils who came largely from the middle classes, leaving the less fortunate in secondary modern schools, led to the concept of the comprehensive school. The twenty per cent average concealed very wide regional differences and was a key argument against the eleven-plus examination.

In 1971/2 about 995 grammar schools still existed alongside 1915 secondary modern schools that have a general education of a rather lower standard, leaving the grammar schools to concentrate upon a more academic approach. Some secondary modern schools arranged special streams where selected pupils were trained for CSE and/or 'O' Level GCE examinations, but the majority of GCE candidates came from grammar schools and most of the university places gained by pupils in the public educational sector were gained by the grammar schools. A few technical schools still existed at the secondary stage, offering education with a practical bias towards industry and commerce.

The Labour Government elected in 1964 decided to allow the development of comprehensive education by local authorities, who considered the needs of their own area and then put forward a plan to the Department of Education and Science. According to Circular 10 issued by the Department of Education in June 1965, LEAs were expected to submit a plan for a comprehensive system of secondary education, but by 1974 there was still a minority of local councils that had not complied, and no comprehensive education was available in their areas. The Conservative Government elected in 1970 back-pedalled over the question of extending comprehensive education. In its White Paper, *Education: a Framework for Expansion* (December 1972), very little was said upon the subject of secondary education and only an extra £10 million a year was allocated for spending upon the worst secondary schools in 1975–6 and 1976–7. The White Paper was followed by a letter to all education authorities requesting them to limit their bids for money for secondary school improvements to one project which the LEA regarded as outstandingly urgent. The main criterion suggested by the Department of Education was that improvements should be made where most of the teaching accommodation was constructed before 1903. The most important change in secondary education in recent years has been the growth in comprehensive education (see Table 4.7). The Labour government elected in 1974 expressed its determination to withdraw the state subsidy from direct-grant schools.

Year	Number of comprehensive schools	Percentage of 11 to 18 year old pupils in comprehensives
1950	10	0.3 (7988)
1960	130	4.7 (128 835)
1968	748	20 (606 362)
1969	976	26 (777 082)
1970	1250	31 (973 701)
1971	1520	35 (1 183 703)
*1972	1585	41 (1 236 678)
*1973	1825	46 (1 487 375)

* approximate figures

Table 4.7   The expansion of comprehensive education in England and Wales

Advantages of Comprehensives

1   The abolition of the eleven-plus examination took a great strain away from pupils who were being carefully prepared for this examination, often to the exclusion of more socialising influences. It also allowed the schools to enlarge their educational horizons, and not to concentrate such a large proportion of their resources upon securing eleven-plus passes.

2   The three-tier (sometimes called tripartite) system of secondary education (modern, technical, grammar), had revealed many problems: selection at eleven was by no means infallible and there had been considerable wastage of educational ability, especially among working-class children; the system had failed to provide the equality of opportunity envisaged in the 1944 Act.

3   Comprehensive schools are able to provide greater resources and the *economies of scale* which accompany large institutions: a small secondary school would not be able to afford a language laboratory, a full-time nurse, common rooms for pupils or extensive career-guidance facilities.

4   The expansion of the comprehensive school system has been accompanied by the concept of the Open Sixth (or New Style Sixth) where young people are able to remain at school in voluntary attendance after the age of sixteen to increase their number of CSE or 'O' Level passes, or to prepare themselves for further educational advancement. The Open Sixth is open to students without academic bar; the only requirements are a sound attitude and a willingness to benefit from the opportunities offered.

5   Comprehensive schools by the nature of their large size are able to offer higher salaries to attract teachers of the best calibre. Also, teachers are attracted to a school which challenges them with a sense of newness, experiment and excitement.

Disadvantages of Comprehensives

1   It is often said that an individual pupil loses his or her identity in such a large institution. Although the comprehensives attempt to overcome this difficulty by dividing into lower, middle and upper sections, and by having year tutors and form tutors (see Figure 4.6), nevertheless there is difficulty in developing individuality.

2   There are also diseconomies of scale especially where a comprehensive school is not purpose-built: it may take some pupils ten minutes to travel from one part of the school to another.

3   It is contended that where there is no streaming and selectivity and all the pupils in one age group are taught as a unit, the brighter pupils are held back. In the early seventies it was apparent that in spite of substantial achievements the comprehensive schools were not securing as large a proportion of university entries (especially to Oxbridge) as were the traditional grammar schools.

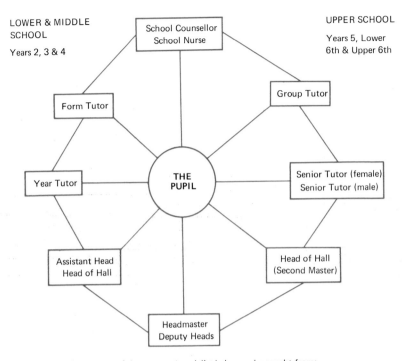

At any one of these stages, specialist help may be sought from:
The School Counsellor
The School Nurse
The Careers Teachers or Advisors
or other outside specialist services if required

Figure 4.6   *Pastoral care—the tutor system in practice at the Hewett Comprehensive School, Norwich*

4   In spite of their attempts to provide an egalitarian society, comprehensives have been accused of being just as meritocratic as the old selective schools. In an article in *Comprehensive Education* (Number 13, 1969) Marsden suggests that the continuation of streaming in a comprehensive school is damaging to pupils' morale and educational performance.

5   It is difficult to ensure the full recognition of parents' choice and still establish schools containing pupils from all the ability ranges; even when comprehensives are neighbourhood schools, they may be made up of pupils either from middle-class or working-class families, tending to reinforce class consciousness.

The secondary schools have to face problems connected with raising the school-leaving age (1972–3). There were nearly 300 000 more pupils between the ages of fifteen and sixteen in the mid-1970s. Many LEAs were unable to offer secondary schools any more financial help towards going comprehensive except from monies available for raising the school-leaving age. Therefore, the advent of the comprehensive schools and the raising of the school leaving age to sixteen have both been retarded in their scope by the lack of financial resources. Secondary schools will have to broaden their outlook and change their methods to cope with the challenge of the raising of the school-leaving age. The Government Social Survey carried out in 1968 revealed that teachers' ideas of the aims of education were very different from those of their pupils and of their pupils' parents. It is still necessary for the schools to impart a general basic education, but young leavers will expect courses geared to their vocational and social needs and to the activities which are provided for them outside the school. Pupils leaving at fifteen, and their parents, placed great stress, according to the Government's report, on the school's function to help towards a good job and teach them such useful aspects of life as how to handle money sensibly and speak easily. The teachers tended to place the greatest emphasis on developing character and personality, and thought that their pupils rated earning power above job satisfaction. The government survey indicated a gap here between the ideas of the school and the ideas of the pupil. The schools are not entirely to blame. When the school-leaving age was raised to fifteen in 1944, there were great hopes of clear-cut educational advancement especially in the secondary modern schools. Unfortunately, because of patchwork changes, lack of money and old-fashioned curricula, the expected progress has not been maintained. Secondary modern schools were not given the beneficial staffing ratios, laboratory and athletic facilities which would allow the potential benefits of the raising of the school-leaving age to be fully realised. There are cynics who believe that the Government raised the school-leaving age in 1972/3 as a cheap way of reducing unemployment. However, this is an unfair criticism because the schools had planned, or ought to have planned, for this move over a period of eight years from the time the scheme was announced. There is still much hope to be gained from the way in which many schools are tackling the challenge of RoSLA. The Schools Council, which receives about £2 million a year from central and local government, commissioned a secondary school curriculum survey in order that methods of teaching should be re-thought and the educational diet offered to secondary school leavers should be more in tune with the requirements of society. There is a need to tap the vocational incentives of young people, for smaller realistic teaching units, for further experimentation in new types of teaching methods such as *team-teaching* and *thematic teaching* and for teachers to have the advantage of *in-service training* as recommended by the James Report and accepted by the 1972 White Paper.

13.2 Further education

Further education is a very exhaustive term covering all types of education that extend beyond the secondary stage. It may be:

1 full-time or part-time
2 vocational or non-vocational
3 academic, liberal or technical
4 social or scientific.

Further education includes a multifarious range of activities extending from the part-time day-release course of a sixteen-year-old youngster attending a technical college to the top levels of higher education including the universities. There are 700 major institutions of further education in England and Wales, including agricultural colleges, colleges of art, colleges of commerce, technical colleges, colleges of education, polytechnics and universities. There were 311 000 full-time and sandwich course students and 1 648 000 (including evening part-time students) in further education colleges in Britain in 1970. We have already considered (see Topic 11.1) the courses that are provided mostly at technical colleges, eg Ordinary National Diplomas, Higher National Diplomas and the like. There are about 140 colleges of education in Britain (1975/6) and their purpose is to turn out qualified teachers with a sense of vocation. The colleges of education normally take students at the age of eighteen, although their role will be modified by the Government's acceptance in 1972 of the six main proposals of the James Report:

1 a large expansion of in-service training for Britain's 400 000 teachers
2 a planned reinforcement of the process of induction during the teacher's first year at school
3 the progressive achievement of an all-graduate teaching profession
4 improved training for further education teachers
5 improved arrangements for the control and co-ordination of acceptance for teacher training
6 the whole-hearted acceptance of the colleges of education into the family of higher education.

By 1981, three per cent of teachers could be seconded for training at any one time. Colleges of education will be expected to move into a closer relationship with the other further education institutions and the period of their time devoted to pre-service training will diminish.

One of the most interesting developments in the field of further education is the establishment of polytechnics. The first three 'polys' were designated in January 1969 and by 1973 all of the thirty proposed polytechnics were operational (see Figure 4.7). A polytechnic is similar to a university in many ways except that it puts stress upon the utilisation of knowledge as well as upon its generation, transmission and distribution. Therefore, although they can award degrees and range over the whole field of human knowledge in the same way as universities, polytechnic courses often tend to be more outward-looking so that a student's knowledge is applied in the fields of business, industry and science. The Secretary of State for Education has stated that polytechnics will be parallel in status to the universities; the main difference is that polytechnics are more orientated towards students' careers. Polytechnics have a more comprehensive student-body than the universities because they include full-time and sandwich-course students with part-time students from the surrounding areas. On successful completion of his course, a polytechnic graduate is often better qualified for a job in society than a university graduate because polytechnics afford extra practical training. Polytechnics are contributing to our society by offering the opportunity

Lanchester Polytechnic

1	Newcastle upon Tyne Polytechnic	16	Oxford Polytechnic
2	Sunderland Polytechnic	17	Hatfield Polytechnic
3	Teesside Polytechnic	18	A Polytechnic to the north of London
4	Leeds Polytechnic	19	North-East London Polytechnic
5	Huddersfield Polytechnic	20	City of London Polytechnic
6	Sheffield Polytechnic	21	Polytechnic of North London
7	A Polytechnic in Central Lancashire	22	Polytechnic of Central London
8	Liverpool Polytechnic	23	Thames Polytechnic
9	Manchester Polytechnic	24	Polytechnic of the South Bank
10	Trent Polytechnic	25	Kingston Polytechnic
11	City of Leicester Polytechnic	26	Brighton Polytechnic
12	North Staffordshire Polytechnic, Stafford.	27	Portsmouth Polytechnic
13	Wolverhampton Polytechnic	28	Plymouth Polytechnic
14	City of Birmingham Polytechnic	29	Bristol Polytechnic
15	Lanchester Polytechnic	30	Glamorgan Polytechnic

Figure 4.7   *New polytechnics and proposed college groupings*

of further educational qualifications to students who may not have the necessary 'A' level grades required by a university. The polytechnics believe that they can overcome the less high-powered academic background of students by more practical teaching methods geared closely to contemporary society and by offering longer courses of study in some cases.

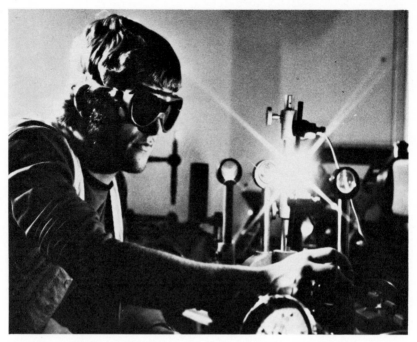

Student at Brighton Polytechnic working in a spectroscopy laboratory

There are forty-four universities in the United Kingdom offering degrees in a wide variety of subjects at many varying levels. A useful division of the universities (though decreasingly important as the 'levelling up' in society continues), comprises the following three groups:

1   Oxbridge: the two old universities of Oxford and Cambridge established in the twelfth and thirteenth centuries.

2   The 'redbrick' or 'city' universities which began with the establishment of London University in 1836 and include such universities as Bristol, Durham, Manchester, Nottingham and Sheffield.

3   The 'new' universities such as East Anglia, Essex, Keele, Kent, Lancaster, Surrey, Sussex, Warwick and York.

The question is often asked, 'What are universities for anyway?' and this was the title of Lord Annan's first Dimbleby lecture in 1972. Lord Annan believed the answer was simple: 'Universities exist to promote the life of the mind.' This definition may seem woolly to some people, but nevertheless it is right that there should be a place in every society for people who are able to discover new knowledge through research or reflection. This knowledge will then be transmitted to society at large by teaching students whatever is considered to be intellectually important, so that the students themselves may ponder upon the knowledge, possibly adding to it in the pondering. Universities are not factories of knowledge. Their highest mission is the seeking after truth so that society as a whole shall benefit from new wisdom and changing knowledge.

In 1971, the first 25 000 students were enrolled in the Open University, which awarded its first degrees in 1973, to students who had completed degree courses by using a combination of television, radio and correspondence courses together with a network of seminars, tutorials and short courses. It would be wrong to regard the Open University merely as a cheap substitute for more formal institutions of higher education. The learning process goes on throughout the whole of life, and the Open University offers opportunities to members of society who have missed opportunities at some point in the educational process: the latent potential of a generation that had fewer chances should not be lost for ever. Polytechnics and universities tend to reinforce the existing structure of society because middle-class youngsters are more able to take advantage of the opportunities offered, whereas Open University facilities allow increased opportunities to an older group and could marginally loosen the structure of society. The Open University should be regarded as an opportunity for learning 'between generations rather than within them' (Alan Hartley, 'Open Doors', *The Guardian*, 26 September 1972).

Finally, there are the broad liberalising courses of adult education supplied by the Workers' Educational Association (WEA), local education authorities, certain residential colleges and the extra-mural departments of universities. The Russell Report of 1973 produced guidelines for transforming the rather patchwork Cinderella activities of the present adult education service into a more meaningful system. Maturity and motivation mean that those over the age of about twenty-two years often have more to offer to society provided their horizons are broadened. Adult education should be seen both as a way of tempting people to spend their increasing leisure more fruitfully, and as a method of making them more useful members of society.

13.3   Youth culture

Since 'teenager' became a vogue word, a distinct youth culture has developed, especially in the affluent capitalist societies. It is difficult to assess the extent to which this distinctive culture has been artificially produced by commercial enterprises seeking the annual £1500 million which young people have to spend, or how far it is a natural phenomenon associated with the so-called generation gap. Many modern youngsters believe that parents ruin the first half of their life; perhaps they may find later that their own youngsters will ruin the second half. When the youth of society is given more freedom some will seek permissiveness and promiscuity, whilst others will decide to rebel against the imperfect society in which they find themselves, indulging in campus revolts or even deciding to drop out of conventional society altogether. It is not necessarily a bad thing for young people to challenge the very basis of society; a few years later they have so often settled down and accepted almost completely and apathetically the very ideals of the society which they once thought were so bad. There is little doubt that in a few years we shall be asking, 'Where have all the Hippies gone?'

The social implications of a *youth culture*, however temporary the phase, provide sociological problems. It is a time when a distinctive group is more separate from the rest of society than at any other time in their lives. The youth have their own groups, amusements, and other interests. They frequent the same discotheques, football matches, pubs and youth clubs. Youth clubs are going through a difficult period because they are stamped with the hallmark of so-called 'respectable society' from which the youth are trying to separate themselves. The increased affluence, especially of the young working classes, has been a significant factor contributing to a segregated youth culture; the middle-class youngster relying on a government grant for further education and frequently dependent upon parental contributions, is often less able to indulge in the expensive activities of working-class counterparts. Business enterprises sponsor a distinctive non-adult culture by using the mass media to promote incessantly the sale of motor scooters, motor bikes, stereos, pop records, drinks, teenage magazines, youth gear, transistors and cosmetics. About a third of the average teenage boy's expenditure goes on cigarettes, drink and general entertainment whilst the average teenage girl spends about forty per cent of her money on cosmetics and clothes. 'This is distinctive teenage spending for distinctive teenage ends in a distinctive teenage world' (Dr Mark Abrams, *Teenager Consumer Spending*).

Do you think that there has been a lowering of morals in society at large as religious and ethical standards have declined? It is wrong to think of a promiscuous younger generation without realising the part played by an apathetic and cynical older generation.

Our youth of today love luxury; they have bad manners, contempt for authority and disrespect for older people. They no longer rise when adults enter a room, they contradict their parents, chatter before company, gobble their food and tyrannise their leaders.

Ask your parents if they agree with that statement, and then tell them that it was said by Socrates about 2000 years ago.

Nevertheless there are some undesirable traits shown by the youth of today, that were not mentioned by Socrates, and they are far more dangerous to society than gobbling one's food. Can you add to this list of modern sociological problems:

1 drug-taking
2 cowardly violence (eg mugging)
3 soccer hooliganism
4 sexual promiscuity.

However, similar problems have always existed in some form or another. What can be done about the problems of youth and the generation gap? A sense of understanding, a degree of tolerance, personal care, good example and improved education will all help young people to get through an exciting yet difficult period, in a way by which society will benefit rather than suffer. Do you think that older people give the young sufficient credit for all their community care work at home and their Voluntary Service Overseas (VSO)?

The official Youth Service aims to encourage development of young people by helping them to broaden their interests, enjoy recreational pursuits and mix socially in their leisure time. The youth service does valuable work through local education authorities and in helping voluntary youth movements such as the Scouts and Girl Guides Associations (over 1 200 000 members), the National Association of Boys' Clubs (162 000) etc. The traditional youth movements provide opportunities for many young people, but more imaginative ideas are required if society is to cater adequately for today's youth. John Ewen (*New Society*, February 1972) and the Dennis Stevenson report (*Fifty Million Volunteers*, HMSO, 1972) both advocated special co-ordinating machinery for youth work, attached to the Prime Minister's Office and under the control of a cabinet minister. Such is the importance that some sociologists attach to modern youth problems. Other ways to improve the present situation include:

1 more public funds
2 providing activities more in keeping with the demands of modern youth
3 'teach him how to promote change within established systems', (Harry Kidd, *The Trouble at LSE 1966–67*, Oxford University Press, 1969)
4 encouragement for self-help. Pete and Suzie in *The Paint House* tell the story of London skinheads who came to smash up their self-programming youth club and then stayed to plaster and paint it before calling it their own. (*The Paint House*, Penguin Books, 1972)

Terms used in this chapter

formal education   socio-cultural factors
élite   deferred gratification
basic education   public language
peer group   formal language
scholastic achievement   culture

Questions

1   The word education is often used in a broad sense to include all the influences to which people in society are subjected. In this sense, how has your own
education been influenced by:
a   physical experiences
b   social environment
c   schools
d   youth clubs
e   friends
f   travel?
  2   Remembering that poverty and deprivation retard chances of equal
educational opportunities, study the graph below.

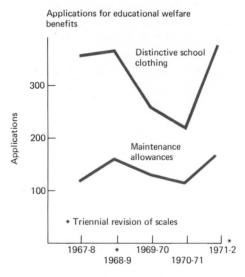

(Source: *New Society*, 26 October 1972.)
Why is it that the three-yearly general revision of scales of assistance for
benefit may spoil the chances of working-class children?

3 What does Basil Bernstein mean when he states that 'children from extreme social groups within societies are exposed from an early age to separate and distinct patterns of learning before their formal education begins? (*Education, Economy and Society*, edited by Halsey, Floud and Anderson). What patterns of learning would you expect to have been passed on by:

a   the parents of professional workers

b   the parents of unskilled manual workers?

4 In 1973 only about one in ten of the $2\frac{1}{2}$ million children between three and five received any nursery education.

a   How many children of this age group should be at nursery school by 1981?

b   What are the advantages of a child being left with its mother rather than attending a nursery school?

5 What is the Dip HE? Who would want to receive it and why should employers be interested in students who gain it?

6 Give some reasons why it was possible for the number of students in higher education in the United Kingdom to double in the ten years up to 1970/71. (*Education Statistics for the UK 1970*, HMSO 1971)

7 The UCCA (Universities Central Council on Admissions) *Tenth Report 1971/2*, revealed that there were probably 2800 unfilled university places in 1972. Think of some reasons for this shortfall in the number of first-year university students.

8 'I teach sociology in a new university. The ethos of the department is what might be called "progressive".' (Writer in *The Times Higher Educational Supplement*, 29 September 1972.) Name some ways in which you think a new university might be progressive.

9 Peter Willmott in *Adolescent Boys of East London* describes how young people withdraw from mixed-age into a one-age (say seventeen to twenty years) society and then return to our society via courtship and marriage. List some advantages and snags of such a move.

10 'The Youth Service is failing to cater for black people,' the retiring chairman told the British Youth Council's AGM in October 1972. In what ways do you think the Youth Service, or young people in general, can help coloured immigrants to Britain?

Questions from GCE 'O' Level Sociology Examination Papers

1 In recent years what additional provisions have been made to secure better vocational training for young people at work? Explain briefly what further measures you would like to see, and why. (AEB, November 1970)

2 Explain carefully what is meant by tripartite and comprehensive systems of secondary education. What factors have tended to make English secondary

education move towards various kinds of comprehensive schemes? (AEB, June
1970)

3   Boys and girls aged 15–17 receiving day or block release for
                         further education, 1969

	Number (in thousands)	% of total age group in work
boys	200	40
girls	55	10

What reasons can you suggest for the sex difference in release for further
education?
b   What changes would you expect during the next few years and why?
(AEB, November 1972)
    4 'Every society is faced with the need to preserve and transmit its culture.'
What does culture mean in this context? What part does education play in
this process of preservation and transmission? (AEB, November 1971)
    5 What are the major social factors affecting educational achievement?
(Oxford Local Examinations, 1972)
    6 What, if any, is the connection between social class and educational
achievement? (Oxford Local Examinations, 1973)
    7 Summarise the sociological arguments for and against raising the school
leaving age to sixteen. (AEB, Specimen Paper for New Syllabus, 1972)
    8 Give a sociological explanation of the important changes in secondary
education which have taken place during the last thirty years. (AEB, June 1972)
    9 'During the nineteenth century . . . public concern with elementary
education was . . . the need to ensure discipline, and to obtain respect for
private property and the social order, and that kind of instruction which was
indispensable in an expanding industrial and commercial nation.'
                    (*Educational and Social Change in Modern England*, D. Glass)
What are the functions of education in the United Kingdom today? (AEB,
June 1973)
    10 To what extent has the aim of equality of educational opportunity been
achieved? (AEB, November 1969)
    11 What do sociologists mean by 'Youth Culture'? How do they account
for the growth of 'Youth Culture' in modern industrial societies? (AEB, June
1973)
    12 Is the function of the educational system in this country mainly to train
people for future employment? (AEB, June 1969)
    13 Summarise what the table tells us about differences in performance at
grammar school between the four groups of boys. How would you explain the
differences?

Performance at grammar school selection, during grammar school, and admission to university, by occupation of father (Boys, England and Wales 1955–1956).

Occupation of father	Top group at entry to grammar school %	Grammar school record of two passes at 'A' level %	Students admitted to university from all grammar schools %	Students admitted to university from all (incl. public) schools %
Professional, managerial and clerical	33.5	52.5	63.5	74.0
Skilled manual	45.3	32.8	30.3	21.7
Semi-skilled manual	16.3	7.1	4.9	3.4
Unskilled manual	4.9	1.6	1.3	0.9
	100.0	100.0	100.0	100.0

Source: R. K. Kelsall, *Report on an Inquiry into Application for Admission to University*, London 1957.
(AEB, Specimen Paper for New Syllabus, 1972)

14 What contribution, if any, has the abolition of the eleven-plus examination made to increasing equality in educational achievement? (Oxford Local Examinations, 1974)

15 'The main factor in educational inequality is not the type of school attended, but the child's home life before he or she even goes to school.' Do you agree? (Oxford Local Examinations, 1975)

16 What difficulties do school leavers experience in making the move from school to work? (Oxford Local Examinations, 1975)

17 'Innate ability is not always the most important factor in producing high achievement at secondary school.'
a   What kind of evidence is there to support this statement?
b   State what other factors are also important and discuss them briefly.

5 Population
Unit 14 Demography

14.1 The study of population

In those days a decree was issued by the Emperor Augustus for a general registration throughout the Roman World. This was the first registration of its kind. (Luke 2: 1–2)

The study of population, sometimes regarded as a discipline of social science on its own, is termed *demography*. Sociologists are concerned with many aspects of demography, especially those which tell us about *social structure* and *social change*.

From the earliest times of civilisation, governments have wanted to know the size of populations, perhaps to calculate the number of fighting men available or to find out how much they might raise in taxation. The Bible records that the Emperor Augustus issued an order for a *census* of the number of people in the Roman Empire to be made. It was because of this census that Bethlehem was Christ's birthplace and not Nazareth. After the Norman conquest, William the Conqueror sent investigators throughout Britain to record details of land use and where people lived: these details were recorded in the famous Domesday Book. In the modern world demography has become more important: a knowledge of the changes in population allows governments to plan ahead. Some of the things that a government may wish to find out from a census are:

1   whether more children are being born, in which case more schools will have to be built
2   whether there are to be more elderly people, so that more money must be set aside for pensions
3   places where the population is increasing, which will need more housing, factories, roads and other amenities
4   whether people are living in overcrowded housing conditions
5   where unemployment exists, and what kind of jobs are in short supply
6   where immigrants have settled, and where emigrants have gone.

Once the government and local authorities have the statistics they are able to make provision for the changes that have taken place in the population.

14.2 The census in Britain

Every ten years since 1801 the Government has appointed investigators to gather information about every inhabitant of the United Kingdom. The last census was conducted in Britain in 1971, and was one of the most detailed surveys ever carried out by a government. This survey was conducted by the Registrar General's department, which appointed several thousand temporary civil servants (mainly local government workers and teachers) known as *enumerators*. Each enumerator was assigned a certain number of households in his locality. Although computers and the most modern techniques of processing are employed, it takes several years for all the information to be processed and analysed by the Registrar General. Today the changes that are taking place in the population and in society as a whole are so considerable and rapid compared with those of a century ago, that it has been found necessary to conduct a small census of ten per cent of the population every five years: this is known as a *mid-point sample survey*.

In April 1971, every householder was bound by law to give details of everyone staying in their household on the night of the census (see Figure 5.1). Included in the census were people in hospitals, hotels, prisons and ships in British ports. The police sought out vagrants to prevent people being omitted, for if each enumerator missed just one household from his list the numbers unrecorded from the census would, it is estimated, equal the inhabitants of a town the size of Nottingham.

There was some concern expressed in Parliament at the time of the last census about the kind of questions that were asked. Some people felt that it represented an intrusion into their private affairs. In particular, the questions relating to a person's country of origin and their parents' country of origin were thought by some to be a potentially dangerous statistical exercise, as the information might be used later against the coloured immigrant community and their children. Yet the personal details and results of the census are to be kept strictly confidential by the Census Office, and not even other government departments may have access to the individual forms.

Census data is one of the most precise forms of demographic material, but other sources of information on population are available to the Government. Since 1837 the registration of births, deaths and marriages has been compulsory. These figures do provide some guide to population

PART B	Complete a line in Part B for **every person present,** that is every person who
	a spends Census night 25/26 April 1971 in this household
	or b joins this household on Monday 26 April and has not been included as presen

*For any **other** person who usually lives in this household complete a line in Part C on the back page.*

B1 Fill in this column first for **every person present.** (see note above) Write **name and surname.** Begin with the head of the household (if present). *For a baby who has not yet been given a name write 'BABY' and the surname.*	**B2** Write the **date of birth** of the person.			**B3** Write the **sex** of the person, (M for male, F for female).	**B4** If the person usually lives here, write 'HERE'. If not, write the person's **usual address.** *For boarders write 'HERE' only if they consider this their usual address.* *For students and children who are away from home during term time give their home address.* *For persons with no settled address write 'NONE'.* BLOCK CAPITALS PLEASE	**B5** Write 'HEAD' for the head of the household and **relationship** to the head for each of the other persons; for example 'Wife', 'Son', 'Daughter-in-law', 'Visitor', 'Boarder', 'Paying Guest'.	**B6** Write 'SINGLE', 'MARRIED', 'WIDOWED' or 'DIVORCED' as appropriate. *If separated and not divorced write 'MARRIED'.*
	Day	Month	Year				
1st person JOHN CITIZEN	6	3	39	M	HERE	HEAD	MARRIED
2nd person JANE CITIZEN	20	11	41	F	HERE	WIFE	MARRIED
3rd person ALAN JOHN CITIZEN	12	6	64	M	HERE	SON	
4th person MARY JANE CITIZEN	7	10	68	F	HERE	DAUGHTER	
5th person EMILY MAY SMITH	22	9	14	F	10, LONG ROAD NEWTOWN LANCS.	MOTHER-IN-LAW	WIDOWED
6th person	Day	Month	Year				

If there are more than six persons present continue on a new form.
(The enumerator will supply you with one if he has not already done so.)   2

Figure 5.1   Part of the 1971 Census Form

ensus form elsewhere.

	B8 Will the person be a **student** attending **full-time** at an educational establishment during the term starting April/May 1971? (see note B8) This question need not be answered for children under 15 years of age.	B9 a If the person was born in England or Wales or Scotland or Northern Ireland tick the appropriate box. or b If the person was born in another country, write the name of the country (using the name by which it is known today) and the year in which the person first entered the United Kingdom (that is England, Wales, Scotland and Northern Ireland).	B10 Write the country of birth of: a the person's **father** b the person's **mother** *This question should be answered even if the person's father or mother is no longer alive. (If country not known, write 'NOT KNOWN'.) Give the name by which the country is known today.*

h have a **job last week (the week ended 24th** (see note B7)

he person had a job even if it was only part-time on was temporarily away from work, on holiday, or laid off.

did not have a job tick whichever of boxes 2, 3, 4 priate; if box 5 is ticked state the reason; for sewife', 'Student', 'Permanently sick'.

need not be answered for children under 15 years

— in a job at some time during the week
— seeking work or waiting to take up job
— intending to seek work but sick   ☐ YES
— wholly retired
— not seeking work for some other reason, ☑ NO
namely
....

a Born in
☑ England   01 ☐ Scotland
02 ☐ Wales (incl. Monmouthshire)   03 ☐ Northern Ireland
or b
Born in .... (country)
and entered U.K. in .... (year)

a Father born in (country)
ENGLAND
b Mother born in (country)
ENGLAND

— in a job at some time during the week
— seeking work or waiting to take up job
— intending to seek work but sick   ☐ YES
— wholly retired
— not seeking work for some other reason, ☑ NO
namely *HOUSEWIFE*

a Born in
☑ England   01 ☐ Scotland
02 ☐ Wales (incl. Monmouthshire)   03 ☐ Northern Ireland
or b
Born in .... (country)
and entered U.K. in .... (year)

a Father born in (country)
ENGLAND
b Mother born in (country)
SCOTLAND

— in a job at some time during the week
— seeking work or waiting to take up job
— intending to seek work but sick   ☐ YES
— wholly retired
— not seeking work for some other reason, ☐ NO
namely
....

a Born in
☑ England   01 ☐ Scotland
02 ☐ Wales (incl. Monmouthshire)   03 ☐ Northern Ireland
or b
Born in .... (country)
and entered U.K. in .... (year)

a Father born in (country)
ENGLAND
b Mother born in (country)
ENGLAND

— in a job at some time during the week
— seeking work or waiting to take up job
— intending to seek work but sick   ☐ YES
— wholly retired
— not seeking work for some other reason, ☐ NO
namely
....

a Born in
☑ England   01 ☐ Scotland
02 ☐ Wales (incl. Monmouthshire)   03 ☐ Northern Ireland
or b
Born in .... (country)
and entered U.K. in .... (year)

a Father born in (country)
ENGLAND
b Mother born in (country)
ENGLAND

— in a job at some time during the week
— seeking work or waiting to take up job
— intending to seek work but sick   ☐ YES
— wholly retired
— not seeking work for some other reason, ☑ NO
namely *PRIVATE MEANS*

a Born in
☐ England   01 ☑ Scotland
02 ☐ Wales (incl. Monmouthshire)   03 ☐ Northern Ireland
or b
Born in .... (country)
and entered U.K. in .... (year)

a Father born in (country)
SCOTLAND
b Mother born in (country)
SCOTLAND

— in a job at some time during the week
— seeking work or waiting to take up job
— intending to seek work but sick   ☐ YES
— wholly retired
— not seeking work for some other reason, ☐ NO
namely
....

a Born in
☐ England   01 ☐ Scotland
02 ☐ Wales (incl. Monmouthshire)   03 ☐ Northern Ireland
or b
Born in .... (country)
and entered U.K. in .... (year)

a Father born in (country)

b Mother born in (country)

3

PLEASE TURN OVER TO THE NEXT PAGE ➡

trends, but all sources need to be supplemented by the census material. In some countries, particularly those under totalitarian regimes, registration goes much further than in Britain. In most countries in Europe, citizens are required by law to register their address with the police, and in some countries all adults must carry an identification card which contains some demographic data. The controversy that accompanied the last census was over whether Britain was becoming too 'continental'. Was the individual citizen's freedom being eroded by the introduction of questions of an economic nature, such as those about car ownership and housing conditions? There are very few people, however, who do not recognise the importance of gaining statistical information from a census; much of our knowledge of society in Britain today and in the past has been obtained from the census as well as from other government departments.

Unit 15 The Size of a Population

15.1 The population of Britain

It has been estimated that at the time of the Norman invasion in 1066 the population of Britain was 1.5 million. An increase of one million each century would bring us to the figure of 10.5 million when the first national census was conducted. The 1971 census showed Britain's population to be 55.6 million: one hundred years ago it was 28 million, so our population has just about doubled during the past century. Although demographers estimate the population will be approximately 63 million by the year 2001, we are likely to see some variation in the actual numbers as different trends occur (see Figure 5.2).

In 1798, Thomas Malthus advanced one of the first important theories of population. Malthus believed that the population increased at a faster rate than a nation's ability to produce food; consequently the population increase was threatened and limited by periodic famine. The high birth rate meant that in theory a population would double itself every twenty-five years, increasing at a *geometric rate*, but food production could not match this increase as it only rose at an *arithmetic rate*. According to Malthus, no normal increase in food production would be sufficient to sustain a population at a constant rate of growth.

Apart from the Irish potato famine of 1845–7 the population did maintain a steady growth rate (Figure 5.2), and people are better fed now than ever before in Britain. Although Malthusian theory has not applied

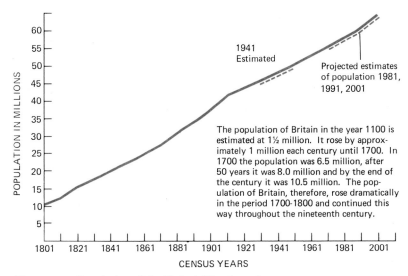

Figure 5.2   Population of the United Kingdom 1801-2001

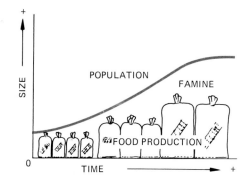

Figure 5.3   Malthus's projection of food production and population growth in theoretical terms

in this country, it has some validity in countries like Mauritius or Puerto Rico where food supplies barely keep pace with the population increase. Many demographers accept the broad principles of Malthusian theory for the underdeveloped countries, yet advanced industrial nations have been able to match population increase with sufficiency in food production through imports, and in some cases have obtained a surplus of agricultural products. The demographic factors of birth rate, death rate, immigration and emigration will affect the size of a population. Social and economic conditions influence these four factors and help to explain why

Malthus was wrong in his predictions when they are applied to the technologically advanced countries of the world.

15.2   The birth rate

Demographers usually express the birth rate in numbers of live births per thousand of the population. This is termed the *crude birth rate* because it is only an approximate measure of fertility: a more accurate figure would be obtained if only the numbers of women of child-bearing age were considered. The crude birth rate (see Figure 5.4) will tell demographers and sociologists something about family sizes in a country: a decline in birth rate will mean that the size of families is decreasing, although the overall population may be increasing due to people living longer, or more people entering the country than leaving it. The effect of family size on the socialising function of the family has been mentioned in Chapter 3, but its wider importance in demographic terms must also be understood.

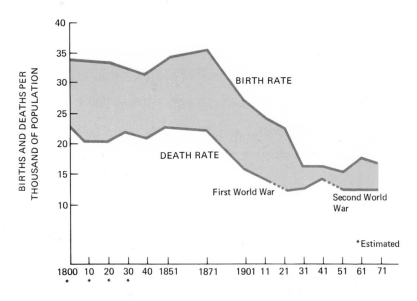

Figure 5.4   Crude birth and death rate in Britain 1800–1971

During this century the birth rate in Britain has declined steadily, except during the periods which followed war-time in 1920 and 1947, when servicemen returned to their wives from whom many had been separated for some time. The birth rate remained fairly constant at sixteen live births per 1000 in the inter-war years; after the last war it rose slightly but the latest figures show a decline to a rate of 14.8 per 1000 live births. It would be difficult to give precise reasons for the stability on the birth rate this century, yet we may reasonably assume a number of factors:

1   The general rise in standards of living has been attributed to, and recognised as being made more possible with, smaller families.

2   As women have improved their status and have gone out to work in greater numbers they have not wished for large families and constant child-bearing.

3   Improved contraceptive techniques and the greater availability of these devices have allowed better family planning.

4   The provisions of the Welfare State have meant that parents need not rely upon their children to support them in old age.

The slight rise in the birth rate during the 1960s may have been due to improved economic conditions: the upper professional classes have always tended to have larger families, and better material circumstances and upward social mobility for some could have caused them to follow this trend, yet most recently a decline in the birth rate has occurred. Perhaps another reason for the slight increase in birth rate during the 1960s was the younger age at which people were getting married. As people marry earlier they also have their family at an earlier age, thereby making it appear that the birth rate is increasing. Most recently, largely economic factors, such as the dramatic rise in the cost of housing for young married people in the early 1970s, may have caused the latest decline in the birth rate, so that we have a zero growth rate in population; in other words the population now is neither increasing nor decreasing.

15.3   The death rate

The overall increase in Britain's population has been caused by the gradual decline in the death rate: as life expectancy increased, so too the population increased in spite of the declining birth rate.

The *crude death rate* is the number of deaths as a proportion (per 1000) of the total population in a given year. A century ago the crude death rate was twenty-two per 1000; by the turn of the century it was sixteen per 1000; since World War I it has remained more or less constant at around twelve per 1000. In 1972 the figure was 12.1 per 1000.

The reasons for the decline in death rate may be directly attributed to such things as:

1   advances in medical science
2   improved hygiene and sanitation
3   better feeding
4   improved living conditions and housing

Advances in medical science and better social and economic conditions
have helped to raise the life expectancy of people from fifty years in 1900
to an average of seventy-three years today (see Table 5.1).

1841	41 years
1871	43 years
1901	50 years
1931	61 years
1971	71 years
1975	73 years

Table 5.1   Life expectancy in Britain

Four Stages in Britain's Population Growth

Stage one: until 1750   Until about 1750 the rate of growth was slow. This
period was one with a high birth rate and a high death rate. Poor agriculture and diet, lack of knowledge of medicine and hygiene, and occasional
plagues were the principal factors influencing the slow population growth
of about one million each century from the year AD 1000. After 1750 the
brown rat predominated over the black rat, leading to the elimination of
plagues.

Stage two: 1750–1870   During this time Britain's population trebled
owing to a high birth rate and a falling death rate. Agriculture improved
with higher yields and better stock through breeding. The discoveries of
the industrial revolution and the development of the factory system
brought people to the towns. From 1840 onwards public health measures
controlling sanitation and water supplies were beneficial as people lived
in cleaner conditions with less risk of disease.

Stage three: 1870–1920   A falling birth rate and falling death rate
slowed down the rate of population growth. Plentiful food from imports
as well as home production ensured adequate feeding for most people.
Bye-laws and government control of hygiene and sanitation became more
stringent. Medicine made significant advances and life expectancy increased. Family sizes fell as birth control became widely practised. Living
standards rose.

Stage four: 1920 till today   The modern period has a low birth rate and

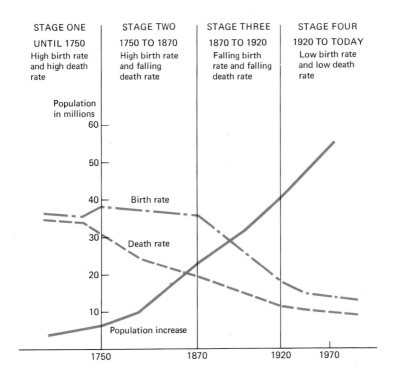

STAGE ONE	STAGE TWO	STAGE THREE	STAGE FOUR
UNTIL 1750	1750 TO 1870	1870 TO 1920	1920 TO TODAY
High birth rate and high death rate	High birth rate and falling death rate	Falling birth rate and falling death rate	Low birth rate and low death rate

Figure 5.5   Four stages in Britain's population growth

a low death rate. Infant mortality is negligible, and life expectancy has greatly increased. A gradual, slow increase in population has occurred, due primarily to the increased life expectancy. The Welfare State and higher living standards have meant a minimum provision of welfare for all and better material well-being. Epidemic diseases have been almost eradicated, while concern about the environment has grown.

15.4   Infant mortality

Infant mortality is the death rate of children born alive but who die before the age of one year, normally expressed per thousand live births. The considerable decline in infant mortality is an important factor of increased life expectancy. The infant mortality rate is used frequently as an index of social and economic progress. Although social and economic advances were made in late Victorian times, the infant mortality rate remained around the figure of 150 per 1000. The failure to apply knowledge of medical science and the poor living conditions of a great number of the working class did not help to alleviate conditions until the first decade of the twentieth century. Only when poverty decreased, standards of hygiene improved, and the midwifery services were extended, was there a noticeable decline in infant mortality (see Table 5.2).

The introduction of penicillin, and the development of more effective vaccines during the war further lowered the infant mortality rate. Since 1945 the figure has continued to fall, but not so dramatically.

Date	Rate	Date	Rate
1851	154	1941	49
1891	153	1951	30
1901	128	1961	22
1921	72	1975	17

Table 5.2 Infant mortality in the United Kingdom per 1000 live births, 1851–1975

Other industrial countries have experienced similar trends in their infant mortality rates; Britain lags behind certain European countries, but is better than others:

Sweden	13.6	France	23.4
Netherlands	15.8	USA	24.7
Norway	18.7	Eire	26.8
Denmark	18.7	India	140.0

Table 5.3 Comparison of infant mortality rates
(Source: *UNO Demographic Yearbook*)

In South Africa there are marked differences in the rates for different races:

Whites 27.7   Blacks and coloured 106.8   Asians 65.0

These figures reveal the importance of social and economic conditions to survival in infancy. The poorer nations have the highest infant mortality and the lowest life expectancy. In most countries of Africa, Asia and South America it is estimated that half the children die before reaching fifteen years, while in Europe the average figure for child deaths before fifteen years is about five per cent. The situation in India today can be compared to Britain a hundred years ago in terms of infant mortality.

15.5   Emigration and immigration

During the nineteenth century, and for the first thirty years of the present century, the number of people leaving Britain (an estimated 20 million) exceeded the numbers entering. Over the twenty-year period of 1931–51 some 465 000 immigrants entered Britain, and since 1951 there has been an excess of about 100 000 immigrants over emigrants. Some controversy has arisen over the actual numbers of immigrants in Britain, particularly those coming from Commonwealth countries since 1945, and it is important therefore to establish as accurately as possible the amount of migration to and from Britain.

For almost four centuries Britain welcomed migrants from other countries. Most of these immigrants were refugees from religious and political persecution in Europe, such as the Huguenots from France in the seventeenth century and Jews since the time of Oliver Cromwell. Since the middle of the last century, Irish immigrants have come in an almost constant flow to England and Scotland. Even since the creation of the Republic of Eire some thirty years ago, southern Irish immigrants have continued to enjoy free access to the United Kingdom, where they may immediately take advantage of political and economic rights. Jewish migration occurred in two main phases, during the 1880s and 90s when the Jews escaped from the pogroms in eastern Europe, and during the 1930s when they were refugees from Nazi persecution in central Europe. Various other national groups, such as Poles and Czechs, came to Britain to serve with British forces during the war and remained afterwards. After the war a number of Europeans returned to Britain as former colonial countries like India and Kenya were given their independence.

To many people the term 'immigrant' is synonymous with the coloured immigrants from Commonwealth countries in the Caribbean, India and Pakistan. According to the Institute of Race Relations, 620 000 immigrants from India, Pakistan and the Caribbean entered Britain between the years 1955 and 1967 (see Figure 5.6). An Act of Parliament in 1962 gave the Government power to restrict the number of people entering Britain from the Commonwealth: this and subsequent restrictions have reduced the number of Commonwealth immigrants to a tiny fraction of the numbers that entered Britain on British passports before 1962. The coloured population of Britain is less than two per cent of the total population: this is the same proportion as that of coloured people in

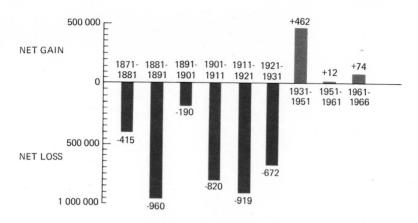

A. TO AND FROM THE U. K. 1871-1966

Note: The number of people migrating is a very small percentage when
compared with the total population for each period. For example,
net gain through migration 1961-66 represents only 0.14% of the
total population.

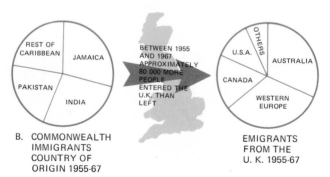

B. COMMONWEALTH
IMMIGRANTS
COUNTRY OF
ORIGIN 1955-67

EMIGRANTS
FROM THE
U. K. 1955-67

Figure 5.6   Migration

Britain (mainly freed slaves) at the beginning of the nineteenth century,
who had been almost totally absorbed by the local population at the end
of the century some four or five generations later. Not as immediately
recognisable as Commonwealth immigrants, are several thousands of
immigrants of European origin from Australia, Canada, New Zealand and
South Africa who have entered Britain in the past twenty-five years.
Excluding those on the diplomatic staff and in the armed forces, some
25 000 United States citizens are resident in the United Kingdom, and a
further 75 000 citizens of other European countries. In 1973 Britain
entered the European Economic Community, membership of which
provides for the free mobility of labour throughout the nine member

countries, so the number of European immigrants in Britain is likely to increase.

As the lands of Canada, Australia and the United States were opened up many people emigrated from Britain. Frequently during the last century, poverty and economic recession in Britain were the causes of emigration. Because of Highland 'clearances' thousands of Highland Scots crossed the Atlantic to Canada and others went to Australia (see John Prebble, *The Highland Clearances*, Secker & Warburg, 1963). When the lairds tried to raise men for the Highland regiments to fight in the Crimean War the native population had so declined and had suffered so terribly at the hands of their masters, that the lairds were told to recruit the sheep that had taken the place of the men. The harsh conditions that followed industrialisation in many towns caused thousands to leave the cities in search of a new life abroad. Agricultural recessions caused others to emigrate rather than to face starvation in Britain. It has been estimated that some 20 million people, including many Irish, left the country between the years 1830 and 1930. Some returned later, but most remained abroad.

Thousands have left Britain since World War II, about one-third emigrating to Australia, one-third to Western European countries, one-sixth to Canada and one-tenth to the United States of America. In this period the total number of people emigrating from the United Kingdom has almost exactly matched those immigrating.

Most migration to and from Britain since 1951 has been motivated by a belief in better material conditions in the new country. Until the 1962 Act which severely restricted the kinds of people who could immigrate into Britain, most immigrants were unskilled or semi-skilled workers. Since 1962 more than half the immigrants from Commonwealth countries have professional skills, usually in medicine and teaching. At first Commonwealth immigrants undertook work, which was often poorly paid with few chances of promotion, in industrial areas. The National Health Service could not function without the large number of Commonwealth doctors and nurses, while the London education authorities rely heavily upon teachers from Australia, New Zealand and other Commonwealth countries.

Migrants from Britain now tend to be skilled workers and many are professionally qualified. While many of the doctors in Britain come from the Asian Commonwealth countries, several hundred doctors leave Britain annually for the United States. In terms of the qualifications of those entering and leaving Britain, the balance is roughly even. The United States operates a restriction upon numbers of immigrants, but it has been calculated that America has gained far more in economic terms from European migrants with skilled and professional qualifications who were trained in Europe than the United States has ever spent or loaned in foreign aid.

Unit 16 Population Distribution

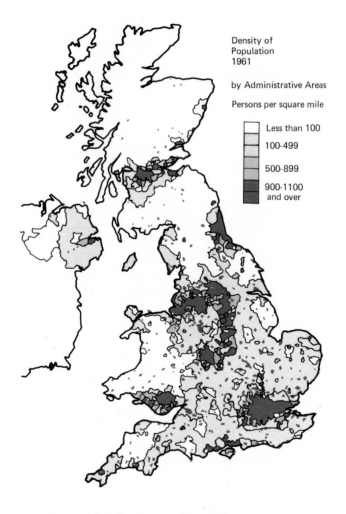

Figure 5.7   *Geographical distribution of population in the United Kingdom*

When a government conducts a census it is concerned to find out not only how many people there are, but where the population is spread or distributed. Distribution also means the proportion of males to females, and the proportion of different age groups within the population. Where people are concentrated and live is a *geographic distribution* (Figure 5.7); distribution by age or sex is *demographic distribution*; if the census records the occupations and such things as the housing conditions of people an *economic distribution* can be calculated.

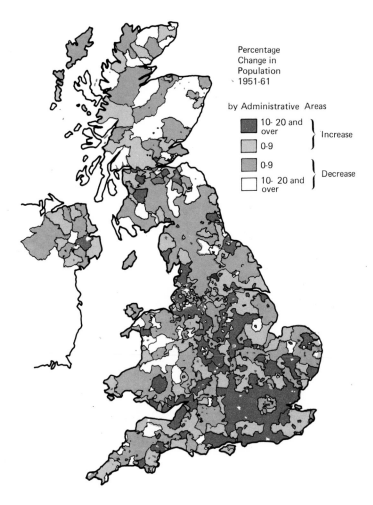

Percentage
Change in
Population
1951-61

by Administrative Areas

10- 20 and over } Increase
0-9

0-9 } Decrease
10- 20 and over

Reproduced by courtesy of the Central Office of Information

16.1   Sex distribution

For every 100 girls born in Britain today there are on average 106 boys born. As boys are often weaker than girls at birth and in infancy, in earlier times the numbers evened themselves out as more infant boys died. The advances in medical science have ensured that more boys survive than in former times, but there are more females in Britain than males. There are a number of reasons why there is a greater proportion of females: the most important one is that the expectation of life for women is, at seventy-five years, six years more than for males at sixty-nine years (Figure 5.8).

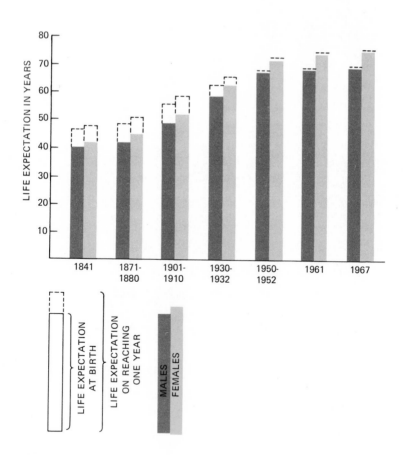

Figure 5.8   Expectation of life 1841–1967 in England and Wales

Non-biological reasons for the greater longevity of females, which causes women to outnumber men in the thirty-five year and older age groups (Figure 5.9), may be the more hazardous lives that men lead. To give some examples:

1   In World War I three-quarters of a million men were killed serving in the armed forces, and in the last war some 250 000 died.

2   Men are engaged in more dangerous occupations such as mining, deep-sea fishing or the building industry.

3   Men are the majority of drivers; over 1000 motorists are killed annually.

4   Because they smoke more than women, men are more prone to diseases associated with smoking such as lung cancer which claims eight times as many men as women.

The risks to women in pregnancy and child-birth have been greatly decreased.

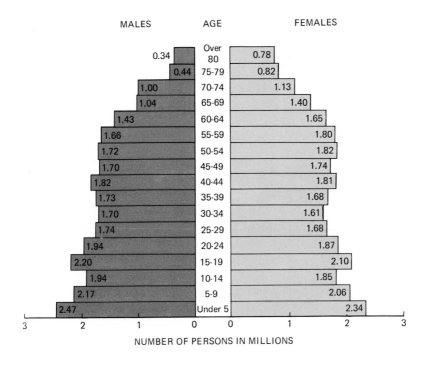

Figure 5.9   Age distribution in the United Kingdom
(Source: Registrar General, 1966 Census)

16.2   Age distribution

Age distribution is of considerable importance to demographers, sociologists and economists in the prediction of future trends, and in planning for governments.

In 1971 the age distribution in Britain was:

Age group	percentage
under 16	25.09
15–64	61.56
over 65	13.35

Those under sixteen are either infants or at school and people over the age of sixty-five are usually retired, therefore most of the working population is between the ages of sixteen and sixty-five. It is the working population who undertake the task of providing the elderly with economic goods and services and of providing for the needs of dependent young people: society always has the job of looking after those at the top and lower ends of the age scale.

Since 1871 older people have formed a growing proportion of the population as a result of increased life expectancy. In 1900 the number of people over the age of sixty-five was about five per cent of the population; today the figure is over thirteen per cent, and this percentage is expected to be the same at the end of the century.

Since the last war the fastest growing proportion of the population has been the under-sixteen age group, ie there has been a slightly higher birth rate. If this trend continues we shall have a more balanced population in terms of age distribution by the end of the century, as more than half the population will be of working age and roughly a quarter of the population will be infants or of school age.

When estimates of the working and non-working sectors of the population are made, factors such as the raising of the school leaving age and developments in education (such as more people taking advantage of higher education) must be taken into account. Improved technology and automation may mean that people will work fewer hours and choose to retire earlier. (These matters will be discussed in Chapter 9.)

16.3   Geographical distribution

One of the most important features of Britain's population is that most of us live in towns, cities or other urban areas. The reason is simple: most of the jobs are in the towns and most of us like to live near our place of work. More than a third of the population live in just seven areas: Greater London, Manchester, Birmingham, Leeds, Liverpool, Newcastle and Glasgow. Because some urban areas may not be separate local government units, but a mixture of different authorities which border one another, we refer to them as *conurbations*. Some 16 million people live in conurbations, and 22 million in other urban areas: forty per cent of the population live on just four per cent of the land area. If a line were drawn from Chester to Hull the land area of Britain would be divided in halves, but two-thirds of the population live south of that line. This concentration of population within a defined geographical area is termed *density*, usually expressed in terms of the number of people living within a square mile or kilometre. England, which has four-fifths of the United Kingdom's population, has a density of about 900 to the square mile; Scotland, with a tenth of the population (5.2 millions), has a density of 170, and Wales with 2.7 million inhabitants, has a density of 300 people per square mile. The population of Northern Ireland is 1.5 millions. The average density for the United Kingdom is 564 people per square mile.

International statistics of density are expressed in people per square kilometre (see Table 5.3).

Birmingham is the largest conurbation outside London

	Persons per square km (1968)
United Kingdom	227
Netherlands	379
West Germany	234
France	91
United States	21
Australia	2
Hong Kong	3797

Table 5.4 Population densities
(Source: *United Nations Statistical Yearbook.*)

16.4 Internal migration

Demographers are often concerned with the movement of population within a country. The numbers involved and rate at which this internal migration takes place have important consequences. In some places there has been considerable depopulation, while elsewhere the population has risen considerably within a short space of time. The principal motive for internal migration, as for immigration into and emigration from Britain, is an economic one. Where traditional industries such as mining or ship-building have lowered production or closed down, people have chosen to move away to where there are jobs in places where industry is expanding. Because the data on internal migration has been rather inadequate in the past, the 1971 census sought to remedy this deficiency by asking a question on the movement of home within the past five years.

The North of England, Scotland, Ireland and Wales are places where the highest losses through migration have occurred since the 1930s. In some of the highland areas of Scotland and Wales a considerable depopulation has resulted from a failure of the birth rate to match the outward flow of people: because the migrants are often young adults the decline is even more marked because they have not stayed to bring up children. The Midlands and South of England have gained in population through migration from other parts of the country and also from the natural increase in population. This trend was most marked during the economic depression of the inter-war years as unemployment caused many to move to the newer light industries of the Midlands and South. After the war the drift to the South continued, although it has been government policy to encourage investment in areas whence migration occurs.

East Kilbride New Town

Movement of population to the towns and cities began in Britain in medieval times. London's population more than trebled during the reign of Elizabeth I. This movement to the towns accelerated considerably in the industrial revolution of the last century. In the 1920s *suburbanisation* occurred around many of the larger towns: residential suburbs grew up where housing estates were built within easy travelling distances of the cities and larger towns. Since 1945 some thirty-two towns have been built or are being built to carry 'overspill' city populations and thereby relieve the overpopulation pressure in the cities. These new towns were planned to give their inhabitants the pleasures and benefits of living close to the countryside together with the facilities of town life. The movement to suburbs and new towns is known as *urban dispersal*. After the war the planning of urban dispersal by central and local government authorities ensured that the countryside was protected from excessive exploitation and at the same time provided accommodation. Before the war suburbanisation was often a haphazard affair as builders spread the houses along routeways into the towns and cities. This 'ribbon development' is much better organised and planned today, although there are still exceptions.

Of late, the demand for housing has grown considerably, particularly around London, so that some local authorities are faced with the problem of either protecting the green belt around cities or of providing more homes. Some commuters to London have been known to travel up to 100 miles to get to work each day. Surprisingly, the number of inhabitants of Greater London has declined by about three-quarters of a million since 1950. People have left the city centre mainly for the home counties of Essex, Hertfordshire, Surrey and Kent. The old centres of many of the large cities have been left almost to decay. The poorer housing conditions of these places are often inhabited by the elderly and the less well-off, and in many places Commonwealth immigrants have moved into these central city parts.

Unit 17 The Future Population

17.1 A population policy for Britain?

Until the mid-1950s demographers and politicians were expressing some concern that Britain's population was ageing. Since 1956 the census reports have shown that the birth rate has been higher than expected (taking the demographers by surprise), and of late some concern has been expressed that the population of Britain may become too large. Yet, once again taking the demographers by surprise, the latest figures of the 1971 census show a slight decline in the birth rate. Hitherto, government policy on population was principally concerned with the economic effects of migration away from the less prosperous regions. A generally hopeful attitude towards immigration and emigration (this is not including internal migration) was that fewer skilled working people would emigrate and that further Commonwealth immigration would be restricted, while those immigrants already in Britain would be successfully assimilated.

Recently, expert opinion has suggested that some consideration should be given towards the overall growth in population numbers. Concern with such matters as the environment, pollution, the preservation of natural amenities, conservation of natural resources, the availability of housing and overcrowding, all seem to point towards the desirability of maintaining or even reducing the size of Britain's population.

Experience of nations such as France after the war has shown that it is fairly easy to encourage population growth through generous state benefits and allowances for people who have large families, but to achieve the reverse poses many more problems. If benefits and child allowances were not given to large families, the poor, who tend to have the larger families, would suffer more, and it would become harder to escape the poverty trap than at present. Only a few extremists seriously suggest compulsory family limitation. The only apparent answer appears to be the prevention of unwanted children through greater knowledge and availability of family planning. Local authorities are now able to run family planning centres where advice about contraceptive methods is freely available, and the Government has decided to make family planning available on the National Health Service with prescription charges for appliances provided.

17.2   World population trends

The world population is currently estimated to be 3500 millions, and this figure is expected to double by the end of the century, giving therefore a growth rate of just under two per cent annually. This massive increase has been a fairly recent phenomenon in terms of world history, and it creates problems (primarily for the poorer nations of the world). Although the populations of advanced technological countries in Europe and the United States stabilised during the inter-war years, the populations of the underdeveloped nations continued to increase. In the richer, developed nations there is a fairly even age distribution with about a quarter of the population under fifteen years, but in underdeveloped countries the percentage of children is much greater at forty to fifty per cent. This is one of the reasons why there will be a high population growth rate over the next generation.

The reasons for the growth in world population are similar to those which caused Britain's population to rise a century ago. The death rate is falling due to a better knowledge of hygiene and medicine, and particularly as epidemic diseases today can be controlled, through immunisation and vaccination, at relatively low cost. The lower infant mortality and higher birth rate in underdeveloped countries have resulted in many more children surviving to adulthood, but contraception is not nearly as widely practised as in developed countries. There may be many reasons for this: ordinary people are often unaware of the advantages of family limitation (in many of these countries the desire to have sons outweighs all considerations of family size); contraceptive techniques may be expensive or unknown; possibly there are religious objections to contraceptive devices, as in Roman Catholic countries; to some extent improved farming methods have helped to feed some of the growing numbers, for example a 'miracle rice' which yields twice as many grains has been successfully introduced to some countries (although periodic famines do still occur).

Whether the world's resources of minerals and foodstuffs will be able to support such a large increase in population is still in doubt. Some economists and scientists maintain that there are not enough resources to give even half the world's population a standard of living equivalent to that of the average European at the present time. Feeding and controlling the world's population growth are perhaps the greatest and most urgent problems facing mankind today, but there is also the difficulty of distribution of resources which may bring problems of ecology and environment. Malthus's dreadful predictions of a century and a half ago are a reality in some parts of the world today, and many more may suffer in the future.

Abandoned children in Bogota

Terms used in this chapter

census
enumerator
life expectancy
infant mortality
migration

distribution
demography
ageing
conurbation
density

Questions

1 Suggest reasons for the questions asked on the 1971 census form (Figure 5.1).

2 Explain why Malthus was wrong in his predictions about Britain's population but right about the populations of some underdeveloped countries.

3 Account for the increase in Britain's population during the nineteenth century, and for the stability in population since 1945.

4 Why do demographers place so much emphasis on comparative infant mortality statistics?

5 What problems arise from:
a an excess of emigration over immigration
b an imbalance of age distribution
c an imbalance of sex distribution?

6 Suggest reasons for the concentration of Britain's population in the southern half of England.

7 Are demographic problems essentially economic problems?

8 Is it necessary to have a population policy for Britain?

9 What are the causes and likely consequences of the world population explosion?

10 Write briefly on *three* of the following:
a life expectancy
b immigration since 1950
c density of population
d internal migration
e Britain's population since 1870
f conducting a census.

Questions from GCE 'O' Level Sociology Examination Papers

1 How useful is the population census to the sociologist? (Oxford Local Examinations, 1972)

2 The population of the United Kingdom is now about 56 million. Describe some of the important differences it would make if the population rose to 80 million. (AEB, Specimen Paper for New Syllabus, 1972)

Vital statistics

3   United Kingdom (per 1000 population)

	1902	1932	1967
Birth Rate	28.6	16.3	17.5
Death Rate	17.3	12.2	11.3

(*Source*: Registrar General U.K.)

a   What are the causes of the changes in the birth and death rates since 1902?
b   Discuss the important consequences of these trends. (AEB, June 1973)

4   The projected increase in the population of the United Kingdom 1969 to 2001

Increase due to	Per cent change	Change in millions
a declining mortality rates	$+2\frac{1}{2}$	$+1\frac{1}{2}$
b excess of births over deaths	$+17$	$+9\frac{1}{2}$
c effects of immigration and emigration	nil	nil
Overall increase	$+20$	$+11$

i   What is the most important cause of the increase in population projected?
ii   Explain clearly what is meant by the three kinds of increase *a*, *b* and *c*.
iii   What are the most important consequences that may result from an increase in population in the United Kingdom? (AEB, June 1972)

5   What social consequences would you expect from a rise in the proportion of elderly people in the population? (Oxford Local Examinations, 1975)

6   Give a sociological explanation for the following figures:

Deaths of infants under one year of age in England and Wales

Year	Deaths per 1000 legitimately born	Deaths per 1000 illegitimately born
1918	91	186
1935	56	89
1945	44	65
1955	25	32
1965	19	25

(Source: *Registrar General's Statistical Review*, HMSO)

(AEB, June 1970)

7   What are the major factors affecting fertility in contemporary Britain? (Oxford Local Examinations, 1974)

8   Suggest some causes that could account for a marked increase in the population of:
a   a simple agricultural society
b   a modern industrial society.
(AEB, November 1969)

9   *Infant mortality rates per 1000 legitimate live births, by*
                   'social class' 1921, 1939 and 1950

		1921	1939	1950
i	Professional and managerial	38	27	18
ii	Intermediate (clerical and lesser professionals)	55	34	22
iii	Skilled	77	44	28
iv	Semi-skilled (manual)	89	51	33
v	Unskilled (manual)	97	60	41

Discuss the above figures and explain
a   why there are differences between one group and another and
b   why changes have taken place since 1921. (AEB, June 1971)

10   Changing distribution of the population of
                           England and Wales (percentages)

| | Age groups | | |
Year	0–14 %	15–64 %	65+ %
1851	35	60	5
1901	32	63	5
1951	22	67	11
1964	21	67	12
1979 (estimate)	20	65	15

a   Account for changes in the distribution of population by age-groups
since 1851.
b   What effects do such changes have? (AEB, November 1970)
   11 Describe the main changes in the geographical distribution of the
population in Britain during this century. (Oxford Local Examinations, 1975)
   12 What do you understand by the phrase 'population explosion'? What
are its causes and possible consequences? (AEB, November 1970)

Country	Population	Birth rate	Death rate	Infant mortality	Expectation of life Male	Female
UK	55 million	18.4	11.5	19.0	68	74
USA	200 million	19.4	9.4	24.7	67	74
India	500 million	38.4	12.9	139.0	42	41
Brazil	80 million	43.0	11.1	170.0	39	46

   13 a   Explain briefly the precise meaning of the following: birth rate, infant
mortality, expectation of life.
   b   In which country on the Table is the population likely to be increasing

most rapidly? What problems are often aggravated by a rapid increase in population? (AEB, November 1971)

14

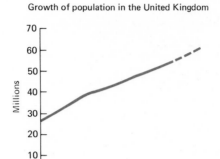

Growth of population in the United Kingdom

a   What was the cause of the increase between 1871 and 1901? What are the reasons for the continued increase in population today?

b   What consequences are likely to follow from a rise in population in the United Kingdom up to the year 2000? (AEB, November 1972)

15   *Population of Great Britain*
                              People born overseas

Birthplace	1931	1951	1961	1966
Number of people (thousands):				
Foreign countries	347	722	842	886
Canada, Australia, New Zealand	75	99	110	125
Other Commonwealth	137	218	541	853
Irish Republic	362	532	709	732
Total born overseas	921	1571	2202	2596
As percentage of population:				
Foreign countries	0.8	1.5	1.6	1.7
Canada, Australia, New Zealand	0.2	0.2	0.2	0.2
Other Commonwealth	0.3	0.4	1.1	1.6
Irish Republic	0.8	1.1	1.4	1.4
Total born overseas	2.0	3.2	4.3	5.0

(Source: *Social Trends* 1972)

Make use of the above figures in writing an essay on immigration and population in the UK.

6 Communications and the Mass Media

Unit 18 Communications

18.1 The importance of communicating

It is not possible to participate in the society in which you live without communicating with other people. For any kind of communication to take place, from the simplest to the most complex form, two things are essential. Messages must be:

1 transmitted by the person wishing to pass on the information
2 received by the people for whom the messages are intended.

The town crier was one of the few means of information before the communication explosion began in the nineteenth century. He was limited by:

1 the local content of his news
2 the small audience attracted by his bell
3 the volume of his voice.

A great deal of communicating is still performed on a person-to-person basis by the simple means of speech. If we travel in buses, stand in football match queues, or eat in restaurants, we are likely to engage in conversation whereby we impart information or ideas, receive news or comment, and very likely have our opinions challenged by other members of society.

One of the first sociologists to appreciate the importance of communications in society was Charles Horton Cooley. He directed attention to *primary groups* and *secondary groups*. Primary groups, such as families, have very close relationships between their members; secondary groups, such as casual acquaintances, communicate infrequently and therefore have less influence upon each other. No doubt you have more acquaintances than friends, but the friends exert the greater influence upon you because of frequent personal confrontation.

Face-to-face contact is by no means the only form of communication and during the last 200 years the art of *mass communication* has become one of the dominating factors of contemporary society. Two things, above others, have promoted the enormous growth of the communication industry:

1   Inventiveness has led to advances in printing, telecommunications, photography, radio and television.
2   Speed has revolutionised the imparting and reception of communications so that local news often takes a back seat to national news, which itself is often almost eclipsed by international news. The French students' revolt in 1968 was followed by six books about the subject within one month of the event.

No longer is the possession of information the prerogative of a privileged minority. In the last century the wealthy man with his own library was indeed fortunate, but today the public library provides a free service. Forty years ago people flocked to the cinema, but at the present time far more people sit at home watching a programme that is being channelled into millions of homes. Technological progress in the field of mass communication has given rise to many social problems such as:

1   a dull uniformity of programmes that pander to majority tastes
2   the *conditioning* of people *en masse*
3   a frequent neglect of minority groups
4   an excess of power wielded by controllers of the means of communication
5   the possibility of political interference by the rulers of the day.

Can you add to this list of problems brought by mass communications?

18.2   What do we communicate?

Communication is no longer merely concerned with the imparting of information. The modern communications industry influences the way people live in society and broadens their horizons by allowing access to:

1   information
2   education
3   entertainment.

The printing, broadcasting and advertising industries are all involved with informing, educating and entertaining. Although it is not possible to establish exact proportions, nevertheless it is fairly certain that the largest sector of the communications industry is devoted to entertainment. It is no accident that the *News of the World* is the only newspaper in the United Kingdom to top the 6 million circulation mark.

A great deal of the material which is communicated by the mass media is very valuable to the individual and to the society of which he is a part, but the vast modern network of communications is open to abuse. Some of the advantages and disadvantages have been tabulated below. No doubt you can add to the list.

Advantages	Disadvantages
1 People are much better informed than ever before	1 People are conditioned by the controllers of the media
2 Experiences previously enjoyed by the minority are available to the masses	2 Standardisation by mass production has meant a dull levelling down
3 A wide variety of material is available to cater for all tastes	3 Much synthetic and trivial material is communicated

Table 6.1 Advantages and disadvantages of mass communication

A great deal of the material which is communicated is very valuable to the individual and to society
Brian Inglis with a mountain of scripts from All Our Yesterdays

18.3   The need to compromise

Sociologists distinguish two main ways by which the communications media can influence society. The mass media can be used to produce either:

1   a *cultural class system*, or
2   a *cultural democracy*.

A cultural class system tends to emerge when the media encourage class distinction, for example between:

1   classical and pop music
2   learned commentaries and human-interest stories
3   high-brow and low-brow tastes
4   'U' and 'non-U' cultures.

A cultural democracy arises when the voice of the people prevails and the demands of the masses dominate the channels of communication for most of the time. Thus a continuous diet of pop-music may be provided on Radio 1. Can you think of any disadvantages of this? For instance would it be a good thing to encourage people to take an interest in ballet and the opera, even though they may have preconceived notions which make them dislike these things?

In Britain, we pride ourselves on a natural ability to compromise, so that neither a cultural class system nor a cultural democracy develops. An attempt is made to gear the system of mass communications to *the tastes of the majority*, without *minority interests* being neglected. We can see this compromise at work when we study our next topic (the press). The quality and popular newspapers provide for all tastes so that no one is forced to read one side of a case. With all communication and mass media there are two sides of a reciprocal relationship at work (see Figure 6.1).

Unit 19   The Press

19.1   What is the press?

The term 'the press' is used frequently as being synonymous with important daily newspapers; it is most probable that these newspapers exert more influence upon people's knowledge, opinions and attitudes than all

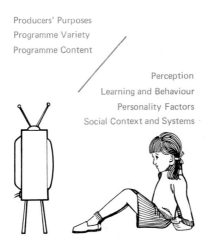

Producers' Purposes
Programme Variety
Programme Content

Perception
Learning and Behaviour
Personality Factors
Social Context and Systems

Figure 6.1   *Communication is double-edged*
(Source: J. D. Halloran, The Effects of Mass Communication, *Leicester University Press)*

the other forms of communication that are produced by the printing presses. But in the broadest sense, the press includes:

1 national daily newspapers   4 press agencies
2 Sunday newspapers   5 periodicals, magazines and journals
3 provincial newspapers   6 books of reference and fiction.

Can you add to this list?

The Newspaper Press Directory of 1971 recorded that 1174 weekly newspapers and thirty-five daily or Sunday newspapers are published in Britain. In proportion to its population, there are more newspapers bought in Britain than by the citizens of any other nation.

However, the choice of papers in Britain is relatively limited owing to the modern tendency for press mergers and closures. (In recent years, the *Daily Herald*, the *News Chronicle* and the *Daily Sketch* have been forced by economic circumstances to cease publication, while *The Sun* is the only new national daily paper to have built up a large enough circulation to enable it to survive.) There are five very important newspaper publishers in Britain:

1 Associated Newspapers   4 News of the World
2 Beaverbrook Newspapers   Organisation
3 International Publishing Corporation   5 Thomson Organisation

All the media of communication are closely linked. For example, most of the major newspaper proprietors have shares in independent television contracting companies and are influenced by the advertising industry. The main national daily and Sunday newspapers are given in Table 6.2.

Title	Controlled by	Circulation average Jan.–June (incl.) 1974
DAILIES		
Daily Express (1900)	Beaverbrook Newspapers Ltd	3 226 936
Daily Mail (1896)	Associated Newspapers Ltd	1 768 207
Daily Mirror (1903)	International Publishing Corporation Ltd	4 192 491
The Daily Telegraph (1855)	Daily Telegraph Ltd	1 427 439
Financial Times (1888)	Pearson Longman Ltd	198 574
The Guardian (1821)	Guardian Newspapers Ltd	364 635
Morning Star (1966)	People's Press Printing Society Ltd	49 842
The Sun (1969)	News International Ltd	3 302 990
The Times (1785)	The Thomson Organisation Ltd	351 205
SUNDAYS		
News of the World (1843)	News International Ltd	5 872 028
The Observer (1791)	The Observer Trust	832 983
The Sunday People (1881)	International Publishing Corporation Ltd	4 386 861
Sunday Express (1918)	Beaverbrook Newspapers Ltd	4 059 983
Sunday Mirror (1963)	International Publishing Corporation Ltd	4 570 712
The Sunday Telegraph (1961)	Daily Telegraph Ltd	776 783
The Sunday Times (1822)	The Thomson Organisation Ltd	1 505 385

Table 6.2 National Newspapers (Source: *Britain 1975*, HMSO)

19.2 Who reads what?

It is too easy to make simple distinctions between types of newspapers. Do you read:

1 a national daily and/or a Sunday paper
2 a national daily and/or a local paper
3 a tabloid and/or a broadsheet format paper
4 a popular and/or a quality paper?

All these divisions are over-generalised because of the essential links between the various branches of the press. Nowhere is the arbitrary nature of these classifications more apparent than in the description of newspapers as *popular papers* or *quality papers*. It is not insulting to be labelled as a reader of either of these types of paper but it would not be so acceptable to use terms such as:

1 popular or unpopular (or less popular)
2 quality or inferior.

The popular papers are frequently of the tabloid type and are likely to concentrate upon sensationalism, human interest stories, sport, prominent headlines and many photographs, while the quality press is of the large broadsheet format and concerns itself with informative journalism and commentaries upon politics, economic problems, literature and the arts. A suggested division into popular and quality newspapers is given below.

Popular	Quality
Daily Mirror	*Daily Telegraph*
Daily Express	*The Times*
The Sun	*The Guardian*
Daily Mail	*Sunday Times*
News of the World	*Sunday Telegraph*
Sunday People	*Observer*
Sunday Mirror	
Sunday Express	

The most popular papers in order of circulation figures are: *News of the World, Sunday Mirror, Sunday People, Sunday Express, Daily Mirror* and *The Sun*. These newspapers find their largest readership among people of working-class origins, nevertheless it would again be too sweeping a statement to say that the popular press is confined to working-class readers or that only the middle and upper classes read the quality

The Daily Express *goes to press*

papers. This can be seen from Table 6.3, prepared with the help of a survey conducted by the Joint Industry Committee for National Readership Surveys (JICNARS).

	Upper Middle Class and Middle Class	Lower Middle Classes	Skilled Working Classes	Lower Working Classes
Estimated per cent of	%	%	%	%
adult population	14	22	33	31
Daily Mirror	5	18	42	36
Daily Express	14	27	32	27
The Sun	5	17	44	37
Daily Mail	16	30	29	24
The Daily Telegraph	42	34	15	9
Daily Record	3	15	44	38
The Guardian	42	34	15	8
The Times	51	27	13	9
Financial Times	53	29	12	5
News of the World	5	16	41	38

	Upper Middle Class and Middle Class	Lower Middle Classes	Skilled Working Classes	Lower Working Classes
The Sunday People	5	19	41	36
Sunday Mirror	6	20	43	31
Sunday Express	22	31	28	19
Sunday Post	8	19	36	37
The Sunday Times	43	30	19	8
The Observer	36	34	20	10
Sunday Mail	5	19	40	36
The Sunday Telegraph	40	32	18	11

Table 6.3 Readership profiles by social grades (based on July 1974 to Dec. 1974 data) (Source: Joint Industry Committee for National Readership Surveys)

Whether or not a person takes a certain newspaper will depend a lot upon his own attitudes and interests and upon the coverage given to these interests (see Table 6.4).

	Political, social, economic, arts	Person-alities	Disaster and crime	Sport
News of the World	20	5	36	39
Sunday People	13	4	38	45
Sunday Mirror	25	11	13	51
Daily Mirror	31	17	14	38
Sunday Express	43	11	11	35
Daily Express	38	3	17	42
Daily Mail	45	8	12	35
The Sun	51.5	19	9.5	20
Daily Telegraph	57	5	3.5	34.5
Sunday Times	61	9	1	29
Daily Sketch	33	17	14	36
The Observer	71	6	1	22
Sunday Telegraph	64	3	2	31
The Guardian	70	1	1	28
The Times	70	6	1	23

Table 6.4 Approximate percentage distribution of news (Source: Roger Manvell, *This Age of Communication*, Blackie, 1967)

Which paper will you choose?

19.3   How does the press influence people?

There are many ways in which newspapers use their power to mould the views, opinions, attitudes and even morals of society. Some of these ways are listed below.

Selectivity

Newspaper editors and sub-editors select material to be included in the paper. The basis of selection will depend upon such things as:

1 the political leanings of the proprietors and editors
2 the policy of the paper on issues of the day such as immigration problems
3 the necessity to reflect in some measure the views of its readers
4 the emphasis which a paper places upon news-values, eg whether it is a
paper which gives pride of place to violence and sex (see Figure 6.2 from *The
Guardian*, 19 January 1973).

Figure 6.2   *How different papers interpret the news*
(Source: The Guardian: *19 November, 1973)*

NB   There is little evidence to prove that advertisers exert much influence
upon the content of a newspaper although one would hardly expect
cigarette manufacturers to advertise, on a large scale, in a newspaper
which constantly printed articles attempting to prove a close connection
between cigarette smoking and the incidence of lung cancer. Advertisers
supply about half the revenue of a newspaper and as Lord Williams has
pointed out in *The Dangerous Estate* (Arrow Books, 1959), '*The Times*,
read by professional and business groups with relatively high incomes,
. . . commanded advertisement revenue out of all relation to circulation
figures because each unit in their circulation totals represented considerable individual buying power.'

Omission

The selection of some news items entails the omission of other material.
This truism is far more important than it may seem at first sight. It is now
known that Geoffrey Dawson used his power as editor of *The Times* to
omit many references to Nazi atrocities before the war. If these omissions
had not taken place the British people would have been aware at an earlier
date of the Nazi danger to civilised society.

Comment

C. P. Scott, a once-famous editor of the *Manchester Guardian*, declared that news is sacred but comment is free. By this he meant that although he did not think newspapers should be untruthful and tamper with the news, nevertheless they should be free to comment fearlessly upon the news.

Newspapers must be very careful that they do not offend against the Official Secrets Act. The Services, Press and Broadcasting Committee issues Defence ('D') notices advising editors of news items that ought not to be publicly known. There are no legal sanctions to enforce 'D' notices but they are usually accepted as a voluntary form of censorship.

Editor gets warning under Secrets Act

By a Staff Reporter

Mr Harold Evans, editor of *The Sunday Times*, was warned by Scotland Yard detectives yesterday that he may have committed an offence under the Official Secrets Act by publishing a report of a confidential railway study.

He said Det Supt Croucher and Det Sergeant Barker interviewed him for an hour at the newspaper's offices.

He said : " They asked about the source of the document, which I refused to give. I was asked whether I had spoken with the chairman of the British Railways Board on October 8, when the report was published, and I said I was not prepared to comment."

Mr Evans was asked whether he took responsibility for the

NEWSPAPERS PETITION HOME SECRETARY

Reporters are refused appeal

Journalists have no special privilege

TWO REPORTERS GO TO PRISON

MPs asked to take up case

By our own Reporter

Two Fleet Street journalists were sen to prison last night because refused to disclose sources of information. It has never happened ...

APPEAL TO PREMIER

Press institute "dismayed"

The British committee of the International Press Institute has written to Mr Macmillan calling ...

Figure 6.3   *Controversy between the Government, the law and the press*
  a)   *Newspapers must not offend against the Official Secrets Act*
(Source: The Times, *8 December, 1972)*
  b)   *Journalists refuse to disclose their source of information*
(Source: The Guardian, *26 January, 1973)*

The triangular controversy between the Government, the law and the press began in 1962 when a Tribunal of Enquiry was set up to investigate the case of a spy called William Vassall. Two journalists who had written about the case went to prison because they refused to disclose the source of information which they regarded as confidential.

A great danger to unthinking readers is that it is so easy for a reporter to begin an article with a simple factual statement and then to insidiously introduce biased comment so that readers hardly know where the news ends and the comment begins. News and comment may be cunningly interwoven; merely one word can cause the reader to be unwittingly influenced. A correspondent who begins an article '*Even* the Conservative Party', or '*Even* the Labour Party', may be endeavouring to suggest that the Party has a low standard of morality, but that even the members of *this* party are capable of showing a small measure of virtue on some particular issue.

Editorials

It is frequently asserted that the press of the Western World is a 'free press' mainly because there is no government censorship and no papers controlled by the state. The freedom of the press is something of an illusion: consider for example the opinion columns of leader writers and editors. The viewpoint expressed may be that of a millionaire proprietor or a wealthy group in society. Would it be fair to assert that the Labour Party had no views to offer in the fight against inflation when a Labour Government had succeeded in limiting price rises to about five per cent a year from 1965 to 1969 while a Conservative Government elected in 1970 immediately abolished the National Prices and Incomes Board and was faced with a twenty per cent rate of inflation during the next two years? Yet the following extract was taken from *The Daily Telegraph* on 15 February, 1973:

The Prime Minister is now in a position of considerable political strength. Everyone knows that neither the TUC nor the Labour Party has anything to offer in the battle against inflation.

Such views, presented in a forceful manner, may well become the opinions of thousands of readers. Students of sociology should ask themselves whether there is more danger to freedom in a society where people's views may be dominated by wealthy press magnates and editors who could be their mouthpieces, or in a communist country such as the USSR where the Government airs its views in *Pravda*. In both cases the writers who influence public opinion have a vested interest in maintaining the type of society (whether capitalist or communist) of which they are important parts. Although editors may contend that they reflect the views of readers the only evidence indicating that this may be so are trends in circulation statistics of the paper; even these are misleading because many people buy the paper only because of comprehensive sports coverage, cartoons, pictures etc. Do you think that editorials attempt to influence, more than reflect, the views of their readers?

Embellishment

Students should search for their own examples of newspaper reports that exaggerate stories. Have you witnessed an incident where you thought the newspaper built up a story almost out of nothing? Human-interest stories lend themselves to embellishment and often the mingling of fact and fiction plays a large part in the accounts of such stories.

Character assassination

The public may be persuaded to adopt a biased and low opinion of a person whom they know only through the influence of the press and other agencies of the media. One of the reasons for the defeat of Richard Nixon in the 1960 electoral battle for the US presidency was the slur campaign of certain organs of the media culminating in the slogan 'Would you buy a second-hand car from this man?' It is impossible to assess the effect that similar character assassination had upon Harold Wilson's credibility in the early nineteen-seventies.

Before he became leader, Mr Wilson was seen as a tricky customer, a short-term tactician, a PR man supreme. After ten years he is seen as a schemer, a short-term tactician and a slightly worn PR man supreme. (Robin Oakley writing in the *Sunday Express*, 11 February 1973)

Special campaigns

The persistent campaign conducted by *The Sunday Times* against the Distillers Company (Biochemicals) Limited and its manufacture and distribution of the drug thalidomide aroused a great deal of public support. In 1972, the Attorney General, Sir Peter Rawlinson QC sought an injunction restraining *The Sunday Times* from publishing an article while the legal battle for compensation for the thalidomide children was still being fought. There can be little doubt that the campaign conducted relentlessly by *The Sunday Times* resulted in more realistic compensation to these unfortunate children (see Figure 6.4).

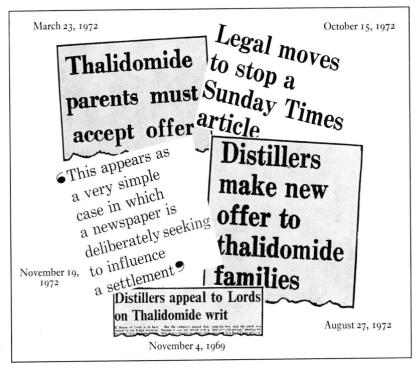

Figure 6.4   *The* Sunday Times *Thalidomide Children campaign, which began in 1969*

19.4   The Press Council

For over twenty years the Press Council has supervised the professional standards of the British press although its main influence is the weight of opinion which is given to reports upon the cases it investigates. The Press Council was set up by law in 1953; it has a lay chairman and twenty-five members. Some of its main aims include:

1   to preserve the established freedom of the British press
2   to maintain the character of the British press in accordance with the highest professional and commercial standards
3   to keep under review any developments likely to restrict the supply of information of public interest and importance
4   to deal with complaints about the conduct of the press or the conduct of persons and organisations towards the press
5   to report on developments in the British press which may tend towards greater concentration or monopoly

6 to make representation on appropriate occasions to the Government, or
to organs of the United Nations and to press organisations abroad
7 to publish its adjudications and periodical reports recording its work
8 to review from time to time developments in the British press and the
factors affecting them.

The Press Council carries out centralised research work into the
communications industry generally and publishes annual reports.
Although there has been a decrease in the number of complaints against
the press in recent years it would be rash to conclude on the evidence
available that British newspapers are more circumspect or that readers
are becoming more tolerant. The Press Council's eighteenth Annual
Report, *The Press and the People* (Autumn 1971) disclosed that 370
complaints had been received compared with 497 in the previous year.
The majority of complaints were later withdrawn or not pursued. In
1969–70 adjudicated cases fell to forty-five, their lowest level for ten
years. In 1970–71 adjudications fell to thirty-eight of which thirteen were
upheld as the following table indicates (see Table 6.5).

	Upheld	*Rejected*	*Total*
National mornings	1	6	7
Sundays	1	4	5
London evenings	—	1	1
London weeklies	—	—	—
Provincial dailies	3	9	12
Provincial weeklies	5	1	6
Scottish	2	1	3
Irish	—	—	—
Periodicals	1	3	4
Agencies and individuals	—	—	—
Total	13	25	38

Table 6.5   Press council adjudications, 1970–71

It would be a useful piece of investigation if students were to look up
outlines of the council adjudications which are possibly kept at their local
libraries. Here are two summaries of case studies from the 1971 Report.

Case I Allegations of inaccuracy

Mr Ian Lloyd, MP for Langstone, objected to criticisms of his voting
record in the Commons. Adjudication:

The Crossbencher column in the *Sunday Express* frequently singles out individual MPs and other public figures for criticism and has every right to do so. In this case the validity of the criticism rested upon an interpretation of figures including the figures for official pairings on Parliamentary business, and since the newspaper's figures were challenged by the complainant, he should have been given a reasonable right of reply. On this point only the complaint is upheld.

Case II Objections to comment

Mr R. A. Hewitt of Matlock complained about the phrase 'the little black dogs of the Commonwealth'. Adjudication:

Although the phrase complained of may seem offensive to some, the language was still within the discretion of the Editor. The complaint against the *Derbyshire Times* is not upheld.

Unit 20 Radio and Television

20.1 Radio

In 1972, the BBC celebrated fifty years of broadcasting. The organisation began as a company but was established as a public corporation in 1927 when J. C. W. Reith, who had been managing director of the previous company, was appointed Director-General of the BBC.

In *Only The Wind Will Listen: Reith of the BBC* (Hutchinson, 1972) Andrew Boyle describes how, from the moment Reith took over at the BBC, he was a law unto himself. He was an authoritarian who was determined that the BBC should give what he called 'a conscious social purpose to the exploitation of this medium' and that broadcasting in Britain should be a public service, not dominated by commercial interests or government control. You should read his autobiographical books, *Into The Wind* (1949) and *Wearing Spurs* (1966).

Controversy still rages about whether it was right for Reith to encourage programmes aimed at an upper middle-class culture, in an attempt to raise standards of taste according to criteria that he alone established. Also, is it desirable or ethical to use a monopoly in broadcasting to shape the pattern of listening in accordance with what one man, or a small group of people, regard as the best public interest?

Until the establishment of local commercial radio stations in 1972 (see *An Alternative Service of Radio Broadcasting* published in March 1971), radio broadcasting in Britain remained the monopoly of the BBC, but although a public monopoly, the BBC remains comparatively free from interference by the Government of the day. The Queen appoints the twelve governors of the BBC, including the chairman, on the recommendation of the Government, but from this stage on government influence takes a back seat and the Governors are responsible for the entire broadcasting system, including the content and culture of the programmes. The Governors appoint the Director-General as the BBC's chief executive officer: he is chairman of the BBC's Board of Management and discusses all major policy matters with the Governors. Antagonism to the monopolistic position of the BBC in radio broadcasting was first expressed in tangible form when pirate radio stations, such as Radio Caroline and Radio London, took to the air. Although they were made illegal in 1967, the pirate stations proved:

1   that there was an enormous demand for non-stop pop music
2   that many firms were willing to pay to advertise on commercial radio.

Pressure from this competitive source had three main results:

1   the introduction in 1967 by the BBC of a fourth network to supply a continuous service of pop music
2   the division of the BBC's service into four main channels catering mainly for
pop music (Radio 1)
sports coverage and light music (Radio 2)
classical music (Radio 3)
speech programmes—news, drama, talks, etc. (Radio 4)
3   the establishment of local commercial stations operating under the control of the Independent Broadcasting Authority (previously the ITA).

20.2   Television

The main pattern of television services in Britain was established in 1954 when the Conservative Government authorised the setting-up of the Independent Television Authority (ITA) to provide an additional television service to that provided by the BBC. The Television Act of 1964 extended the life of ITA to 1976 and authorised the BBC to run a second television channel called BBC 2.

In 1936 the BBC launched the first regular television service. The earliest regular European colour television service was transmitted in

1967 on BBC 2, whilst in 1969 BBC 1 went into full colour. About 16 million households are equipped with television sets capable of receiving BBC and ITV programmes. The BBC has to take the utmost care that it is not influenced by any commercial interests. In 1973 doubts were expressed about the wisdom of the BBC proposing to accept money from British Petroleum, in order to provide half the production costs (including the salaries of the BBC staff) to make *The Web of Life*, a conservation film which made little mention of the Alaskan ecological controversy concerning a proposed pipe-line to be constructed across the Tundra by a consortium of oil companies.

Commercial television is now controlled by the Independent Broadcasting Authority (IBA). Whereas the BBC is financed by government grants related to licence fees, the costs of independent television are met entirely from advertising revenue. The overall responsibility for administering the independent part of the television system is in the hands of the IBA appointed by the Minister of Posts and Telecommunications. The independent television programmes and the accompanying advertisements are provided by separate programme companies. The IBA performs four main functions:

1 selects and appoints the programme companies
2 transmits the programmes
3 determines the programme output
4 controls the advertising.

It is sometimes assumed that the working classes are more inclined to watch commercial television programmes than are the middle classes. There is some evidence that comedy and light entertainment programmes appeal more to the working-class audiences whilst informational and educational programmes are viewed more by the middle class. Anthony Piepe and Anthony Box, two sociologists engaged in research at the Portsmouth Polytechnic, reported their findings in *New Society*, 25 September 1972. The results of their investigations of 272 families are set out in Tables 6.6(a) and 6.6(b). The inquiry indicated that *home-centred* families spend less time watching television than *traditional* families. Rather than use the term middle-class, Peipe and Box called a family home-centred when it:

1 was involved in home ownership (including mortgages) compared with living in rented property
2 owned at least four durable consumer goods
3 enjoyed a superior standard of home decoration and furnishing.

Traditional families had at least two of the above attributes.

	Southern TV		BBC		About Same		Total
	No.	%	No.	%	No.	%	No.
Weekday							
traditional	76	40	31	16	82	44	189
home-centred	20	24	20	24	43	52	83
Weekend							
traditional	54	28	54	28	81	44	189
home-centred	19	23	20	24	44	53	83

Table 6.6a   Choice of channel

Type of Programme	Traditional		Home-centred	
	No.	%	No.	%
comedy, light entertainment	4 834	43.0	1 584	41.0
information, educational	2 271	21.0	982	25.5
sport	935	8.4	379	9.8
children's	1 380	12.4	404	10.5
religious	124	1.1	37	0.9
films	1 265	11.4	357	9.3
plays	314	2.7	115	3.0
total	11 123	100.0	3 858	100.0
average per family		58.5		46.4

Table 6.6b   Number and type of programme watched

The fifteen programme companies appointed by IBA are shown in Figure 6.5. The IBA is required by law to:

1   provide services which cover information, education and entertainment
2   ensure that programmes are of a satisfactory standard and properly balanced
3   control the frequency, amount and nature of the advertisements.

The IBA has a great responsibility concerning the moral standards of its programmes. Great controversy raged in 1973 over the interim injunction granted by the Court of Appeal to Mr Ross McWhirter against the showing of a film by David Bailey about the American pop artist, Andy Warhol. It is most important that public taste is not unduly offended but it is also important that modern works should not be excluded from the TV screen because they are considered daring or incomprehensible by contemporary standards. The Director of the banned ATV documentary

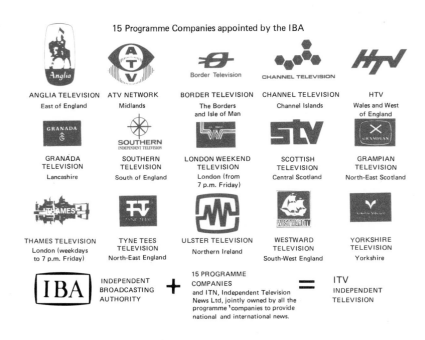

Figure 6.5   *The ITV companies*
(Source: ITV, *Independent Broadcasting Authority, 1973)*

considered it to be a momentous film, and argument will continue for a long time concerning whether or not three legal experts should have been able to postpone the showing of a television documentary without having seen it, and about the right of one individual to secure an injunction against showing the film. Clearly the rights of the minority must be protected but the majority also have their standards and attitudes, and whether or not they are prepared to accept new ideas can only be determined by subjecting these ideas to their scrutiny. The members of the IBA cannot be expected to see every programme and must inevitably trust their appointed executives to use initiative in making some important but controversial decisions. Eventually the judges decided in favour of the IBA's right to make its decisions unimpeded.

Before we turn to advertising in the next unit, study Figure 6.6 which shows the division of average ITV output. As sociologists we are vitally concerned with the proportion of TV time devoted to the various facets of social life (education, religion, documentaries, etc.) and with the general pattern of programmes.

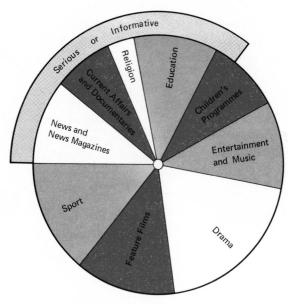

Figure 6.6   *Division of ITV programmes*
(Source: ITV, *Independent Broadcasting Authority, 1973)*

One aspect of the influence of television which has been much publicised is the influence of television upon crimes of violence. In spite of all the subjective 'guesstimates' that are made about the adverse effect of television and cinema programmes, comparative studies 'lead us to doubt very strongly whether screen violence has any *direct* effect on the real behaviour of young people' (*Violence on the Screen,* by André Glucksmann, 1971). The world in which we live is probably no more violent than the world of yesteryear; it is merely that through the medium of television in particular, the horrors of Vietnam and Northern Ireland appeared on television screens often within a few minutes of their happening.

As sociologists we must be objective and therefore be wary of those who continually stress, usually without research or evidence, the supposedly bad effects of television especially upon young people. Sociological research has suggested that 'any connection between the mass media and overt behaviour will be indirect' (L. Bailyn, *Mass Media and Children*). Perhaps the soundest contribution to the controversy about the influential effects of television has been made by James Halloran in *Television and Delinquency* (Leicester University Press, 1970); Halloran's approach to the research into the importance of television in shaping

Making a TV documentary

social values has been to place TV's influence in relation to all the other factors in modern society.

It does seem likely that the more a person is exposed to television, the less likely that person is to be much moved by what he sees. Certain of Dr Hilde Himmelweit's investigations (*Television and the Child*, Oxford University Press) suggest the more used a child is to films, the less he seems alarmed by them.

Study Table 6.7. Why do you think class C view longer than classes A and B? What information can you find from Table 6.6 about viewing by age groups?

United Kingdom

	February					August				
	1968	1969	1970	1971	1972	1968	1969	1970	1971	1972
Average weekly hours viewed										
Age groups:										
5–14	19.4	21.1	21.9	20.7	21.0	14.8	15.4	17.0	18.8	20.1
15–19	15.6	16.3	16.7	16.6	16.6	12.0	13.3	13.4	13.9	14.7
20–29	15.6	15.8	16.6	17.0	18.3	11.2	13.4	13.9	14.0	14.3
30–49	17.4	17.8	18.4	18.4	18.4	11.4	12.8	13.2	14.2	13.7
50 and over	17.5	18.3	18.4	18.9	18.9	11.6	13.4	14.3	14.7	14.7
Social class of adults (15 and over):										
A (top 5%)	13.9	14.6	14.6	14.0	13.3	10.2	11.2	11.4	12.7	11.5
B (Next 25%)*	15.9	16.5	16.5	16.8	17.0	10.7	11.9	12.5	13.1	13.1
C (Bottom 70%)	17.9	18.3	19.0	19.1	19.3	11.8	13.7	14.4	15.0	14.9
Overall average weekly hours viewed by all persons aged 5 and over	17.6	18.2	18.7	18.6	18.9	12.0	13.5	14.2	15.0	15.3

Table 6.7   Television viewing in the United Kingdom
(Source: *Social Trends* No. 3, 1972, HMSO)

* Inserted by the author.

Unit 21 Advertising

21.1 The persuaders

The sociologist is interested in all forms of persuading people, from the brutal brainwashing described by George Orwell in *Nineteen Eighty-Four* to subtle methods of propaganda such as *subliminal advertising*. (Subliminal advertising is the fast flashing of information introduced into cinematic or televised programmes so that the subconscious mind registers what the eye does not.) The most obvious persuasion to which the ordinary citizen is exposed is the medium of advertising.

Although it is not possible to determine the percentage of advertising which is solely *informative* (giving details of an article's price, use, size and colour), it is almost certain that in a modern sophisticated society there is far more *persuasive advertising*. The advertisers appeal to such motives as sex, snobbery and status in their endeavour to expand the sales of their

The caption underneath this photograph reads 'The Ormarin Bath is for ladies who want to do a little more than keep clean.'

products. Expenditure upon advertising is steadily increasing in almost all countries. Table 6.8 is based upon reported changes in measured media advertising expenditure for selected countries.

Country	Total reported measured media advertising expenditures (in millions of US dollars)			Percentage increase or decrease	
	1966	1968	1970	1966–8	1968–70
Argentina	133.2	200.7	217.2	+51%	+ 8%
Australia	320.0	385.4	456.4	+20	+18
Austria	72.2	77.8	102.5	+ 8	+32
Belgium	89.7	94.8	123.8	+ 6	+31
Ireland	17.2	25.2	32.5	+47	+29
Israel	13.4	15.3	23.0	+14	+50
Mexico	197.6	195.7	214.7	− 1	+10
Netherlands	147.2	219.8	271.2	+49	+23
Turkey	15.5	43.5	41.2	+181	− 5
United Kingdom	1226.4	1158.8[1]	1238.5	− 6	+ 7
United States	7524.8[2]	11870.5[2]	13016.0[1]	+58	+10
West Germany	1221.1	1489.4	1795.7	+22	+21

[1] reflects 14% devaluation   [2] cinema expenditure not reported

Table 6.8 Changes in advertising expenditure (Source: 'World Advertising Expenditures—1970', International Advertising Association)

As would be expected, the developed nations of Western Europe and North America spend far more on advertising than do the poor under-developed countries of Asia and the Middle East. Table 6.9 lists the

Country	Advertising expenditures as a percentage of Gross National Product
Eire	2.23
Switzerland	2.18
United States	2.11
New Zealand	1.65
Denmark	1.64
West Germany	1.56
Australia	1.44
Netherlands	1.38
Sweden	1.32
Austria	1.30
Argentina	1.28
Canada	1.25

Table 6.9 Countries in which advertising expenditure exceeded 1.25 per cent of GNP in 1970

countries spending over 1.25 per cent of their GNP upon advertising in 1970. Contrast these with Indonesia (0.01 per cent), Iraq (0.06 per cent) and Pakistan (0.08 per cent) which are examples of less developed countries with very low percentages of advertising expenditure.

In Britain about £600 million is spent annually upon advertising. The newspapers still lead in advertising expenditure as Figure 6.7 shows.

How much money is spent on advertising?
£323 million was spent on advertising in all forms in Britain in 1960 (pale red bars) and £591 million in 1971 (red bars). The diagram shows you how this money was spent.

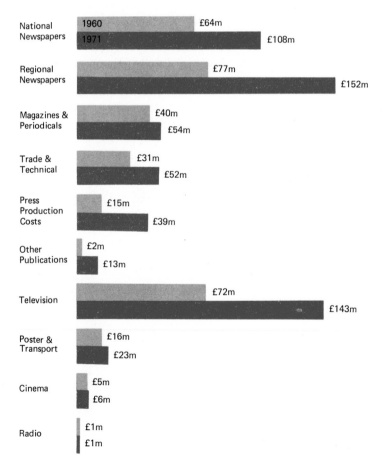

Figure 6.7   *Total advertising expenditure by media*
(*Source: Issue numbers 32 and 33 of the* Advertising Quarterly, *1972*)

Finally here we must consider the ethics of advertising and the sociological influences it has upon the attitudes of people. Critics of the
morality of much advertising believe that:

1 advertising can appeal too much to the emotions and to unworthy motives
2   people are exploited because of their gullibility
3   an appeal is made to greed and private materialism
4   children are unable to recognise the falsity of some advertising claims
5   consumers may be persuaded to purchase things that they do not really
need and cannot afford
6   inferior products are sold merely by high-pressure salesmanship.

Father Thomas Garrett believed that 'advertising has an importance
far greater than that of mere salesmanship. It is in a sense a moral guide',
and that ethically advertising may be defended on the following grounds:

1 People's standards of living have been raised so that the gap between the
'haves' and 'have-nots' has been lessened.
2 Advertising is not merely of products but promotes the aims of worthwhile organisations such as Oxfam.
3 People need a guide through the bewildering kaleidoscope of changes in
products. 'Consumer advertising is the first rough effort of a society becoming
prosperous, to teach itself the use of the relatively great wealth of new resources,
new techniques and a reorganised production method.' (Leverett S. Lyon,
The Encyclopaedia of Social Sciences, Macmillan, 1937)
4 All advertising in Britain is subject to the requirements of the Code of
Advertising Practice established by the advertising industry.
5 Advertising promotes competition so that 'In today's world of mass
production there is hardly such a thing as "a bad product".' (David Williams,
Advertising and Social Conscience, Foundation for Business Responsibilities,
1972)
6 People are liberated from 'Puritanism, parsimoniousness and material
asceticism' (Otis Pease, *The Responsibilities of American Advertising*, Yale
University Press, 1958).

21.2 Advantages and disadvantages of advertising

The main advantage of advertising is that potential customers can compare similar commodities. Advertising promotes competition between
firms and therefore could result in reduced prices in the long term. The
expense of advertising has to be borne by somebody and it is likely that a
large proportion of the cost will fall upon the consumer, but this does not
mean that prices will be higher, because large-scale manufacture may
mean lower production costs. The price of newspapers would be much
higher if it were not for the revenue supplied by advertisers. The

percentage of advertising space averages about a third; see Table 6.10 where three typical newspapers are compared.

Newspaper	1937	1955	1961	1965	1974
The Times	33	40	32	36	35(est.)
Daily Mail	41	36	32	39	38
Daily Mirror	26	34	33	35	34

Table 6.10 Percentages of advertising space (Source for 1937 to 1965 figures: *Communications*, Raymond Williams)

It is claimed that advertising improves the general standard of living in a community although that will not necessarily make for a happier society. Motor cars, soapless detergents and deep freezers would not have been developed to their present level of efficiency, or so that so many people benefit from them, without the stimulus of advertising. Increased production means more opportunities for employment.

An examination of Table 6.11 will give an indication of some advantages of advertising, because it lists reasons why members of a group of 1260 people approved of advertising. When people approve of something it suggests that they consider that it has advantages.

Number of adults who approve of advertising	Total Weighted: 848 100%	Sex Male 401 100%	Female 447 100%
		Percentages	
tells about product/prices	32	26	38
tells about new products	13	11	15
helps people choose products	10	9	10
helps sell products	19	20	17
lower costs	1	—	1
helps business/trade	12	14	10
helps employment	4	6	1
supports TV	1	2	—
supports the press	1	1	—
essential/useful	7	4	9
interesting/educational	7	7	7
amusing	2	2	3
other reasons	3	2	5
ambiguous answers	3	2	4
don't know/not stated	3	3	3

Table 6.11 Reasons for approval of advertising

Tables 6.11 and 6.12 are the results of a survey undertaken by the British Market Research Bureau on behalf of the Advertising Association; fieldwork for the survey was conducted in 1972. Those interviewed formed a representative sample of people aged fifteen and over. The points listed in Table 6.12 indicate some of the disadvantages of advertising.

Number who disapprove of advertising	*Total Weighted:* 295 100%	*Sex*	
		Male 152 100%	*Female* 143 100%
		Percentages	
products should sell on merit	6	3	5
too much advertising	14	18	9
too much repetition	5	3	7
misleading	23	18	29
puts prices up/wastes money	32	33	30
makes people spend more	3	3	4
people buy what they don't want to	10	11	8
makes up your mind for you	2	3	2
aims at lowest intelligence	5	9	1
gets on your nerves	4	3	6
spoils TV	7	5	8
other answers	5	3	7
ambiguous answers	5	1	10
don't know/not stated	—	1	—

Table 6.12   Reasons for disapproval of advertising

Some of the most important disadvantages of advertising are:

1   wasteful use of resources
2   over-production of 'luxury' things
3   under-production of many 'essential' things
4   creation of monopolies that act against the public interest
5   undesirable consumer loyalty.

Terms used in this chapter

conditioned	quality papers
cultural class system	minority interests
cultural democracy	majority interests
class distinction	anti-social attitudes
popular papers	subliminal advertising

Questions

1 Professor Marshall McLuhan invented the catchphrase 'the medium is the message'. Can you think of something where the *way* in which something is communicated is more important than *what* is communicated?

2 In its issue of 6 July 1972 *New Society* published an article entitled 'The Social Influence of Fiction—can fiction ever change people's opinions or behaviour?' Compile a questionnaire to be used in an attempt to determine an answer to this question. Diana Spearman in *New Society* suggested the following questions:

a Have you ever been influenced by any novel or play (including television plays, but not documentaries)?

b If you were influenced, please give author and title of work and say whether the work:

i made you behave differently

ii altered your general outlook

iii changed your attitude to some particular aspect of your life (for example, politics, sex).

c How do you think this change was produced?

i by giving you models to imitate

ii by making you understand yourself better

iii by making you understand other people better

iv by giving you a better understanding of the society in which you live.

Add three questions of your own and give the questionnaire to ten of your friends.

3 Give three reasons for the decline of the cinema as an instrument of the mass media.

4 Name a specialised periodical which caters for the interest of each of the following:

agriculture	Methodists
angling	music
birds	nursing
economics	opera
education	radio
electronics	rugby
gardening	science
golf	soccer

5 Give two reasons why weekly periodicals appealing to women (eg *Woman*, *Woman's Weekly*, *Woman's Own* and *Woman's Realm*) are the magazines with the highest sales in Britain.

6 By browsing through the contents of recent issues, attempt to assess which of the following journals have a tendency towards a left-wing or a right-wing bias (or is politically independent):

New Society	*Spectator*	*Tribune*
New Statesman	*The Economist*	

7

Commons TV rejected again

MPs last night rejected on free vote a motion
to allow experimental televising of the Commons. The vote was 191-165 — majority 26.
Only 356 MPs voted.

Press cutting   (20 October 1972)
Give reasons for and against debates in parliament being televised.

   8   In its issue of 21 January 1973, *The Sunday Times* carried a story entitled
'Radio Clothes Line' by Peter Dunn about the snags involved in starting
commercial radio broadcasting. What difficulties would you think might be
experienced by people wanting to set up a national commercial radio network
in Britain?

   9   Read the following cutting from a newspaper (December 1972)

Daily Mail altered sense of letter

The Daily Mail altered the
sense of a letter from a former
Metropolitan magistrate and
omitted a main point, the Press
Council says in an adjudication
published today.

   The council recalls its earlier
recommendation to newspapers
that it is desirable, when prac-
ticable, to obtain the consent of
a correspondent to any substantial alterations to a letter.

   Mr T. F. Davis, of Newchapel
Road, Copthorne, Sussex, complained that the Daily Mail
mutilated and distorted a letter
from him following the publication of an article which he
claimed was intended to attract
sympathy for people who offered
themselves as sureties for bail.

Mr Davis's letter to the chief
crime reporter was published in
a different form several days
later.

   He said that the implication
of the altered letter was that
he must have allowed many
sureties to undertake their
liabilities without asking them
if they were worth £X after all
their debts were paid and without a declaration on oath being
obtained. He asked for an
apology and publication of a
correction in an equally prominent place.

   Mr Dennis Holmes, assistant
editor, replied that he was sorry
Mr Davis was distressed by
publication of a very slightly
condensed version of the letter.

a   In what ways can a newspaper alter the sense of a letter?
b   Why should an editor wish to alter a reader's letter?
c   What can the Press Council do to ensure that justice is done?

10 What emotions and/or motives are appealed to by the advertisement on page 165?

Questions from GCE 'O' Level Sociology Examination Papers

1 What do you understand by the words 'mass media'? Why are sociologists interested in the mass media? What kind of work have sociologists done in this field? (AEB, November 1971)

2 Newspapers often refer to the generation gap. How acceptable or useful do you find this phrase? (AEB, June 1972)

3 Make use of the following figures to help you write an essay on the influence of newspapers in Britain today.

Average daily circulation of national newspapers

	1960	1964	1968
Daily Express	4 270 000	4 190 000	3 787 000
Daily Mail	2 825 000	2 400 000	2 039 000
Daily Mirror	4 649 000	5 085 000	4 949 000
Daily Sketch	1 075 000	847 000	886 000
Daily Herald	1 418 000	—	—
The Sun	—	1 414 000	1 009 000
The Guardian	212 000	278 000	270 000
Daily Telegraph	1 206 000	1 324 000	1 379 000
The Times	260 000	255 000	415 000

(AEB, June 1970)

4 If you wanted to conduct a survey in your school or college to find out more about the students' television viewing habits, how would you go about this? Describe what preliminary work would be necessary, what methods you would use, and what kinds of conclusions you would be justified in coming to. (AEB, June 1970)

5 Do you agree with the statement that radio and television represent the single most important factor in the formation of opinions and attitudes? (AEB, November 1969)

6 Discuss the sociological arguments for and against introducing commercial radio in this country. (AEB, June 1971)

7 What evidence is there to support the view that the mass media are influential in forming or changing attitudes? Make quite clear what kinds of attitudes you are discussing. (AEB, June 1972)

8 To what extent is it true that youth culture is simply the result of the mass media catering for working-class tastes? (AEB, November 1969)

7 Government and Politics
Unit 22 Government

22.1 The meaning of government

Government is the means by which different societies or groups are led and organised. When we talk about the Government we usually mean the people who control the affairs of the nation. The kind of government that we have in power is important because it can directly change our lives and the way in which society is organised. People who have various ideas about what should be done to lead and organise society become involved in another discipline of social science, the discipline of *politics*. Politics, therefore, is the study of people who have power or who seek to exercise power in society and the way in which they are able to influence events.

Many of the words used in government and politics are taken from the language of the Ancient Greeks, whose civilisation was one of the first to experience many different kinds of government and to produce writing about political ideas. The word politics comes from the Greek *polis* meaning a city; the ways in which different city-states were governed introduce us to some of the concepts of politics. When Athens was at its highest point of civilisation and power in the fifth century BC it was governed by an assembly of male citizens who decided all matters of policy and leadership by vote. Because Athens was governed by the citizens (even though women and slaves were excluded) it was known as a *democracy* from the word *demos* meaning people. In the rival city-state of Sparta a small group or *élite* made most of the decisions in government; since this was rule (*archia*) by a few (*oligos*) Sparta was known as an *oligarchy*.

Just as Athens and Sparta were traditional enemies, so too there is a constant conflict between the political philosophies of democracy and élitism in the writings of political theorists. In ancient Athens it was possible for all the citizens to gather in one place, for each to be heard, and for them all to take decisions, but in modern states with populations numbering millions no such direct participation in democracy is possible. In democracies today representatives are chosen to conduct the affairs of government on behalf of the electors. The method of choice the electors exercise, and the composition of the representatives, is the subject of the study of *political sociology*.

Who are the electors?

Who are the representatives?

Why and how do people vote in a certain way?

The answers to these questions can be categorised and analysed in a sociological manner, but first we must understand the workings of our Government.

22.2   Government in the United Kingdom

Government in the United Kingdom (see Figure 7.1) has evolved during the course of our history. The central Government meets in the Houses of Parliament at Westminster. Parliament is divided into two chambers: the House of Commons, and the House of Lords; of these the House of Commons is the more important as the Lords have had their powers considerably reduced since 1911.

The House of Commons comprises 635 Members of Parliament who have been elected by the adult population. Each MP represents an area or constituency in the United Kingdom which contains an approximate average population of some 60 000 electors. Since 1872 voting for MPs has been by secret ballot. Almost all the MPs belong to one of the three major political parties: Labour, Conservative, or Liberal. The party

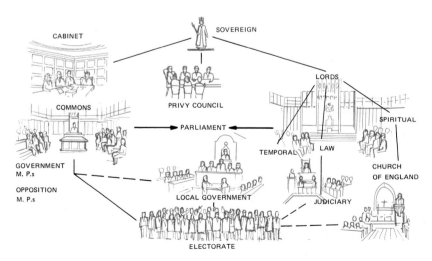

Figure 7.1   Diagrammatic representation of government in Britain

which has the largest representation in the Commons usually forms the government because, being in the majority, it is most able to secure the success of its policies. After an election the leader of the party which has the most MPs is asked by the Queen to become Prime Minister, and to select members of his party to form the Government.

The Government consists of MPs who have been chosen by the Prime Minister to run various ministries or departments of state. Each minister or secretary of state is responsible for introducing any new laws in the form of Acts of Parliament (known as bills until they have passed through Parliament) concerning his department, and for carrying out the wishes of Parliament with the help of civil servants in his department. Ministers and their Civil Service departments are termed the *executive* because they execute the wishes of Parliament. Parliament is known as the *legislature* because it makes changes in the law and may introduce new legislation. If there is any dispute about the interpretation of the law the *judiciary* or judges decide the dispute. The highest court in the land is found in the House of Lords.

The second largest party in Parliament is known as the Opposition, since its members seek to criticise and oppose many of the measures that the Government may introduce. Although they rarely succeed in defeating the Government in a straight vote, they are constantly ready to take over and form a government should they win in an election. As an alternative government their leaders are sometimes referred to as the Shadow Cabinet.

The House of Lords contains three types of peer (lord): the Lords Spiritual, who are the two Archbishops of the Church of England and another twenty-four senior bishops; the Lords Temporal who hold hereditary titles (dukes, marquesses, earls, viscounts and barons), or who are people who have been given peerages for life only, under the Life Peerages Act of 1958, and who do not pass their title on to their heirs. The third group of peers are the Law Lords who are the most senior judges of appeal. Altogether about a thousand hereditary peers are entitled to sit in the Lords, yet only a minority choose to attend. Most of the business in the Lords is conducted by the life peers who are usually elder statesmen and who came to prominence in political life when they were MPs in the Commons. The principal function of the Lords is to have a second look at legislation from the Commons and to suggest constructive amendments to it. All financial measures pass through the Lords without a vote, and they are unable to hold up any matter approved by the Commons which has been passed in two successive sessions; the Lords have the power to delay a bill for only one year, but this is rarely used.

22.3 The passage of legislation

Almost all new legislation originates from the *Cabinet*, which consists of the Prime Minister and his most senior colleagues. Not all members of the Government form the Cabinet, but only some twenty or so of the most important ministers and secretaries of state who meet regularly at 10 Downing Street to discuss important matters of policy under the chairmanship of the Prime Minister. It is possible for an individual MP (known as a private member) to introduce new legislation, but he has little chance of success unless the Government is prepared to lend its support to the measure.

Before a bill becomes an Act it is considered on three occasions, known as *readings*. The first reading is just a formality; at the second reading the general principles of the bill are debated in the Commons; then it passes to a committee of MPs for further examination before it passes back to the Commons for a third and final debate. If the measure has been approved in all its three readings in the Commons it goes to the Lords where the same procedure is employed. Finally it is sent to the Queen for formal signature (known as the Royal Assent), when the bill becomes an Act of Parliament and hence law.

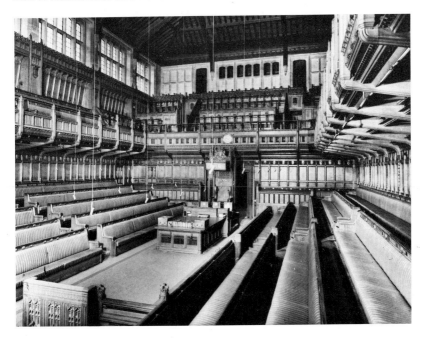

The Chamber of the House of Commons

The Monarch plays very little part in government. The Sovereign is the symbolic Head of State, whose most important governmental function today is the selection of the Prime Minister and the right to advise and warn governments on various aspects of their policies.

22.4   The separation of powers

Eighteenth-century political philosophers on the Continent often admired the system of government in Britain, although by modern standards we should have regarded it as corrupt and undemocratic. The reason for their admiration was the way in which the three branches of government (legislative, executive, judicial) were at once complementary and yet distinct. Although Parliament (the legislature) is theoretically supreme, the Government (executive) is able to function efficiently because it commands a majority of supporters in the Commons. The judiciary is technically independent of the legislature and executive, and therefore we are free from tyranny—for if there were no legislature (or just a puppet parliament) the executive would be answerable to no one, and would in all likelihood control the judiciary. In other words, we would have a dictatorship. As it is, while the executive is given considerable power to govern it is, nevertheless, ultimately answerable to the legislature, the Sovereign, and possibly to the judiciary. For the most part majority government has meant efficiency in government. Should a government seek to extend its authority and become no longer answerable to the legislature (ie to members of Parliament and, hence, the electorate) it would become undemocratic. A general election *must* be held every five years, though rarely do governments remain in office for the full period. The electorate, therefore, is able to express its approval or disapproval of the Government's policies at regular intervals.

22.5   Local government

The central government at Westminster directs and controls the affairs of the nation as a whole, but a large number of the functions of government are either shared with local authorities or directed entirely on a local level. Not only does this make for greater administrative efficiency, but the variations of regional and local needs are met by local democracy. The basic functions of local government may be divided into three categories:

1   personal: education, health and welfare

2   environmental: planning, housing and roads
3   protectional: weights and measures, the police and fire services.

Under the Local Government Act of 1972 a major reorganisation of local government was planned, to take place in 1974. Greater London which had been reorganised ten years earlier was not affected by this Act. The changes in population distribution, together with the desire to spread more evenly the administrative tasks, led to this reorganisation, and a two-tier system of local government has now been introduced in England and Wales. The top tier consists of some fifty-two county councils, the lower tier of 333 district councils. The six largest conurbations, apart from London, were formed into units known as metropolitan county councils, these are Newcastle (Tyneside), Leeds (West Yorkshire), Sheffield (South Yorkshire), Liverpool (Merseyside), Birmingham (West Midlands), and Greater Manchester. The responsibilities of the top and lower tier are broadly:

a   county councils: overall planning, education, personal social services, refuse disposal, libraries, police, roads, fire service
b   district councils: housing, environmental health (sewerage, drains, hygiene, food, clean air), museums, playing fields, public transport.

There are several sources of income to meet the costs of local government: more than a third of the revenue comes from government grants, a quarter from the rates, another quarter from loans, and the rest is made up from services that councils provide and charge for, such as car parking. By far the greatest proportion of expenditure is on education, which accounts for half of local government spending. Although local government expenditure is annually over £12 000 million, and so much of our daily lives is affected by the decisions taken in council chambers, very few people seem to take much interest in local politics and government. The average percentage of the local population voting for the councillors, who serve for four years, is between thirty and forty per cent: in some places it falls to as low as ten per cent. A survey conducted for the Committee on Management of Local Government found that a quarter of the electorate were unable to name just one service provided by their local authority, while more than a third felt indifferent about influence on their local council.

Lack of interest in local affairs is coupled with a lack of knowledge about local government. The better informed may be aware of the functions of local government, but many feel that all the real decisions taken in government are made in Whitehall and not the Town Hall. The recent

Local government—a council chamber

reorganisation of local government may help to improve the situation as there will be greater publicity given to the political conflicts, and the larger authorities will be seen to have real powers, but as yet it is too early to tell how effective this will be. A healthy democracy requires that there is public interest and participation in all levels of government, both national and local.

Unit 23   The Electorate

Subjects of the United Kingdom over the age of eighteen years who are not serving prison sentences, who have not been certified as insane, and are not peers, are entitled to vote in parliamentary and local government elections. Over the past 150 years the right to vote (franchise) has been gradually extended from a few male property holders before the Reform Act of 1832, to the present electorate (Figure 7.2). In the nineteenth century the electorate divided its support between the Conservative and Liberal Parties; since World War I the Labour Party has gradually replaced the Liberal Party as the main contender for power against the Conservatives.

The study of the way in which people vote is also a minor discipline of

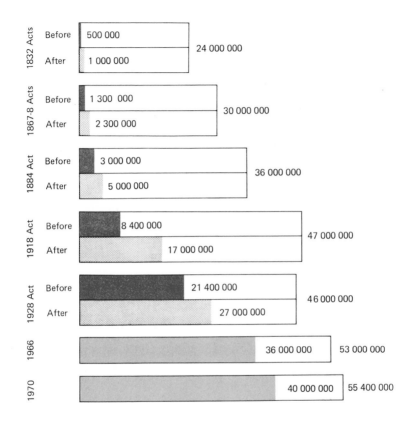

Figure 7.2   Electorate and population, 1832–1970 (after 1918 the figures do not include the Republic of Ireland)

social science, known as *psephology*. The techniques of psephological analysis of voting behaviour have become quite refined since World War II, with various ways of surveying and sample analysis in opinion polls, while a considerable degree of accuracy in prediction has been achieved for some elections since 1945.

The electorate in Britain consists of approximately 40 million people. On average since 1945 three-quarters of the electorate have cast their vote in general elections. This turnout as a percentage is shown in Table 7.1.

Date	Percentage	Date	Percentage
1945	73.5	1964	77.0
1950	84.0	1966	75.8
1951	82.5	1970	72.0
1955	76.7	1974 (Feb.)	78.7
1959	78.7	1974 (Oct.)	72.8

Table 7.1   Percentage voting at general elections 1945–74

The percentage of people who vote in British general elections is quite high compared to that of many other parliamentary democracies: in the United States only half the electorate cast their vote in the presidential election. In Australia, voting is compulsory under the threat of a fine. In Britain there is no compulsion and a certain percentage deliberately choose to stay away from the polling stations on election day. These people are termed *positive abstainers*. Those electors who made no deliberate choice to abstain but who fail to vote are known as *negative abstainers*.

23.1   Abstentionism

Over the past twenty-five years the margin between the major parties has been narrow in terms of votes cast at general elections:

	Conservative	Labour	Liberal	Others
		'000s		
1955	13 287	12 405	722	346
1959	13 750	12 216	1639	255
1964	12 002	12 206	3093	349
1966	11 418	13 066	2327	453
1970	13 144	12 179	2117	900
1974 (Feb.)	11 928	11 661	6056	1695
1974 (Oct.)	10 458	11 458	5348	1909

Table 7.2   Votes cast at general elections 1955–74 (thousands)

Because the difference is often so small (eg 20 400 votes difference between Labour and Conservative out of an electorate of 36 million in 1964) the rate of abstentionism can have a profound effect upon the outcome of the election. Mr Wilson's Labour government had a majority of four in 1964, and one seat, in Brighton Kemptown, had a majority of only seven votes. The much lower turnout in local elections makes the effects of abstention even more marked.

Under our system of election the candidate who gains a simple majority wins, even if the combined votes of his opponents total more. For example, we may have three candidates Smith, Brown and Jones; on election day the results are: Smith: 12 000; Brown: 11 750; Jones: 11 500. Smith wins with a majority of 250 even though Brown and Jones have a combined anti-Smith total of 23 250. The Liberals argue that this was the reason they were only able to elect fourteen MPs in 1974 although nationally they polled more than 6 million votes. In 1951 more Conservative MPs were returned than Labour, although the Labour Party polled nationally 231 000 more votes than the Conservatives. In February 1974 the Conservatives polled 267 000 more votes than Labour. Although there was no clear majority for either party then, the difference between more votes polled nationally yet less seats in Parliament is explained by the differences in size of majorities obtained in the constituencies. Even if a candidate gets just one more vote than his nearest opponent he is still elected. Four-fifths of all the seats in Parliament are considered safe, ie the sitting member's majority is high enough more or less to guarantee his return at the next election. Where the majorities are below four figures the seats are *marginal* and it is in these constituencies where a swing of five per cent or so in the other direction can unseat the sitting member; naturally psephologists usually concentrate their studies in these marginal constituencies. According to Jean Blondel in *Voters, Parties and Leaders* (Penguin Books, 1969), about eighty-five per cent of the electorate show continuous allegiance to the same party at each election, the remaining fifteen per cent of *floating voters* who change their vote or who abstain usually make the difference in outcome in a general election. Because a one or two per cent abstention rate of a party's supporters may put the other party in power, the abstainers and floating voters merit further attention.

Positive abstainers are thought to be a smaller group than negative abstainers. The positive abstainer may choose deliberately not to vote for a number of reasons. These usually are:

1   He may not be able to vote for the party that he supports in his constituency (for example if he supports the Liberal Party and there are only Labour and Conservative candidates).

2   He may have a personal dislike of the candidate standing for the party of his usual choice.

3   There may be some aspect of the policy of the party that he usually

supports that he has considerable disagreement with, but he cannot bring himself to vote for one of the other parties.

4   He may be cynical about the whole idea of elections.

5   Possibly he may think that the result is a foregone conclusion anyway, particularly in a safe seat.

The negative abstainers are perhaps more numerous. They tend to be the least interested and least informed about political matters. They are usually found among the youngest, oldest and poorest members of the community. There may also be practical reasons for abstaining. If the polling stations are in remote places, as in some rural areas; if a mother cannot leave her very young children to vote; or possibly if someone is ill and has not got a postal vote, then abstentionism is inevitable.

If we assume a failure of twenty-five per cent of the electorate to vote, from this figure between five and eight per cent are not true abstainers: they are people who have died since the electoral register was compiled; people who are on holiday or away on business at the time of the election, or people who have moved out of the constituency and have not obtained a postal vote. This leaves a real abstention rate of just under twenty per cent, or on average about one-fifth of the electorate in general elections since the war.

The *floating voters* who change their allegiance from one election to another, and who are thought to number about fifteen per cent of the electorate, are similar to the abstainers: they tend to be the least politically minded and are easily swayed by election propaganda. It is remarkable that the outcome of such an important thing as a general election in the United Kingdom is usually decided by the rate of abstentionism and the fickle floating voter who is often unaware of the serious issues involved, simply because the two major parties are so evenly balanced. Psephologists are often amazed, if not amused, by the high degree of political ignorance found among floating voters and negative abstainers: for example many such people are unable to name three cabinet ministers nor could they name the candidates in their constituency.

23.2   The voters

Male and Female

If women were still without the franchise it is quite possible that we should have had a succession of Labour governments over the past three decades; certainly the proportion of the Labour vote would have been much higher. Blondel suggests that women tend to vote Conservative more than men, in a ratio of 60:40, and there are more women electors. The main reason for the Conservative bias of women, particularly those who do not go out to work, is thought to be that they are less influenced by industrial conditions and trade union activity. In an industrial situation the differences between the classes are often more noticeable: women, who often work in offices, are in a more middle-class situation and do not experience conflicts of the kind found on the factory floor. It has also been suggested that women are more passive than men and therefore more conservative in temperament.

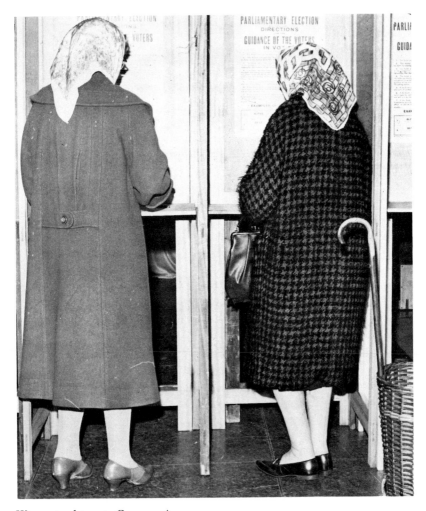

Women tend to vote Conservative

Age

Another factor linked to voting behaviour is that of age. The young tend to be more radical in outlook and the old more conservative: this may be because the young are more idealistic, while the middle-aged are more complacent about matters. The young, particularly the young married couples with small children, are more likely to have problems establishing themselves economically and thus tend to seek more immediate political solutions for their problems and be more radically-minded.

The eighteen-year-olds vote for the first time (April 1970)

Religion and Region

Compared to most other European democracies, religion plays very little part in Britain's politics—with the significant and tragic exception of Northern Ireland. Communicant members of the Church of England tend to vote Conservative, but Labour draws much of its strength from the non-conformist areas of England as well as from Scotland and Wales. On the results of previous voting figures, if Scotland and Wales had their own parliaments Labour would have held power there for half a century. In England, where most of the population is concentrated in the southern half of the country, the Conservatives usually hold the majority, except in the heart of industrial towns and cities. Catholics in England and Scotland usually vote Labour as most are of Irish descent and have an historical antipathy towards the Conservatives.

Class

The greatest determining factors of voting behaviour are the environment and social class of the elector. In simple terms, the higher up the social scale someone is, the more likely they are to vote Conservative. Three-quarters of the middle class vote Conservative, and two-thirds of the working class vote Labour. More than seven-eighths of voters (ie those who vote Labour or Conservative) identify their class-interest with the two major political parties. There are of course exceptions: the working-class Conservative voter has greatly interested political sociologists (such as Mark Abrams, *Class Distinction in Britain*) who found in 1958 that thirty per cent of the solid working-class voted Conservative. It has been this group who have sustained the Conservative Party since the war (the working class is greater than the middle class numerically, therefore the working-class Conservative vote is of considerable significance). Most working-class Conservatives are found in the more prosperous middle-class areas and regions of England, such as the Midlands and the South East. In the predominantly working-class industrial towns and conurbations of the North West there is a more solid Labour vote as is shown in Figure 7.3.

Two explanations are offered to account for the large Conservative working-class vote; they may be summarised as the *deferential* and the *pragmatic* explanations. Many of these voters are from the lowest economic level: the deferential voters consider that the country is best run by those who were born to it and who received the best (ie public school) education; the pragmatic working-class Conservative voter admires someone who

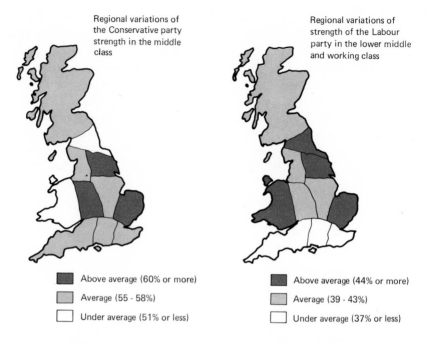

Regional variations of the Conservative party strength in the middle class

Regional variations of strength of the Labour party in the lower middle and working class

Above average (60% or more)
Average (55 - 58%)
Under average (51% or less)

Above average (44% or more)
Average (39 - 43%)
Under average (37% or less)

Figure 7.3   Regional variations of voting behaviour in two social classes, General Election 1959
(Source: Blondel, Voters, Parties and Leaders, Penguin, 1969)

has achieved a position of power through his own efforts and ability, and like the deferential voters he has a good deal of respect for political leaders of high social status. Many of the more extreme views associated with the Conservative Party are held by their working-class supporters and concern such groups as strikers, students and coloured immigrants.

Unit 24 The Political Parties

24.1 The Conservative Party

The Conservative Party was born in 1834. Originally the *Tories* were the party who opposed the Hanoverian succession in the eighteenth century. Before the 1867 Reform Act extended the franchise, the political groupings in Parliament were loose: MPs frequently changed sides on one issue or another, and this did not really matter as MPs were usually of the same upper and professional classes and were responsible only to a small wealthy section of the population: as long as the interests of the voters were not seriously threatened, a loose political association with one party or another was sufficient. After 1867 the working-class voter was able to exercise some influence, and it was recognised by the Conservatives that a tightening up of party discipline was needed in Parliament and that a national organisation was necessary to secure the election of their MPs. At the beginning of this century the Conservative politicians were primarily concerned with two aims: to keep Ireland as part of the United Kingdom, and to protect British industry from ever-increasing foreign competition. Today the Conservative Party is identified with the interests of businessmen and property owners. Its basic philosophy is to support business, and to keep state interference to a minimum in economic matters.

24.2 The Labour Party

The Labour Party was officially formed in 1906, although various socialist groups combined together five years earlier to provide trade union and socialist representation in national and local government. The first Labour government, although not possessing an overall majority of MPs, held power for nine months in 1924. Despite a split in the party in 1931, when the leadership found itself at odds with the mass of its supporters, Labour began to replace the Liberals as the second major party in the inter-war period. The Labour Party's philosophy differs from the Conservatives' in its belief in more state intervention to alleviate any stress caused by the economic system. Socialists believe that the wealth of the nation should be distributed more evenly among all sections of the population through a progressive taxation system and the national-isation of certain major industries. Clause 4 of the Labour Party's constitution perhaps best sums this up:

To secure for the workers by hand or by brain the full fruits of their industry and the most equitable distribution thereof that may be possible, upon the basis of the common ownership of the means of production, distribution and exchange, and the best obtainable system of popular administration and control of each industry or service.

The Labour Party held power immediately after the war from 1945 to 1951, from 1964 to 1970, and latterly since February 1974.

24.3   The Liberal Party

The Liberal Party grew out of the eighteenth-century Whig faction and transformed itself at about the same time as did the Conservative Party in the nineteenth century. Since World War I the Liberals had until recent times declined in strength. Liberal candidates have now polled 6 million votes since 1945, but their representation in the Commons has been limited to under a dozen because the mechanism of our electoral system does not favour minority third parties. If membership of the House of Commons were to be shared out proportionally to the number of votes cast for each party, the Liberals would have more than 100 seats. In February 1974, when there was no overall majority for either Labour or Conservative, the fourteen Liberal MPs (and the Nationalist parties) had an influence in politics far beyond their numerical strength in the Commons. Ironically, when the minority Labour government fifty years ago proposed a system of proportional representation it was the Liberals who voted the measure down. By and large it can be said that the Liberal Party stands somewhere between the Conservative and Labour parties in terms of its political philosophy. Its electoral weakness perhaps also lies in its inability to appeal to any particular class. Whereas the Labour Party has the support of most of the working class, and the Conservatives the support of most of the middle classes, according to D. E. Butler in an article 'The Floating Voter' (*The Sunday Times*, 17 March 1973) the Liberals derive their strength in about equal proportions from the working and middle classes without obtaining the overwhelming support of either.

24.4   Membership of political parties

Membership of political parties is divided between those who are active in their party's affairs, and those who give only limited support—usually merely providing a financial contribution. Unless a trade unionist has deliberately chosen to opt out of a political levy (known as 'contracting out') part of his union contribution goes towards the Labour Party. For this reason membership of the Labour Party is apparently high as indirectly very many trade unionists in the Trades Union Congress are affiliated members of the Labour Party. The Conservatives obtain financial support from some businesses and from their claimed party membership of three million. If trade unionists are included, the Labour Party numbers just over six million members; of these only one million are individual party members. About two-fifths of the Labour membership participate in their party's activities, whereas something between a quarter and a third of the members of Conservative associations participate in their party's activities.

Most of the business conducted by the constituency parties is concerned with local politics. At election time, agents (who are often full-time, paid officials) and volunteers seek to persuade the voters to come to the polls in support of their party. Each of the political parties holds an annual national conference, usually in the autumn, to debate issues of national policy. The influence that constituency parties and associations have upon MPs, the Government and the Opposition, will vary from party to party, issue to issue, and according to the strength of demands. The parliamentary party, consisting only of MPs, elect their own leadership, and naturally will have a considerable influence on party policy as most of the leading politicians in a party are MPs or members of the Government. Yet the parliamentary parties cannot really afford to ignore the wishes of the ordinary constituency members on too many issues. In the first place, the candidate is selected by the local organisation, and there is always the threat that he will not be re-adopted, although this is

Lady Douglas-Home and Mrs Reginald Maudling at a Conservative Women's Conference

a very rare occurrence. When elected, the MP must pay some attention to the party workers in his constituency if only to maintain their enthusiasm and support, just as he must look after the people in his constituency who may or may not have voted for him.

Blondel in Chapter 4 of *Voters, Parties and Leaders* points out that even in solid working-class areas more than half the officers of the Labour Party are middle-class, and in the Conservative Party more than three-quarters of the local associations' officers are middle-class. Of the ordinary membership more than half are middle-class, while in the Labour Party the proportion is somewhat lower. This will mean of course that people of middle-class origins and occupations predominate in all the major political parties. The MPs are even more solidly middle-class: more than half of them have been to university and only a very small minority have not received a secondary education at a grammar or public school.

24.5 Political motivation

Because our political parties are mass parties they must contain members with quite widely differing views within the same party. On almost every issue there will be some who disagree with the majority of their political colleagues. Disagreement does not mean that they will leave the party, unless they consider the issue to be extremely serious, as there are many more issues on which they share a common approach. The voting on whether Britain should join the Common Market provides an example of this: several prominent Labour politicians, including the then Deputy Leader, Mr Roy Jenkins, voted with the Conservative Government and Liberals; on the other side a number of prominent Conservatives, including Mr Enoch Powell, voted with the Labour Opposition. Obviously, if the issue is felt to be very important, or if there arise many other matters where someone is not happy with the way in which his party is going, then resignation may be the best course. Mr Dick Taverne resigned his seat in Lincoln when he disagreed with the Labour Party's policy on the Common Market; he fought and won the seat again in 1972 with his own Democratic Labour Party; yet resignation is rare. Most party members and party politicians hold strong convictions, or believe in a basic ideology which commits them to their particular party; indeed, that is why most of them entered politics in the first place. Voters too show a strong sense of loyalty to one party, usually for life; we have already given the figure of eighty-five per cent for loyal voters. Young and first-time voters largely follow their parents' lead in voting for the same party. Why is there this strong party-allegiance?

The principal reason for this consistency in voting behaviour is that, rightly or wrongly, the parties are identified with self and class interest. As has been explained, a large number of working-class Conservative voters apparently choose a party which would appear to contradict their class interest, or at least what are regarded as being against their class interests by two-thirds of their fellow working class. At the same time a quarter of the middle class vote Labour, which would seem to be against their own interests. There is perhaps no specific reason for the way in which someone votes. Most probably it is primarily an identification of class interest, combined with approval of the policies of the party, feelings about the leadership of the party, and finally respect for the qualities of the candidate who is standing. The voter has his or her image of the party and its politicians constantly reinforced favourably, or disillusioned gradually, over a period of time. The role of the mass media in determining attitudes and opinions may be considerable in this process.

H. J. Eysenck's scale of political attitudes is interesting from a psychological as well as a political viewpoint (Figure 7.4). In the Conservative,

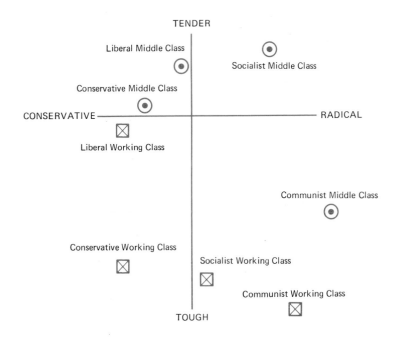

Figure 7.4 Party supporters and the two scales of political attitudes, 1950 (Source: H. J. Eysenck, Sense and Nonsense in Psychology, *Penguin, 1957)*

Labour and Communist Parties, the working class have a *tougher* attitude on political matters than other classes. As we can see from chapters dealing with socialisation and class, simple and direct solutions are to be expected from members of the working class, and politics are no exception. Of the middle classes, the Socialists have the *tenderest* attitudes. The Labour Party may be described as being a coalition of trade unionists and intellectuals (there is a high proportion of teachers and academics in the party), and intellectual opinion usually favours moderation and compromise on issues. The position of the Communist middle class, nearest to mid-point on the tough-tender scale, is perhaps due to the rather curious situation of *being* a middle-class Communist. Certainly this scale does reveal the connection between the socialisation process, environment and the choice of political party. At first sight there may appear to be some anomalies, for example the Liberal working class is more 'Conservative' than the Conservative middle class. Also the Liberal working class is far more 'tender' than the other working-class groups. Of course, this scale was drawn up more than twenty years ago and in politics, just as in everything else, things have changed.

If you had to draw up a similar scale today which positions would have changed and why?

Unit 25   Politics Outside the Parties

25.1   Interest groups

Outside the normal channels of party politics certain groups are able to exercise an influence on government and society. These groups are sometimes known as *pressure groups*, or *lobbies*, however as Professor S. E. Finer in his book *Anonymous Empire: A Study of the Lobby in Great Britain* (Pall Mall Press, 1966) points out, not all exert pressure in a direct sense. We shall refer to them as *interest groups*.

Most commentators agree that interest groups can play an important part in the government and politics of society, although some may have an unfair and undue influence which does not necessarily reflect the interests of most members of the public in society as a whole. Some examples of interest groups are: trade unions, the RSPCA, the Automobile Association, The National Council for Civil Liberties, Shelter, the Confederation of British Industries, and the Clean-up Television

Campaign. The various churches too may be regarded as interest groups. Almost every adult is a member of one interest group or another.

When the Government is preparing a bill to put before Parliament it often consults the interest groups whose members may be affected by the measures contained in the bill: the Government may discuss proposals for new traffic legislation with such groups as the Automobile Association, the Royal Automobile Club, the Royal Society for the Prevention of Accidents, and the Motor Manufacturers' Association. If a private Member of Parliament is fortunate enough to be allowed time to introduce a bill, he may well seek the advice of an interest group concerned with his proposed legislation: a private member's bill to regulate conditions in private zoos might be drawn up by the RSPCA, who will then seek to persuade other MPs to attend the Commons on the day of the bill and vote for it. Interest groups may choose a variety of methods to win support for their cause. They may make direct appeals to MPs by writing to them and inviting them to attend functions where they will put their case. Sometimes interest groups will seek to win over public opinion by placing advertisements in newspapers or by writing to the press. Demonstrations and marches are another means of gaining publicity for their cause.

Interest groups may be divided into two kinds, those who act in a defensive manner to protect their members' interests if these appear threatened, and those who are seeking to promote a cause. The *protective groups* are trade unions, professional associations, and groups who may seek to protect individuals unable to look after themselves, eg the NSPCC was created to prevent cruelty to children. *Promotional groups* are more concerned with getting things done, to promote or amend legislation which they feel will benefit society, or more directly, themselves. The villagers of Wing village ran a successful promotional campaign to prevent the siting of London's third airport near their homes. The Campaign for Nuclear Disarmament seeks to persuade people that Britain should not have nuclear weapons. Broadly, therefore, protective groups are concerned with the interests of individuals, and promotional groups seek a wider appeal for their causes. Sometimes the protective groups undertake a promotional role (for example, the Automobile Association ran a campaign to reduce motor taxation by getting its members to send postcards to MPs) yet their principal function is to keep a constant watch over the interests of their members.

As in the political parties, the membership of interest groups may be people drawn from many different walks of life. The difference between interest groups and the political parties is that they have limited aims and do not seek power at Westminster.

A criticism of interest groups is that they may be undemocratic: protective groups do not claim to represent anyone but their own members; and an interest group which is well organised and well financed is more likely to be successful than one which is poorly led and has a small budget. This means that there is an inequality in the representation of various interests. The motorists are well represented, but pedestrians, who are in the majority, are not able to exercise as much influence upon governments. A strong trade union in a key sector of the economy can make its strength felt very rapidly, but an old age pensioner has only the power of the ballot box and not the strike weapon at his disposal. As in political parties, only the interested (usually meaning the middle class) members participate in the group's affairs, thus a sectional interest is put forward as being the group interest.

There has been some dissatisfaction expressed at the way in which MPs may allow business or trade union interests to prevent them taking an objective view of political affairs. There is no suggestion that MPs are corrupt if they hold directorships of companies or are sponsored (ie have a proportion of their election expenses paid) by a trade union or professional association, yet some concern has been voiced that an MP may be placed in the morally unsatisfactory position of being the unofficial parliamentary spokesman for, say, the drugs industry or the National Union of Mineworkers. On the other hand, in an age of a mass public and a developed technology and bureaucracy governments are informed of matters and sensitive issues which might have escaped their attention had there not been the intervention of an interest group. Interest groups are thus participating in the wider democratic process. Because an elector does not vote specifically for each item on a political party's manifesto, it may be said that his membership of an interest group looks after his needs and enables him to press for action on matters which were not covered in the election manifesto.

There are thought to be some 6000 national interest groups (national in that any citizen may join these groups) and despite the inequalities of representation, this does mean greater public participation in government, which is not a bad thing for democracy. The Government is able to prevent the excessive influence of any one group by questioning whether its interests coincide with the public interest.

25.2   The Establishment

Mention was made at the beginning of this chapter of the conflict throughout political history between élitism and various forms of democracy. We have also outlined some of the theories of élitism in Topic 7.2. The underlying suggestion of most of these theories is that there can never be a true democracy, or that although people may vote every four years or so they do not have any real power. Others suggest that élites are necessary, if not inevitable, in the governing of a nation. In some countries a ruling élite is clearly identifiable: they are members of a military junta or of a single permitted party where there is no opposition. It has been suggested that we have an élite of a kind in Britain: this élite, termed the *Establishment*, is not immediately recognisable as a ruling class, but there are people who, because of their birth, wealth, or position in government are able to exercise considerable power.

One definition of the 'Establishment' is: those circles who are able to exercise considerable influence over the lives of others but who are not democratically answerable in their positions of power.

The Establishment is composed of a number of top people from important institutions, such as financiers from the City, senior civil servants, high-ranking officers of the armed forces, judges, and the directors of the mass media and nationalised concerns. The aristocracy too is part of the Establishment; but as they are insignificant in numbers they do not on their own constitute a ruling class. The Government may exercise power by directly implementing political measures; the Establishment exercises power indirectly (an example might be if the City were to direct investment out of Britain on a massive scale, thereby destroying a government's economic policies). The Establishment does not have any political aims, except those of maintaining its permanence. The Establishment favours a Conservative administration since the Conservatives are least likely to threaten its position; but a Labour government is usually unable or unwilling to effect much change upon its powers.

The public schools have been described as the nurseries of the Establishment. Contacts made at school and university are often useful later on, particularly in business. These contacts between members of the Establishment may be reinforced through marriage. This is not to suggest that the Establishment is some kind of conspiracy (indeed, many of its members would not even recognise its existence) because the Establishment is not interested in rule, only with maintaining its own existence. Perhaps we may describe the Establishment as the most powerful informal interest group in Britain. It may be argued that it is a good thing to have an Establishment, as the only alternative is greater state domination. Equally it can be said that the Establishment is too strong and some form of democratic control is needed in many of its spheres of activity.

25.3   Politics in Britain

After the French Revolution in 1789 the National Assembly sat in a
semicircle with the more extreme revolutionaries on the left and the more
moderate politicians ranged towards the right, where the supporters of
the *ancien régime* were seated. At Westminster the MPs sit on either side
of an aisle, as the chamber was originally a church: the Government and
their parliamentary colleagues sit on the right-hand side of the *Speaker*
(chairman) the Opposition on his left. When political attitudes are discussed we use the words left and right, which originated with the National
Assembly, to denote how radical or how conservative these attitudes are.

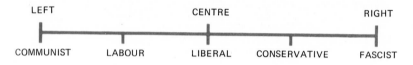

Figure 7.5   A theoretical representation of the wings of the British political parties

Just as there are constant changes in party policies, so too do politicians
move along the left-right axis, sometimes ahead of their party and on
other occasions behind it. In general terms the parliamentary politicians
adopt attitudes which are more to the centre than those of the rank and
file membership of the political parties. Politics is sometimes said to be
the art of compromise, and when the reality of power is felt many politicians tone down their views. Where free debate is allowed, less extreme
opinions will usually prevail. Democracy can only really survive when the
media are free to comment upon and criticise the actions of all politicians.
Although public opinion may be against one or other of the parties on
certain issues at different times, the overwhelming majority of the public
are in favour of maintaining the present political system. As governments
are answerable to the people at each general election they cannot afford to
ignore public opinion too often on too many issues. The principal
difficulties in maintaining democracy in a country of 56 million people
with only 635 representatives are to ensure participation through the
existing system and to enable the public to make its voice heard. We have
seen how such participation may take place within the political parties,
or through the medium of interest groups.

Terms used in this chapter

democracy   dictatorship   psephology

marginal seat	socialist	Establishment
floating voter	interest group	
deferential voter	promotional	

Jean Blondel's book, *Voters, Parties and Leaders* (Penguin) provides an excellent account of the political sociology of Britain if you are interested in further reading on this subject.

Questions

1 Suggest the political and social reasons for the extension of the franchise between 1867 and 1928 (Figure 7.2).

2 Who are the abstainers at General Elections?

3 How much importance are we able to attach to *demographic* factors in voting behaviour?

4 How much influence has the ordinary political party member over his MP?

5 Explain the importance of social class to political attitudes (Figure 7.4).

6 Do interest groups assist or obstruct the workings of democratic government in Britain?

7 Explain the difference between protective and promotional interest groups.

8 Suggest some right-wing and left-wing policies on

a immigration

b unemployment

c prices.

9 What is the Establishment and how does it exercise power?

10 Write briefly on *three* of the following:

political sociology	working-class Conservatives
the separation of powers	political motivation
psephology	participation in democracy.

Questions from GCE 'O' Level Sociology Examination Papers

1 What are the respective functions of central and local government? (AEB, June 1968)

2 What are the arguments for and against the continued existence of the monarchy in the United Kingdom? (AEB, November 1970)

3 Outline some of the most important ways in which an individual can have an influence on the government of this country. (AEB, June 1970)

4   To what extent is it true that the Conservative Party is an upper-class
and middle-class party, whereas the Labour Party is supported by, and
represents the interests of, working-class voters? (AEB, November 1971)

5   *Voting intention by region and class 1963–66*

		London and S.E. England	S.W. England	E. Midlands	N.E. England	Wales
Class	*Voting Behaviour*	%	%	%	%	%
Middle ⎱ Class ⎰	Conservative	74.1	77.4	83.2	72.7	58.0
	Labour	13.0	9.9	8.9	18.6	30.8
Skilled Working Class	Conservative	33.6	38.2	33.5	26.5	15.2
	Labour	56.0	46.9	59.0	69.2	79.9

Source: Table adapted from 'A Sociological Portrait: Politics' by Anthony
King in *New Society*, 13th January 1972.
   Explain clearly what the table tells us about the relation between social class
and voting behaviour. (Point out what information is missing from the table.)
(AEB, June 1973)
   6   Does social class determine the way a person votes? (Oxford Local
Examinations, 1972)
   7   What are pressure groups? Give two examples of influential pressure
groups in this country, describing their aims and how they try to get what
they want. (AEB, November 1974)
   8   Compare and contrast the functions and responsibilities of the Government and the Civil Service. (AEB, June 1969)
   9   Is there any connection between social class position and voting
behaviour in contemporary Britain? (Oxford Local Examinations, 1974)
   10   What are the major social factors which influence how people vote in
Britain? (Oxford Local Examinations, 1975)
   11*a*   What is the role of pressure groups in our society?
   b   Describe, with examples, two *types* of pressure groups showing how
they differ from each other. (AEB, November 1974)

8 The Welfare Society
Unit 26 The Background to Welfare

26.1 Poverty through the ages

The Welfare State grew out of the needs and miseries of those people in society who suffered from great *poverty*. From the beginnings of human life there have always been some people forced to live in poverty, lacking sufficient food, clothes and shelter.

Before the State intervened it was left to voluntary groups to help the poor. Those living in squalor often combined to help themselves and unless rich benefactors were moved to compassion it was largely the poor who helped the poor. Sometimes the poor acted together in violent social revolt as in the Peasants' Revolt of 1381, or sometimes they made peaceful, communal efforts such as Robert Owen's villages of co-operation in the nineteenth century. In the middle ages the monasteries helped to relieve poverty, but after the dissolution of the monasteries by Henry VIII poor relief passed to the State; the 1601 Poor Law placed the responsibility for relieving poverty upon local government and it was largely the parishes who looked after the poor, but they did this in a harsh and cruel manner.

As the State failed to provide adequately for the poor, it was left to individuals to help relieve poverty. After the Great Plague of 1665, many of the poor were without work and in danger of starving. Thomas Firmin believed that the poor should be given the means to help themselves so he provided them with raw materials to enable them to work and escape from their poverty. The *self-help* idea has continued throughout the centuries and Samuel Smiles in his book entitled *Self-Help* (which ran to four editions in the first months of its publication in 1859) echoed thoughts in keeping with the aims of the great friendly societies. These societies did more than anyone else in the late nineteenth and early twentieth centuries to encourage the poor to assist themselves. From 1872 to 1874 alone membership of Friendly Societies (such as the Oddfellows and the Foresters) rose from two to four millions.

Urban poverty began in the growing industrial towns of the early nineteenth century, and has lasted to the present day. The nineteenth-

century towns with back-to-back houses and the terrible squalor so
vividly depicted in Gustave Doré's pictures, were places of horror and
deprivation. The death rate increased considerably from 1821 to 1831 in
some of the expanding industrial towns, even though the overall population of these towns was increasing rapidly: according to Chadwick's
Report of 1842 the average expectation of life amongst the working
classes in Manchester was seventeen years, compared with thirty-two
years in rural Rutland. In Manchester the average expectation of life
amongst the gentry was thirty-eight years.

The Speenhamland System of 1795 had provided poor relief by small
money payments but the deterrent Poor Law of 1834 forced the able-
bodied poor to endure the atrocious conditions of the Victorian workhouse. The Speenhamland System of poor relief was not really *state
welfare* because it arose from a local decision made by magistrates meeting
at the Pelican Inn in the village of Speen, Berkshire. The system was
adopted in most counties, but the 1834 Act established a state system
intended to give paupers the least possible help based upon the principles
of 'less eligibility' and 'the workhouse test'. The only help for the poor

One hundred years ago—Gustave Doré's picture

was to be provided in the workhouse. Investigations and reports of conditions in towns after the passing of the 1834 Act revealed a state of overcrowding, filth and fever never before witnessed in Britain. These reports included:

1   1838: Dr Southwood Smith, Dr Arnott and Dr Kay's report on London
2   1840: report of the Health of Towns Committee
3   1842: Edwin Chadwick's report on an Inquiry into the Sanitary Conditions of the Labouring Population of Great Britain
4   1844/5: report of the Health of Towns Commission.

The various reports on early Victorian life threw light upon the worst period of English poverty. In part of Leeds all the streets and dwellings in one area were:

. . . deficient in sewerage, unpaved, full of holes, with deep channels formed by the rain intersecting the roads, and annoying the passengers, sometimes rendered untenantable by the overflowing of sewers and other more offensive drains, with ash-holes, etc. exposed to public view, and never emptied;

In Westminster, water was so short that in Snow's Rents:

On the principal cleaning day, Sunday, the water is on for about five minutes, and it is on also for three days in the week for one half-hour, and so great is the rush to obtain a modicum before it is turned off, that perpetual quarrelling and disturbance is the result.

The origins of a welfare society sprang from the poverty revealed by these reports. Southwood-Smith and Chadwick were not termed sociologists but some of their investigations and research work followed the best traditions of modern sociological surveys and were directly responsible for measures such as:

1   Public Health Act 1848
2   Sanitary Commission 1869
3   Public Health Act 1875.

The latter Act, passed a century ago, made local councils responsible for the general health of their areas including control of diseases, drainage, sanitation, sewerage, water, etc.

Charles Booth, in *Life and Labour of the London Poor*, showed that one Londoner in three lived in continuous poverty, while about one person in ten lived perpetually on the edge of starvation. Charles Booth started his inquiry in 1886 and published accounts between 1889 and 1907. He covered an exhaustive field of sociological topics including employment,

Providence Place, Stepney, 1908

health, housing, religion and wages. Booth vividly described London's slums: the back-to-back houses thrown up by speculative builders, the sunless courts and the insanitary tenements. The people who existed under these conditions 'lived the life of savages, with vicissitudes of extreme hardship and occasional excess'. When they were able to get work it was very lowly paid and of the most unskilled nature, such as occasional labouring or street-selling, but many were just 'loafers, criminals and semi-criminals'. Charles Booth's most important contribution was to study social problems not as disconnected subjects, but to indicate the extent to which bad health, disabilities, poverty, slums, unemployment and working conditions were related. Practical social workers such as Lord Shaftesbury, General William Booth of the Salvation Army, and Dr Barnado, accomplished much but it was clear that no permanent universal solution to the problem of poverty was possible without massive *state support*. The whole of society had to accept the ideals of welfare provisions. From these origins the Welfare State arose.

Acceptance of welfare principles and efforts to establish a welfare state have not yet led to the disappearance of poverty. The world wars of this century and the sufferings of the poor in the inter-war depression have been major setbacks to the advance of the welfare society. World wars have rendered people homeless and destitute and have led to the mass migration of unfortunate people. The poor condition of the low-paid British working class after World War I culminated in the Great Strike of 1926, soon to be followed by the Great Depression of 1929–33. Three million British people were unemployed in 1933 and street corners were littered with discontented, hungry men many of whom had given up

Unemployed man, Wigan, 1939

hope of ever having a job again. The families of these men were deprived as the dole in 1930 only amounted to £1.50 for a married man with two children. The poverty was aggravated by a means test whereby if someone in the family found work then the state unemployment pay was reduced. Great masses of unemployed marched upon London demanding work rather than charity. The comparative affluence of the middle classes in the 1930s made the lot of the poor even harder to bear. Discontented workers in Europe turned to extreme political movements such as *fascism* and *communism* and World War II was the result. Mass bombing raids rendered people homeless and the Black Market meant that the better-off suffered far less than the poor. There were genuine attempts by the coalition government in Britain to secure equality of sacrifices: rationing, which was not abolished completely until 1954, aimed at fair shares for all at least in the bare necessities of life.

Since World War II pockets of real poverty have remained. Pensioners,

	No. of live illegitimate births as % of all births %	No. of children in care per 1000 population under 18 years %	No. of children supervised under 1958 Children Act per 1000 population under 18 years %
England & Wales	7.9	5.2	0.08
Greater London	11.4	7.9	0.12
Brent	14.6	8.2	1.3
Camden	17.1	14.0	1.0
Hackney	15.6	11.8	1.1
Hammersmith	16.7	15.8	2.1
Islington	14.2	15.0	1.0
Lambeth	17.0	12.2	1.5
Lewisham	13.2	9.8	1.6
Southwark	13.1	11.2	0.6
Tower Hamlets	13.5	26.1	0.5
Wandsworth	14.3	12.4	2.0
Birmingham	11.3	7.4	0.9
Bradford	8.3	9.1	0.4
Cardiff	10.8	5.1	0.5
Coventry	9.0	5.1	0.6
Liverpool	10.3	5.4	0.4
Manchester	16.5	9.6	0.4

Table 8.1 Special need groups (Source: R. Holman, *Socially Deprived Families in Britain*, Bedford Square Press, NCSS, 1970)

the low-paid and widows have all' suffered great hardship. Television plays such as *Cathy Come Home* and *Edna, The Inebriate Woman*, have brought to the mass of the people the plight of the unemployed, the vagrants, the homeless and the unfortunate misfits who exist even in our so-called Welfare State.

Poverty is a relative concept. Even a condemned cottage in Britain would be paradise to those people in Hong Kong who are dwelling in shelters made of petrol tins. People are poor because they are deprived of the opportunities, comforts and self-respect regarded as normal in the community to which they belong. It is therefore the continually moving *average standards* of that community that are the starting points for an assessment of its poverty (Social Science Research Council, *Research on Poverty*, 1968). Compare the percentages in Table 8.1. Note carefully how certain London boroughs and some conurbations have many more *cases of special need* than the average population of England and Wales.

The gap between rich and poor is still rapidly increasing, both nationally and internationally.

> My song is of that city which
> Has men too poor and men too rich;
> Where some are sick, too richly fed,
> While others take the sparrows' bread.
> (W. H. Davies, writing about London)

Why does poverty still exist in advanced industrialised societies? Some possible reasons are given below. They are deliberately controversial. Try arranging them in order of importance and see if you can add to them.

1   There are great inequalities of wealth and income combined with a constant battle to keep up with inflationary conditions.

2   Some people find it difficult to adjust to a modern society. The pace of advanced industrialised societies means that there is a lack in the quality of life so that many become misfits or drop-outs.

3   Government ministers, who are largely products of the middle classes, are unable sufficiently to appreciate or sympathise with the poor.

4   Not enough welfare is provided; eg in some EEC countries family allowances are two or three times as high as in Britain.

5   The welfare services provided are often badly-managed or bureaucratic: too much money may be spent in administering schemes rather than in actively relieving poverty.

6   Many people, especially the elderly, do not receive social security payments to which they are legally entitled because they are unaware of their rights

or incapable of making applications. Some are too proud to apply for what they consider to be charity.

7 More research into conditions of poverty is required, and the findings of surveys which reveal severe social deprivation should be acted upon speedily. Often social survey reports are shelved or not acted upon for many years.

Table 8.2 suggests that low wages and old age are the two most important causes of poverty.

Cause of Poverty	1899	1936	1953-4	1960
	%	%	%	%
old age	1*	15	49	33
sickness	2*	4	7	10
unemployment	2	29	5	7
low wages	55	38*	30*	32*
large family (5 or more children)	22	5*	5*	8*
single-parent family	12*	8	5	10

* Estimated figures.

Table 8.2 Percentage of those in poverty (Source: *New Society*, 1 March 1973)

There is a bare minimum of subsistence recognised by most people, and modern industrial societies (with problems of increasing populations, overcrowding and a large proportion of elderly people because of the longer expectation of life) find it difficult to maintain this minimum standard for everybody in spite of the affluence enjoyed by the many. An often-used standard level for the poverty line is based upon the national assistance (or supplementary benefit) scale. This standard has the advantage that the rates paid 'conformed closely to the Beveridge Standard which in turn bore a close resemblance to the standard used by Rowntree', ie in 1899 (B. Abel-Smith and P. Townsend, *The Poor and the Poorest*, G. Bell & Sons, 1965).

26.2 The origins and development of the welfare society

The term *welfare state* did not come into common usage until after World War II, but we saw in Topic 26.1 that the state responsibility for the welfare of society *as a whole* developed gradually over many centuries. The nineteenth century gave great impetus to welfare provisions as urban slums forced people into the *poverty trap* and as *national economic growth* supplied the financial means for poverty to be more vigorously tackled. The idea of a welfare state suggests social measures imposed from above so that citizens shall be entitled to reasonable conditions of education, housing and employment and to receive state aid when their conditions fall short of a certain level. A welfare society 'recognises its collective responsibility to seek to achieve the maximum welfare of each and every individual citizen and not only to relieve destitution or eradicate penury'. (*The Welfare Society*, ed. Joan Eyden, National Council of Social Service, 1971)

The real origins of the Welfare State were established by the reformist Liberal Governments of 1906 and 1910 and especially in the period from 1906 to the beginning of World War I. The fuller development of the Welfare State started with the Beveridge Report of 1942 ('Report of the Committee on Social Insurance and Allied Services', Cmd. 6404, HMSO) and was put into legislative form by the Labour Governments of 1945 to 1951. Some minor erosions of welfare principles have been made since, but generally, Britain has enjoyed welfare state conditions for about thirty years, although there are always new areas into which social services may be extended.

In Britain the Liberal Government of 1906 began zealously to improve the lot of the poorer classes. Charles Booth had advocated old age pensions and in 1908 pensions of one shilling (5p) to five shillings (25p) a week were given to those over seventy years old, subject to a means test. The most important Liberal measure was the 1911 National Insurance Act based largely upon Bismarck's scheme which had proved successful in Germany. Contributions were made by the Government, employers and employees, and covered all workers between the ages of sixteen and seventy who were not receiving more than £160 a year (ie well above the average wage for this period). The 1911 Act provided for disablement, maternity and sickness benefits, and for some medical services including those of a general medical practitioner. By 1914 nearly 14 million people contributed to, and received benefit from, the National Health Insurance Scheme.

Very slow progress was made in the inter-war years. Orphans' and widows' pensions were started in the 1920s, while the Education (Provision of Meals) Act of 1926 permitted a limited distribution of meals and milk to children at state schools. Local authorities were given further responsibilities for working–class housing including slum clearance and for providing welfare services for particular groups such as the blind, the mentally defective, mothers and young children. The Poor Law Relief (or Public Assistance) was made the responsibility of county and county borough councils. The depression and its aftermath brought a reduction in welfare services and in 1931 unemployment benefits were cut by ten per cent with a means test which many people regarded as a humiliating inquisition. When the war came in 1939, a welfare state did not exist but Britain was advancing very slowly towards it.

The development of the Welfare State as we know it began with the Beveridge Report of 1942. Beveridge advocated welfare services aimed at 'the destruction of Want, Disease, Squalor, Ignorance and Illness'. A new face was given to welfare because 'the scheme as a whole will enhance, not certain occupations and income groups, but the entire population'. This last quotation is taken from the Government's Social Insurance White Paper which was one of four that followed the Beveridge Report. The other White Papers put forward schemes for improvements in Workmen's Compensation, a full employment policy and a free health service. The principles set out in the survey reports of this period gave rise to:

1   Family Allowance Act 1945
2   National Insurance Act 1946
3   National Insurance (Industrial Injuries) Act 1946
4   National Health Service Act 1946
5   New Towns Act 1946
6   National Assistance Act 1948
7   Children's Act 1948.

The Labour Government of 1945–50 passed more social legislation in five years than had been enacted in the previous 500 years; the state was committed fully to the policy of working towards a society where each citizen would have the right to be cared for by the State from the cradle to the grave.

In its broadest context the term welfare state includes a modern government's responsibility for:

1   social services, including all social security measures (see Topic 27.1)
2   comprehensive health service
3   safeguarding the environment
4   full employment
5   equality of educational opportunity
6   special provision for the socially handicapped.

There are those who believe that welfare principles have been taken too far: workers are able to strike knowing that real economic suffering may be long delayed; thrift is less of a virtue and the spirit of enterprise is sapped; some mothers spend family allowances upon cigarettes, while foreigners come to Britain to take advantage of the National Health Service. But welfare services available to the community as a whole cannot be curtailed because the services are abused by a few; there are not many who would be prepared to go back to the pre-1945 system of selective state help of a minimum standard. In the long run, a *welfare society* has some advantages over a *welfare state* in the sense that the former term recognises a sense of caring by the whole of society. We should all be concerned that members of society should have all possible facilities to develop to the utmost, and be looked after if they fall upon bad times.

Unit 27 The Modern Welfare State

27.1 Social services

Social services and benefits are provided by the state literally from the womb to the tomb. An expectant mother receives a maternity allowance, while a maternity grant of £25 (1973) is payable on the birth of the baby. The maternity allowance starts eleven weeks before the baby is expected and goes on for eighteen weeks. Eligibility for maternity allowance depends upon the woman being a contributor to National Insurance and having twenty-six stamps on her national insurance card during the previous twelve months. A mother-to-be can get help and advice from an ante-natal clinic; after the child is born the mother usually takes the baby regularly to a post-natal clinic for cheap foods and a check-up, while health visitors go to the child's home to see that mother and baby are progressing satisfactorily. Where a child is left without parents, guardians' allowances (£5.65 per week in 1975) are paid to those who bring up the child. Family allowances of £1.50 a week for the second and for each subsequent child are paid (since April 1975) to a mother until her children leave school or reach the age of eighteen. The children's officer of the local authority is responsible to the Children's Committee for seeing that no child is without adult care. Controlled adoption, fostering and the provision of children's homes are all part of the services of the Welfare State.

The Government announced in 1972 that there was to be a considerable extension of nursery education (see Topic 13.1) so that schooling is possible from the age of two, although compulsory education does not begin until the age of five. While at school, youngsters receive help from the Welfare State in the form of such services as dental and medical examinations, subsidised school meals and, near the end of school life, the Youth Employment Service.

The transition from school to work is made easier by the Factory Acts which control the hours and conditions of work, while the Government sponsors training schemes at technical colleges. Apart from further education opportunities, councils set up youth committees which appoint youth officers to organise LEA youth clubs and help voluntary youth organisations.

On starting work a young person contributes to the National Insurance Scheme. The majority of workers have a contribution deducted from their wages and to this contribution the employer adds more money. National Insurance Scheme benefits are available (so long as certain conditions are upheld) to people who are:

1   unemployed
2   injured at work
3   sick
4   disabled
5   guardians
6   widows
7   expectant mothers
8   retirement pensioners
9   war pensioners
10 dependants of the dead (Death Benefit).

From the beginning to the end of life, the Welfare State watches and cares. Help and advice is offered in the way of legal aid and citizens' advice bureaux. Can you think of some other social services provided by the state but not mentioned in this topic?

27.2   The National Health Service

Britain has developed an excellent, comprehensive, free national health service (see Figure 8.1), but there will always be improvements that can be made.

The NHS has suffered from:

1   The initial opposition of the medical profession, a minority of whom were preoccupied with the higher remuneration gained from the better-off private patients. There is still resentment from some people who think that the individual's personal relationship with his doctor is lost in a national system.

2   A lack of adequate financial resources so that staff have been underpaid, while there has also been a shortage of modern buildings and equipment.

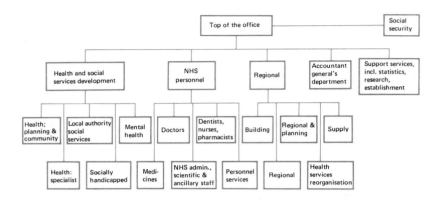

Figure 8.1   *New work-structure for the Department of Health and Social Security, from 1974*
(Source: New Society, *28 December, 1972)*

3   The 'Brain Drain' which has meant the loss of many good doctors, especially to the USA, so that the NHS would not have survived without immigrant staff.

4   It has not been possible to undertake large-scale preventive medicine (except for a few illnesses such as tuberculosis) involving screening whole communities so that disease can be checked. Curative treatment is more expensive in the long run.

5   The existence of private patients able to secure priority in treatment.

The achievements of the NHS include:

1   The establishment of a comprehensive service where hospitals, general practitioners and local authorities combine so that more resources are available.

2   The provision of some well-equipped modern hospitals particularly in specialised medical fields: expenditure on health and welfare services amounts to approximately £2500 million a year (1973).

3   The removal of financial worry about the cost of treatment provided by hospitals, doctors, dentists, opticians, chemists etc. (Although some charges have been imposed since the NHS was started, the bulk of the cost still comes from public funds.)

4   The acceptance by the majority of the medical profession that it is better to work for the service of the whole community than for private gain.

5   The supply of medical attention to all members of society regardless of social classes.

The services provided by the NHS may be divided into three main categories.

The Hospital and Specialist Services

The Department of Health and Social Security, under the Secretary of State for Social Services, is ultimately responsible for the hospital service, although the day-to-day running is controlled by area health authorities and administered through regional health authorities. The NHS inherited a large proportion of nineteenth-century hospitals, but plans made in 1962, and revised in 1966, allowed for about £1000 million to be spent on hospital building in the ten-year period ending in 1977. There are nearly 3000 hospitals in Britain including about forty teaching hospitals, twenty-six of these being famous London hospitals: in actual practice teaching hospitals include groups of hospitals so that very many hospitals are involved in specialised teaching. A very high standard of medical training has been established by the NHS. There are specialised services in all fields of medicine and rehabilitation aids, including physio-therapy, artificial limbs, hearing aids, invalid chairs and vehicles, and surgical supports. Social workers help patients with socioeconomic difficulties which may arise from their illness, resettlement or disability. Other specialised services include abortion (permitted since 1968), bacteriological laboratories, blood transfusion, chest radiography, drug dependence treatment, psychiatric help, etc. There is an increased urgency about the need to provide up-to-date mental hospitals.

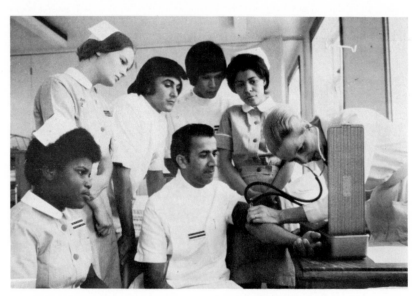

Training to be a nurse requires dedication to the patients' welfare

The General Practitioner Services

The Minister of State for Health has overall responsibility but, since 1 April, 1974, effective administration is conducted by forty Regional Health Authorities and ninety Area Health Authorities. An individual citizen is allowed to choose his own doctor. More than three-quarters of the 24 000 general medical practitioners work in group practices or partnerships because this arrangement has the advantages of always ensuring that there is a doctor available, sharing expenses of surgery, receptionists, etc. and the pooling of medical experience. It is becoming a more general practice for midwives, health visitors and home nurses, employed by the local council, to be attached to doctors' practices. Nearly all GPs in Britain play some part in the NHS. The maximum number of patients allowed to be on a doctor's list is 3500 and the average number is about 2500 (1975). Do you think that this is too many? The family doctor is usually the one to recommend a patient to other parts of the National Health Service, eg hospital, specialist or optical treatment. The health service in Britain also involves about 12 000 dentists, 1000 ophthalmic practitioners and 7000 ophthalmic and dispensing opticians. About 14 000 retail pharmacists dispense NHS prescriptions.

Local Authority Services

Local councils play a vital role in promoting the general welfare of their community. Four groups of people are looked after by local authority health services:

Mothers and Young Children Apart from maternity and children's centres, local councils employ midwives, home-helps and health visitors. About twenty per cent (1975) of mothers have their babies at home, and in these cases the local authority services will combine with the family doctor. Local authorities also make provisions for family planning advice (often given by the Family Planning Association), unmarried mothers and their babies, the distribution of welfare foods and the organisation of day nurseries. About seventy-five per cent of babies receive help at the local authority centres, and there is a great deal of follow-up work in the way of education of mothers, vaccination and innoculation.

The Mentally Disordered Local authorities have a statutory duty in the Welfare State to help the mentally disordered members of society. It is current practice for those with mental illness to be discharged from hospital, where possible, more quickly than in years gone by. It is necessary for social workers to do much rehabilitation work and for the authorities to provide occupational centres for the mentally ill and training centres for the mentally handicapped.

The Physically Handicapped   Local authority welfare services are available to the blind, deaf, disabled, educationally sub-normal and all who are permanently handicapped. This is a sphere where there is intensive co-operation between local councils and voluntary social workers. Assistance given to the handicapped includes social clubs, occupational centres and the provision of various aids to cater for individual needs (such as the provision of guide rails, special toilets and ramps).

The Elderly   The social problems of old age are of a very special nature. Can you add to the following list?

i   So many live on their own that they need special welfare provisions, eg home nursing, domestic helps.

ii   The poor diet and living conditions of so many on a low income make for bad health: hence the demand for meals-on-wheels and special centres where the elderly may be provided with a substantial meal.

iii   The elderly often lack sufficient warmth: even in January 1973 some medical opinion believed that about half a million were suffering from hypothermia.

iv   Special housing is required to cater for the needs of the elderly, especially as they are so easily injured by falls.

v   There is often an inability to communicate with the outside world when medical and other welfare aid is required.

vi   Old people need to feel that some people really care about them.

vii   Elderly people ought not to be classified *en masse*. There are some whose mental health is improved if they are able to disengage from their contemporaries. They are entitled to privacy, but their well-being needs constant checking.

viii   On retirement those over sixty-five years may believe that they have lost their main purpose in life, so there is a need to provide hobbies of an active type.

ix   Loneliness is not just a case of being self-pitying and introspective. 'There are signs that loneliness is now being recognised as one of the major causes of social disaster, and that severe mental illness often has its roots in loneliness.' (*The Times*, 19 July 1971.)

x   As we get older we tend to lose our faculties, especially hearing and sight. Social workers employed by local authorities are often the only contact that an old person has with the outside world.

Local authorities provide facilities such as nursing, domestic help and special laundry services. Under legislation passed since 1962 councils provide clubs, day centres, meals for old people and recreational workshops. Social workers are increasingly engaged in helping the elderly,

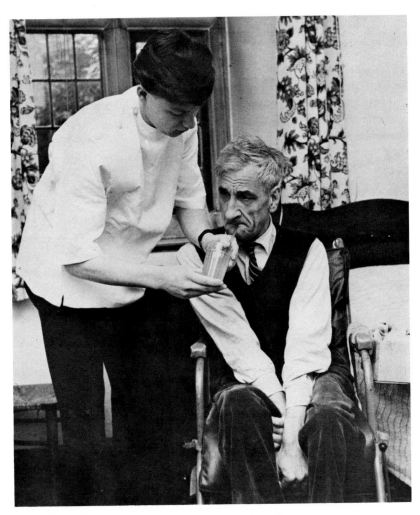

The elderly need to feel that people really care about them

especially as the proportion of old people to the rest of the population is
growing. The majority of old people needing special help receive it in
their own homes, but local authorities provide about 2500 old people's
homes (1975). These homes usually cater for thirty to fifty residents and
house about two per cent of the population over sixty-five. Local authorities also provide special small dwellings for the elderly and the modern
concept is for a warden to be employed to undertake social welfare duties
in a housing complex especially designed with the needs of old people
in mind.

27.3   Housing

Although a Housing Act of 1890 gave local authorities power to build houses for those in the lower income groups, very little was done to improve the housing situation until after World War II.

There are nearly 20 million dwellings in Britain and they may be conveniently divided into three main groups.

Owner-occupied houses account for about one-half of all dwellings and they were mainly built in the inter-war and post-war years. A large number of them are in suburban developments and are bought by way of building society mortgages with repayments extending over fifteen, twenty, twenty-five or thirty years. These houses are owned largely by the middle classes because working-class people find it difficult to save the customary minimum ten per cent deposit or to keep up payments with the interest rates at eleven per cent (1974).

Housing owned by local authorities consists mostly of well-maintained modern dwellings the majority of which have been constructed since World War II (see Figure 8.2). Although local authority accommodation units allow working-class and lower-middle-class people to be housed in better conditions than would otherwise be the case, the tendency for the people from the two or three lowest social classes to be separated on to council estates has many disadvantages. Compare such an estate, for example, with a village where agricultural workers, retailers, teachers, farmers and businessmen all live in close proximity and share a communal life. The standard of local authority housing is continually improving and over ninety per cent of council dwellings built in 1974 had central heating.

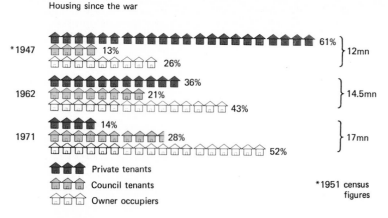

Figure 8.2   *Housing since World War II*
(*Source:* New Society, *28 December, 1972*)

A high proportion of council house tenants have incomes below the national average and include many old age pensioners. Local authorities give preference to those living in overcrowded conditions and to large families. Most councils have waiting lists and require applicants to have lived in the area for a specified time.

In accordance with the Housing Act of 1972, local authorities assessed their own fair rents which were submitted to special rent scrutiny boards. Council tenants no longer had subsidised rents, but were eligible for a rent rebate related to their earnings. The social purpose of the scheme was to check the subsidisation of better-off council tenants and to give rebates to the poorer tenants. If any council had funds in hand at the end of a financial year all but a small proportion were passed to the Exchequer to be redistributed amongst councils that needed help.

Privately rented housing now only accounts for about fourteen per cent of dwellings compared with over sixty per cent in 1947 (see Figure 8.2). An increasing proportion (about one-sixth) of privately rented housing is let furnished. Privately rented accommodation forms a very high proportion of the older property in Britain and about three-quarters is over fifty years old. Four major reasons for the decrease in the proportion of rented dwellings are:

1   Increased availability of local authority accommodation.
2   More people are able to buy their own homes.
3   Many old rented properties have been demolished by slum clearance.
4   Rent restrictions originally introduced in 1915 as a temporary measure have been more severely controlled since the Rent Act of 1965.

The Housing Act of 1972 meant that private and public sector tenants were treated on the same basis. From 1 January 1973, local authorities had to provide rent allowances for needy tenants living in unfurnished private property, following the same basic scheme as the rebates for which council tenants were eligible. Some examples of rebates for private and council tenants are given in Table 8.3.

Conclusion

There is still a severe housing problem in Britain. Apart from the three main categories (see Figure 8.3) of owner-occupier, local authority and private dwellings, there is also the work of *housing associations, house improvement schemes, slum clearance* and *urban renewal*. A slum is a property which has reached the end of its useful life and cannot be reinstated at a reasonable cost. Where it is possible to use the existing structure and improve a dwelling, then urban renewal is very worthwhile.

Type of family	Gross income	Rent payable, after rebate, on dwelling whose rent is:			
	£	£3	£4	£5	£6
married couple	20	2.09	2.49	2.89	3.29
no children	30	3.00	4.00	4.59	4.99
married couple,	20	1.63	2.03	2.43	2.83
1 child	30	3.00	3.73	4.13	4.53
married couple,	20	1.14	1.54	1.94	2.34˙
2 children	30	3.00	3.26	3.66	4.06
married couple,	20	0.45	0.85	1.25	1.65
3 children	30	2.39	2.79	3.19	3.59

NB: In each case, it is assumed that the wife is not working

Table 8.3   Model rebate scheme

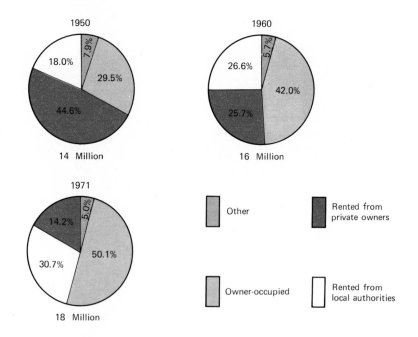

Figure 8.3   Ownership of dwellings in Great Britain, 1950, 1960 and 1971 (Source: Central Office of Information)

Urban renewal—Arlington Development, Norwich

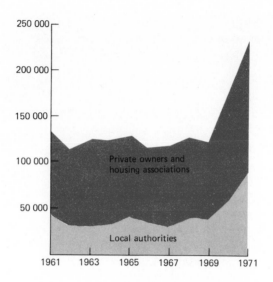

Figure 8.4   *More house improvement grants went to the private rather than to the public sector (1961–1971)*
(Source: Department of the Environment, Housing Statistics)

A major criticism of the 1972 Housing Act was that it left the 8 million owner-occupiers in a highly privileged position. They were excluded from the provisions of the Act, but received over £300 million a year in tax relief. House purchasers received far more aid (about £70 per head in 1972–3 compared with an average of just over £50 for a council tenant), and yet owner-occupiers are mainly in the top three of the five generally recognised social classes. The 1972 Act was an ambitious piece of legislation to restructure Britain's fragmented and often unfair housing system, but it involved stiff increases in council house rents and consequently was repealed by a Labour government in 1974.

27.4   Voluntary organisations

Consider the following reasons why voluntary bodies still exist in a welfare state and see if you can add to them.

1   There is less administrative cost involved.
2   Volunteers give willingly of their own time and this is essential when people are lonely or feel they need someone who really cares.
3   Unpaid workers may be less patronising than professionals.

4 Voluntary organisations are not over-organised and have less rigidity and bureaucracy than agents of the state.

5 Small organisations may be better able to deal with local welfare problems.

6 Volunteers are deeply interested:

a they may have had experience themselves of a certain problem (eg Gamblers Anonymous)

b they are free to act as pressure groups against the Establishment (eg Society for the Aid of Thalidomide Children)

c they are willing to listen patiently to other people's problems (eg Samaritans).

The Welfare State has always encouraged voluntary organisations. It arose out of the voluntary principle and past charitable work mostly conducted by various religious bodies. In the nineteenth century, William Booth left the Methodist church in order to establish the Salvation Army which recognised that spiritual comfort needed backing by practical Christian charity to the starving and homeless. William Booth's *In Darkest England and the Way Out* described the conditions of the down-and-outs in 1890 and several of Booth's suggestions, which were way ahead of their time, are now part of the welfare state services, eg aid for released prisoners and lawyers' advice to the poor. Orphans brought up in good conditions in a local authority's children's home owe much to the pioneering efforts of Dr Thomas Barnardo who worked for the welfare of the poverty-stricken homeless waifs of London, and opened his first home for children in Stepney in 1867. The non-conformist churches were in the fore of voluntary work of a welfare nature: the Methodists concentrated upon the large cities and used their central halls as social missions; the London Missionary Society was mainly supported by the Congregationalists and helped people to start life afresh in British colonies; the Baptists did much social work among the deprived and under-privileged. The religious bodies and individual philanthropists laid the foundations of the Welfare State and gradually in the twentieth century the Government began to take over institutions organised on behalf of the orphans, the poor, the old and the sick.

There are probably over 100 000 voluntary organisations in Britain. The Charity Commissioners were faced with over 70,000 applications for registration when they began compiling a register in 1960. It is very difficult to classify voluntary bodies because of their numerous organisational structures and frequently inter-related aims. There are organisations whose main work is involved with:

1 Religious motivation: Church Army, YMCA, Toc H, Society of Friends.

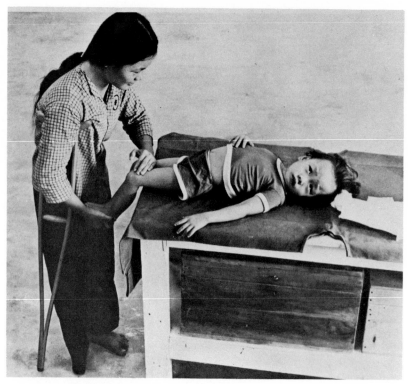

First Vietnamese Physical Therapy Service, organised by the Society of Friends

2   Helping those with personal problems: National Council for the Un-married Mother and Child, National Society for the Prevention of Cruelty to Children.

3   Family problems: Family Welfare Association, National Marriage Guidance Council.

4   Providing services for the sick: British Red Cross Society, St John Ambulance Brigade.

5   Looking after the special needs of the disabled: Royal National Institute for the Blind, National Association for Mental Health, National Society for Mentally Handicapped Children, Royal National Institute for the Deaf.

6   Caring for those who suffer from similar problems: Alcoholics Anony-mous, Narcotics Anonymous.

7   A wide range of services: Women's Royal Voluntary Service assists in hospitals, does relief work in emergencies, provides residential clubs for the elderly and supplies meals-on-wheels.

8   Administering the funds of self-supporting organisations: Carnegie United Kingdom Fund, Nuffield Foundation, Wolfson Foundation.

A Shelter photograph of some contemporary housing in Birmingham

9 Help for special groups of people and acting at the same time as modern pressure groups: Shelter's work for the homeless and badly housed, PROP's efforts on behalf of prisoners.

10 Supplementing the central and local government's own services: Central

Council for the Disabled, National Society for the Prevention of Cruelty to Children.

11 Filling a gap in services provided by the Welfare State: Royal National Lifeboat Institution.

12 Improving the quality of life: Friends of the Earth.

13 Maintaining world peace: United Nations Association, CND.

14 International problems such as aid to the under-developed countries: Oxfam.

15 Providing a central link between voluntary organisations: National Council of Social Service, National Institute for Social Work Training.

The National Council for Social Service brings together most of the principal voluntary associations for consultation and joint action. It is very important to avoid duplication of services with subsequent wastage of resources and additional administrative expense. The NCSS has produced some inspiring literature especially concerned with pioneer work in the field of welfare. You should try to read at least two of the following relatively short booklets.

Creative living: about the work and purposes of a community association (1964)

They can't fit in: a study of destitute men under thirty in St George's Crypt, Leeds (1970)

Youth in action: an account of social service by young people (1971)

Loneliness: a new study (1972)

Service for the elderly at home: a review of current needs and problems (1971)

Physical disability and community care: a study of disability in relation to the environment and social services of a London borough (1969)

The Beveridge Report saw the need for the enlistment of voluntary workers. In the *Voluntary Worker in the Social Services* (Bedford Square Press of the NCSS) five ways in which volunteers may work are suggested:

1 as members of a voluntary body undertaking a particular type of work

2 in a service or scheme provided by a voluntary organisation in association with a local authority or other public body

3 as members of an organisation recruiting volunteers for work of a variety of different kinds within public services such as hospitals

4 as volunteers directly recruited by and attached to a hospital, school, local authority department or other public body

5 in a service provided and staffed by a public body, but operating from premises unconnected with that body and working as a separate entity.

There will always be a need for voluntary organisations to pioneer and experiment in paths of welfare which the state has yet to travel.

27.5 The Welfare State and the family

The Welfare State provides the family with greater security. If the breadwinner is temporarily out of work, then unemployment benefit is available; if the unemployment is of a long-standing nature, such as structural unemployment, then the state provides redundancy payments or the opportunity to learn a fresh job at a Government Skill Centre. When there is sickness in the family, then the free services of the general practitioner or the hospital are available and there is sickness benefit to help the family at a time which could be one of financial hardship. If the family has been relying upon the earnings of the wife, then if she becomes pregnant they can fall back upon maternity allowances and the lump sum grant. Retirement pensions and death grants are entitlements under the National Insurance Scheme. The State pays widows' pensions (however inadequate) and industrial injury benefits. So the Welfare State has helped to make the family more secure.

Yet in many ways the family is less of a unit because the state has usurped, or at least partly taken over, many of the family's original functions. For centuries it has been the responsibility of the father to find a home for his wife and children. Husband and wife together were expected to bring up their children without interference or help, to educate them especially in the vocational sense when it was customary for a son to follow his father in a trade. The family provided guidance on morals and behaviour without the help of State or school. Recreational activities took place within the framework of the family.

However, the modern Welfare State has an influence upon the family from the beginning. Marriage requires legislation by the State even if the marriage ceremony is performed by the church. Divorce needs the State's acceptance and the parties to the divorce have rights which the State protects. Family planning advice and devices are provided by the State; the expectant mother and the young mother can use the assistance provided by the State. It is most likely that confinement will take place at a state hospital.

The family was once the greatest agent of socialisation. During the vital formative years the family is still the primary influence, but with the extension of nursery education in the 1970s, there is an increasing tendency for the mother to get back to work and therefore her influence upon the child is less. Religion plays little part in most family life today: it is left far more to the state school to implant beliefs, ethics and good standards of conduct. With more educational and library facilities, the culture of society is transmitted to a large extent outside the family circle.

Young people tend to leave home at an early age, especially since legal adulthood has been reduced from twenty-one to eighteen years. If young people go away for further education they may only return for fleeting vacational visits to the family; at the age of about twenty-two it is common to secure a job in a different town so that contact with the family is almost relinquished. As the age of marriage has decreased, the young people of the family of origin soon start families of procreation. As another family begins, it is likely that the Welfare State will have more influence upon this new family than will the family of origin. Working-class children are more inclined to stay within the family atmosphere after leaving school at sixteen, until they get married in their twenties, but much of their leisure time, especially in their late teens, will be spent away from the home, possibly at local authority youth clubs or at night school. The middle-class young person of a similar age may have a study where he can disengage from family life, and it is likely that the state school will play at least as great a part in his life as will his family. When a father and mother are elderly, they frequently receive more assistance from the local council's paid domestic help than from their own children, and they may well finish their days in an old people's home provided by the State rather than being cared for by their own children, as was customary in previous generations. The young people of the middle classes rarely provide any substantial economic contribution to the family as they did in years gone by. Even though the Welfare State provides further education at colleges, polytechnics and universities, a parental contribution, depending upon the parents' income, is expected towards a student's grant. The State encourages the young person to remain at educational institutions and provides most of the financial means to allow him to do so: many young people are not an economic asset these days. Apart from youngsters of the working classes, who may be expected to pay about £6 a week for their keep, the young people of today are likely to be an economic burden to other members of the family who are gainfully employed.

So the contemporary family is, in many ways, less of an *economic unit*. Nowadays about sixty per cent of married women are in employment, while the children are cared for at school by school welfare officers, school counsellors and the teaching staff generally. There may be nobody at home during the day so the likelihood of parents not knowing of truancy is greater and if the child becomes unwell during the day responsibility falls on the staff, including the school nurse, and not on the parents. A large proportion of juvenile delinquency takes place between 4 pm and 6 pm when many children are expected to return to an empty home, and then other servants of the Welfare State (eg police officers or probation

officers) have to sort out the problems and exercise guidance which otherwise would have been the responsibility of the parents.

Terms used in this chapter

poverty   slum clearance
social security   urban renewal
Beveridge standard   fair rents
urban slums   under-privileged
poverty trap   national insurance

Questions

1   Use reference books to look up the main contribution made to the relief of
poverty by five of the following:

Octavia Hill   Florence Nightingale
John Pounds   Charles Kingsley
Richard Oastler   Charles Dickens
John Howard   William Morris
Elizabeth Fry   George Bernard Shaw

2   Consider the principle that intervening to help people might interfere
with their private lives and the freedom of the individual in the following
situations:

a   a baby being cruelly treated by its parents
b   a teenage girl asks her doctor for a prescription for contraceptive pills
without her parents' knowledge
c   a drug addict tells you that he has decided to commit suicide
d   an old person is too proud to apply for benefits to which he is entitled.

3   Conduct a survey in the neighbourhood of your school or college on the
causes and consequences of loneliness. What actions can your group take to
help lonely people?

4   What are the special problems connected with the welfare of coloured
immigrants in Britain?

5   What ways can you think of, apart from increasing taxes and national
insurance contributions, to provide greater financial resources for welfare
work?

6   Find out what slum clearance and urban renewal programmes are under
consideration in your nearest town.

7   When you are married will you rent or buy a dwelling? Give reasons for
your answer.

8   Obtain and complete a mortgage application form from a local office of
a building society.

9   Oxfam aid has been categorised in six main groups (1970):

agricultural	27%	medical	30%
emergencies	4%	relief and welfare	23%
feeding	3%	training	13%

Give examples of aid in each of these groups.

Questions from GCE 'O' Level Sociology Examination Papers

1   What do you understand by 'poverty'? To what extent has poverty been reduced in the UK since 1945? (AEB, November 1974)

2   What do you understand by 'the Welfare State'? (AEB, June 1968)

3   What do you understand by 'the affluent society'. To what extent, if any, do welfare services contribute to 'affluence'? (AEB, June 1971)

4   'The development of the Welfare State has made voluntary associations irrelevant to present-day problems.' Discuss. (Oxford Local Examinations, 1971)

5   Assess the contribution made by Sir William (later Lord) Beveridge to the development of the Welfare State. (Oxford Local Examinations, 1970)

6   What do you understand by a 'slum'? Why are slums usually found in central urban areas? (Oxford Local Examinations, 1970)

7   Explain carefully what you mean by the term 'welfare society'. What effect, if any, has the provision of welfare services by the State had on the family, religious bodies and voluntary organisations? (AEB, November 1971)

8   'However comprehensive the services provided by the State there will always be a need for voluntary organisations.' Do you agree? (AEB, November 1969)

9   Is there a housing problem in Britain? Give reasons for your answer. (Oxford Local Examinations, 1973)

10   What are the major social problems of old age? Are present services adequate to meet these problems? (Oxford Local Examinations, 1971)

11   What are the major social consequences of urban renewal? (Oxford Local Examinations, 1972)

12   Is the function of the family being affected by the increasing activity of the Welfare State? (AEB, November 1969)

13   Give a brief account of Charles Booth's *Life and Labour of the London Poor*. (Oxford Local Examinations, 1971)

14   'What counts as poverty varies from time to time and place to place.' Discuss. (AEB, June 1975)

15   Outline briefly the development of the National Health Service in Britain. What have been its major achievements and limitations? (Oxford Local Examinations, 1975)

16   Examine the contribution of Charles Booth and Seebohm Rowntree to the study of poverty. (Oxford Local Examinations, 1975)

9 The Economy and Employment
Unit 28 Work and the Economy

28.1 Why do we work?

We work to satisfy our needs. In any society man must work hard enough
to satisfy his three basic needs for food, clothing and shelter. People in a
primitive society are able to manage with very basic foodstuffs. In 1971,
a party of social anthropologists and sociologists discovered a group of
about twenty-five Tasaday people living in caves in the Philippines on a
diet consisting mainly of natek, which was prepared from the pith of the
palm tree, plus tadpoles, frogs and crabs that were caught by hand and
wrapped in leaves and roasted. Some researchers think that the Tasaday
people have been cut off from communication with other human societies
for about 2000 years but yet they survived. Admittedly, the clothing and
housing needs of the Tasaday society were very sparse: the men's only
clothing was a pouch of orchid leaves worn as a kind of loin cloth whilst
their shelter was a bare cave.

As societies become more civilised, so their needs increase and it
becomes very difficult to distinguish between a *need* and a *want*. A man
does not *need* a car in order to live, but he *wants* one so that he can carry
on the type of life to which he is accustomed and which may include
commuting every day from a village some miles from where he works.
So although we work to produce the essential things which we need, we
are also often striving to obtain things that we want, ie things we should
like to have if we had a little extra money. Some people would call these
things *luxuries* and consider the essential things as *necessities*. It is a
simplification however to separate economic goods into necessities and
luxuries, for not only is the luxury of today the necessity of tomorrow, but
things which some people believe they need so desperately that they
regard them as being necessities, other people would consider as luxuries.
Is a telephone a necessity or a luxury to an elderly, sick woman living on
her own? Is a radio necessary for a blind man living in a modern society?
Some welfare workers would regard both the telephone and the radio, in
these cases, as real needs that ought to be supplied by the State. Decisions

about which goods and services should be supplied by the individual and which by the State are political decisions depending to some extent upon whether capitalism or communism is accepted as the best way of organising the production and distribution of economic goods.

We work to produce goods and services; the more complex the society the more complicated will be the methods of production and the channels of distribution. Professor J. K. Galbraith in *The Affluent Society* (Hamish Hamilton, 1957) suggests that law and order constitute a basic requirement of production. In any society, men will not be encouraged to work

Children playing with matches were the cause of this fire, estimated to have caused £686 000 damage to a Lancashire factory

if the goods they produce are destroyed through theft, violent acts, civil strife or arson. So law and order are essential if people are to work to fulfil their needs and wants. The product of man's work will also be increased by improved educational standards, a good health service and an efficient transport system.

The simpler the society, the easier it is to see a close relationship between a man's work and his needs and wants. If a man tills the soil or works as a hunter, then he and his family (or tribe) will consume the produce of the land or wear the skins of the animals killed in hunting expeditions. It is very easy to see that he works to provide his family (or tribe) with satisfactions.

In a modern industrial society the relationship between work and need or want is not so obvious. Consider this discussion between a lorry driver and an acquaintance whom he has not met for a long time.

Friend: What job are you doing now?
Lorry driver: Driving heavy goods vehicles for sixty hours a week.
Friend: How much do you get?
Lorry Driver: £75 a week.
Friend: Do you like it?
Lorry driver: No. It's just a means to an end.

What is the end that the lorry driver has in mind? He is presumably thinking of earning money and spending it upon food, rent, clothing and other necessities for his family and himself, with something left over for his leisure pursuits. He admits that he does not get any enjoyment from the work; he is often not aware of any direct relationship between his work and his wants. He works merely for his wage, because the money which he is paid enables him to satisfy his wants.

He goes to work
to earn the cash
to buy the food
to get the strength
to go to work
to earn the cash,
            and so on.

In a modern society money is essential so that people can satisfy their needs and wants. A clerk cannot be paid in ledger sheets nor can a policeman be allowed to keep as slaves the criminals that he catches. So money is used as a medium of exchange and as a yardstick (or *unit of account*) by which the value of all work and wants are measured. Unfortunately money sometimes acts as a veil which hides the relationship between the reason why a man works and the wants that he is working to satisfy, but the relationship exists even though it may not be apparent to the worker. Where a person is not working for money it is usually easier to see why he works. If a man digs his own vegetable garden he is working to produce vegetables to satisfy needs. If a young lady makes a dress she is working to provide herself with an article which will give satisfaction. Even if a person indulges in a hobby which costs him money he is still working to provide satisfaction. There are two main reasons why man will always have to work to satisfy his desires:

1   The goods that he makes will be used up. A cigarette is made to be smoked and as soon as a new car is driven the tyres and other components will begin to wear.

2   Man's wants can never be satisfied. It is true that 'keeping up with the Joneses' makes man chase his own tail; he becomes involved in a consumer-orientated society which brings higher living standards but not necessarily a greater degree of happiness. This constant endeavour of man to improve his lot should not necessarily be viewed with disparagement, because it is a motivation which raises man above the higher animals.

We work to make things to use, so we are both *producers* and *consumers*. An automobile worker helps in the production of motor cars and he probably drives a car himself. When man works he merely changes the location and shape of things; he is not able to produce something from nothing. So in an economic sense man does not create goods. He may take iron ore from the ground and work upon it until, when it is combined with other things, he has produced aircraft, bicycles, cars or cutlery. Society is supplied with the things which it demands by man combining his *labour* with things from the land *(raw materials)* and with *capital* (factories and machinery). Economists call labour, raw materials and capital the *factors of production*. Most modern economists believe that the organiser (or *entrepreneur*) is a fourth factor of production; it is he who decides what shall be made and how the other factors of labour, raw materials and capital shall be combined.

28.2   Employment and unemployment

We saw in Topic 28.1 that people work to produce goods and services. These goods and services may not necessarily be beneficial to society: cigarettes, drugs or guns are made because they are demanded by members of society who are willing to pay money for them. These people are prepared to give some of the value of their own work (ie money they have earned) in order to pay for goods and services. In a *capitalist economy* the

Industry or Service	Great Britain	N. Ireland	Total
	Thousands		
Employees:			
Agriculture, forestry and fishing	421	53	474
Mining and quarrying	361	2	363
Manufacturing industries:			
Chemicals and allied industries	424	2	426
Metals, engineering and vehicles	3957	49	4006
Textiles	555	39	594
Clothing and footwear	418	23	441
Food, drink and tobacco	728	26	754
Other manufactures	1582	27	1609
Total: manufacturing industries	7664	164	7828
Construction	1338	49	1387
Gas, electricity and water	335	9	344
Transport and communications	1501	24	1525
Distributive trades	2690	63	2753
Professional, financial, scientific and miscellaneous services	6327	141	6468
National government service	583 ⎫	40	1583
Local government service	960 ⎭		
Total: employees	22 182	477	22 659
Employers and self-employed persons (all industries and services)	1820	71	1891
Total in civil employment	24 002	548	24 550

Figures may not add up to the totals shown because of rounding.

Table 9.1   Total in civil employment in Great Britain (mid-1970)
(Source: *Britain 1975*, HMSO)

variety of goods offered will be determined in the long run by the *effective demand* of the people. Economics is concerned with effective demand because a person's desire to possess something can only be satisfied if he has the ability to pay the price demanded.

Not everybody in society works. The number of employed in Britain totals about 25 millions out of a population of 56 millions (1974). There are four groups of people who do not work (ie whose work is unpaid):

1   children of pre-school age and those undergoing full-time education

2   housewives: married women who stay at home to do housework and/or look after children.

3   retired people: usually women over the age of sixty and men over the age of sixty-five

4   those unemployed because they are physically or mentally handicapped, plus people who are unable (or unwilling, to get a job).

There are also about three-quarters of a million unemployed and over a quarter of a million in HM Forces, making a total *working population* of roughly 25 millions. Those registered as unemployed are included by the Department of Employment in the total working population. The working population may conveniently be divided into three groups:

1   *Primary workers* engaged in the first stages of production such as agriculture, mining and fishing

2   *Secondary workers* who mostly work in manufacturing industries

3   *Tertiary workers* who provide services and in a modern affluent society make up about half the work force, eg over 6 million people are engaged in professional, financial, scientific and miscellaneous services, apart from those working in the distributive trades, transport or for the Government.

About one-third of those in employment are women and in the early seventies women only received on average about half the pay of men. By the Equal Pay Act of 1970, women should have received 'equal pay for the same work' since 29 December, 1975. It is unlikely that equal pay will be implemented fully because there are so many ways (such as the down-grading of tasks of work) by which employers can avoid paying women the same wage as men for 'similar jobs'. The main hope for the fullest possible implementation of equal pay is that 'between now and 1981 . . . women provide the only substantial new source from which

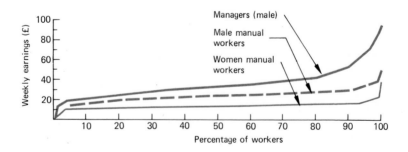

Figure 9.1   *Women workers earn far less than men*
(Source: Lloyds Bank Review, *July 1969)*

extra labour and particularly skilled labour can be drawn'. (The Royal Commission of Trade Unions and Employer's Associations, 1965–8, the Donovan Report) (See Figure 9.2.)

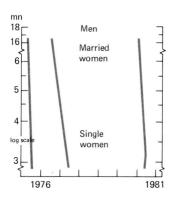

Figure 9.2   Women provide the main source from which new labour can be drawn

Women should have more scope for entry into the professions: according to *Planning for Women at Work* (a document presented to the National Conference of Labour Women, 1969) less than five per cent of those engaged as actuaries, architects, chartered accountants, engineers and solicitors were women. The unequal social and economic position of women is seen in the opportunities afforded to boys and girls. Apart from the fact that less money is spent upon the education of girls, the number of girls' training opportunities is far fewer than those offered to boys. About forty-three per cent of the boys who entered employment in 1970 were indentured for apprenticeships compared with seven per cent of girls. On the other hand, nearly forty per cent of girls entered clerical work, much of it of a routine nature, compared with nine per cent of boys. Three important reasons for these unequal training opportunities are:

1   Girls are less willing to undertake long apprenticeships because they do not look upon the job as a lifelong career.
2   Employers are reluctant to accept girls for apprenticeships because they are likely to get married and not stay the course.
3   Some trade unionists have been prejudiced against females in the past, especially in trades traditionally reserved for males.

The lack of good employment opportunities for girls was one of the issues behind Mr Willie Hamilton's Anti-Discrimination Bill in 1973.

The causes and consequences of the increased employment of married women is of great interest to the sociologist. Some of the possible effects are given in Table 9.2; you should be able to add to the causes and consequences suggested.

Increased Employment of Married Women	
Causes	Likely Consequences
Emancipation of women	Struggle for equal pay
Increased demand for female labour	Less home care for children
Nursery education for under-fives	More women trade unionists
More female career opportunities	Less time spent in looking after the home
Time-saving domestic gadgets	Delinquency amongst children who return to an empty house
Inflation erodes the husband's pay	
Smaller families	Husband helps wife with the domestic chores
Desire for 'pin money' to supplement the family income	Family dependent on joint income

Table 9.2   Increased employment of married women

Since World War II there has been a remarkable change in the employment situation in Britain. In 1931, unemployment was twenty-one per cent and until the outbreak of war in 1939 the percentage of unemployed was nearly always over ten per cent; since the war Britain has had an almost permanent state of *full employment* using this term in the Beveridge sense that more than ninety-seven per cent of those registered for jobs are employed (Lord Beveridge, *Full Employment in a Free Society*, Allen and Unwin). A Government White Paper entitled *Employment Policy* was published in 1944 and since then successive governments have succeeded in maintaining a state of full employment, until 1972 when the unemployed numbered over one million (see Figure 9.3) for the first time since the war. It is usually possible by economic planning and by following principles first laid down by Lord Keynes to see that 'full employment is maintained'. Lord Keynes advocated that extra government spending when necessary should be directed towards useful public works. 'Even three per cent appears as a conservative, rather than an unduly hopeful, aim to set for the average unemployment rate of the future under conditions of full employment.' (Lord Beveridge, *Full Employment in a Free Society*)

A state of full employment has sociological consequences. A state of *over-full employment* may arise where workers find it so easy to obtain jobs that instead of an employer being in the position to say to a worker, 'If

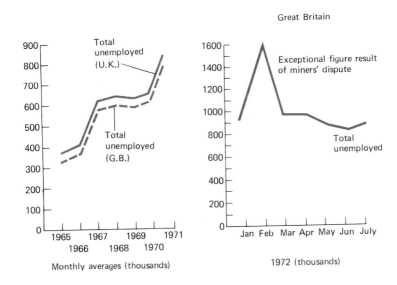

Figure 9.3a   *Unemployment, 1965–1971*
     b   *Unemployment, first half of 1972*
(Sources: Department of Employment Gazette, *July 1972;* Monthly Digest of Statistics, *July 1972)*

you do not work, there are other people ready to take your job,' a worker is able to say to the boss, 'If you don't want me, it will be very easy for me to find work elsewhere.' It is when workers have taken this attitude that some people have argued that a measure of unemployment is good for a society: they have argued that men will work harder if there are unemployed people willing and waiting to take their jobs. So although unemployment over a long period is very bad for an individual, over-full employment may be bad for society in general if it leads to persistent industrial unrest and indiscipline at work.

Full employment may also adversely affect *labour mobility*: a dynamic economy requires that some workers should be willing to move between areas and between occupations. Certain older industries (such as coal, cotton, shipbuilding, wool and railways) are declining and can only use a smaller labour force, whilst expanding industries such as chemicals, computers, electronics, plastics and vehicles may be crying out for a larger work force. Where the staple industry is established in a traditional and localised setting then it is very difficult to get workers to move their homes, leaving old associations and familiar surroundings to take their families to a different area.

Full employment has also led to a more affluent working class and the subsequent expansion of the advertising industry (see Topic 21.1), and of credit purchases. Workers may be unduly influenced by advertisers and the tempting hire purchase offers so that 'the consumer is by no means the key factor in the situation. Rather, it is the producer who as a rule initiates economic change . . .' (S. R. Parker, *The Sociology of Industry*, Allen & Unwin). Modern youth culture (see Topic 13.3) is both a cause and consequence of the very favourable market position in which young people have found themselves in recent years. Those in their late teens have been able to get jobs relatively easily and demand high wages, especially as the proportion of those going on to further education has increased. In this respect girls aged over sixteen are in a slightly more favourable situation than boys of a similar age because:

1   there are more males than females in the population in this age group
2   a greater percentage of males than females go on to further education. (Only just over a quarter of British students are females.)

Young wage-earners have found themselves in a favourable position in recent years

Intensive advertising campaigns and instalment buying (over £2000 million in 1974) have led to:

1   some families spending beyond their means and then being subjected to adverse social pressures
2   manufacturers imposing rapid changes in fashion and *planned obsolescence* with goods not made to last
3   an increase in the employment of married women and teenagers
4   workers choosing to do overtime rather than have more leisure time.

Unemployment is a social scourge, but nevertheless no society can secure 100 per cent employment because there will always be some who:

1   are unable to work because of sickness, either temporary or chronic
2   do not want to work because they find social security benefits sufficient for their particular needs
3   are out of work because of weaknesses or changes in the economic structure.

Eight causes of unemployment which arise from the economic system itself are given below.

Type of unemployment	*Main cause*
1 Casual	Employment offered cannot always be steady and some workers are unspecific, such as manual labourers who move from one unskilled job to another.
2 Cyclical	Trade cycles have brought mass unemployment, eg about 3 million in Britain from 1931–3; these cycles have largely been replaced by milder yet still serious recessions.
3 Frictional	Unemployment is caused by workers with a special skill not being able to get work in one area, but a shortage of the same type of worker existing in another area.
4 International	Unemployment can spread between countries as was seen after the Wall Street crash of 1929. About 20 million workers were out of work in the USA and the effect of their decreased purchasing power on imports caused unemployment to spread throughout the world.
5 Regional	Workers in some regions, such as NE England, suffer from long-standing unemployment because of the decay of old staple industries upon which they had come to place complete reliance; they are loath to move to another area or learn another job.

6	Residual	There will always be a hard core of people who are unable to work: even laziness may be regarded as a disability, especially if it is caused by some deep-rooted psychological upset.
7	Seasonal	A man may find work at a seaside resort in the summer and at a sugar beet factory in winter, but unemployment will be caused by the lag between these seasonal jobs.
8	Structural	Unemployment is caused by the changes in demand for products, eg more people might decide to travel by air, with a consequent increase in unemployment in the shipbuilding industry.

From the sociological aspect unemployment for whatever reason is bad for an individual although obviously long-term mass unemployment is far worse than temporary unemployment from casual or seasonal causes. Long term unemployment, even when state assistance staves off financial worries and material suffering, can lead to a feeling of inadequacy and, if widespread, may result in social unrest. Mass unemployment before World War II led to misery and despair for the one-time breadwinner and for his family. Children suffered deprivation in their home life which was reflected in educational handicaps. Worry over lack of income is a common cause of quarrels within a family and entire families from babies to dependent relatives suffer from a man's inability to hold down a job. In desperation he may drown his sorrows at the pub, or gamble away his unemployment benefit, while his wife and children go hungry and badly clad. In the worst cases the unemployed may be tempted into crime to augment the social security benefits received from the State. After years of unemployment a man may lose his job skills and become filled with despondency as he regards himself as a reject from society.

Modern problems of redundancies brought about by rationalisation, mergers, automation and other technological changes have forced Governments to take measures to alleviate some of the subsequent social problems. Three Government aids for help and retraining are:

1 Twenty-seven Industrial Training Boards that encourage firms to develop training programmes and make grants to promote special technical training in depressed parts of the country such as Development Areas and Intermediate Areas (see Figure 9.4).

2 Fifty Government Skill Centres with courses especially arranged for skilled apprenticeship training.

3 Lump-sum payments to redundant workers from a Central Redundancy Fund.

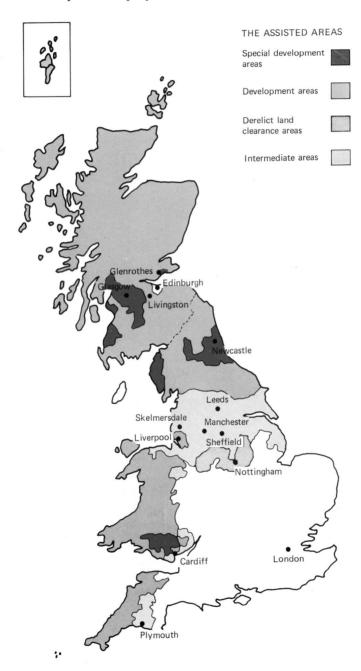

THE ASSISTED AREAS

Special development
areas

Development areas

Derelict land
clearance areas

Intermediate areas

Glenrothes

Glasgow   Edinburgh

Livingston

Newcastle

Leeds

Skelmersdale   Manchester

Liverpool   Sheffield

Nottingham

Cardiff   London

Plymouth

Figure 9.4   Development Areas and Intermediate Areas (1972)

28.3   The distribution of income and wealth

Tables 9.3 and 9.4 indicate the unequal distribution of income and wealth in Britain.

Lower limit £	Cumulative numbers above lower limit (Thousands)				
	1949–50	1954–5	1959–60	1964–5	1969–70
Dc limit*	20 350	20 597	20 955	21 188	21 735
400	7658	12 303	16 000	18 935	20 953
500	3660	8692	13 652	17 023	19 731
1000	835	1167	3245	7937	13 085
1500	395	513	973	2420	6884
2000	235	315	525	1009	2666
5000	43	55	82	154	255

Table 9.3a   Distribution of incomes before tax

Lower limit £	Cumulative numbers above lower limit (Thousands)				
	1949–50	1954–5	1959–60	1964–6	1969–70
Dc limit*	20 350	20 597	20 955	21 188	21 735
250	13 120	17 276	—	—	—
400	—	—	15 530	18 608	20 819
500	3022	8283	12 854	16 402	19 215
1000	483	869	2324	6332	11 013
1500	—	—	615	1367	4156
2000	89	138	298	493	1280
5000	—	—	—	51	78

* The deduction card limit was £135 in 1949–50, £180 in 1954–5 and 1959–60, £275 in 1964–5 and £330 in 1969–70.
Table 9.3b   Distribution of incomes after tax (Source: Inland Revenue, Survey of Personal Incomes 1969–70, HMSO, 1972)

A mere five per cent of the population of the UK hold about forty-seven per cent of the country's wealth. The economist regards income as a *flow* which is received usually weekly or monthly, whereas wealth is the

Years	Percentage of total personal wealth
1911–13	65–70
1924–30	60
1936–38	55
1946–48	50
1951–56	42
1960	42

Table 9.4 Property holding of top one per cent of owners
(Source: S. Pollard and D. W. Crossley, *The Wealth of Britain*, Batsford, 1968)

stock of goods held at a certain time. Wealth includes all things with a money value such as land, houses, cars and furniture. The very unequal distribution of both wealth and income has been brought about mainly by the capitalist nature of our society: one would expect a collectivist system to result in a more egalitarian state if communistic principles were really applied and a new wealthy class was not allowed to emerge and replace the old.

It can be argued that some disparities of wealth and income are justified; the necessary saving required by any progressive society will come mainly from the rich. According to the costs and surplus theory, there is a certain minimum cost of keeping alive and the rest is surplus which can be ploughed back in the form of investment. But it is impossible to determine exactly what are an individual's costs and what is his surplus, especially as in an affluent society expenditure tends to rise to exceed income. We have long shelved Micawber's simple rule that a man who receives £20 a year and spends £19.97½ is a happy man, whereas if he spent £20.02½ he would be an unhappy man. The idea that if the great inequalities of wealth and income are evened out we shall kill the goose that lays the golden egg, has been replaced by the realisation that it is not only the individual within society who can invest; the State as a whole can invest, eg in nuclear power stations or in automated steel plants.

Table 9.3a indicating the unequal distribution of income, leads the sociologist to consider ways of mitigating the inequalities of the social structure. The comprehensive social services available in Britain help to ease the lot of the less well-to-do. The National Health Service, social security benefits, and housing subsidies all help to alleviate poverty. Incomes are evened out to a limited extent by progressive direct personal taxation (see Table 9.3b) whereby the greatest burden of tax falls on those who are more capable of bearing it. Some would say that these measures are only tampering with the sociological problems of inequality and that the real answer is a radical change in the structure of society, from a capitalist one motivated largely by private profit to a communist society motivated (one would hope) by the principle of service. Human nature being what it is, ideals are often not practised; it is very difficult to organise society along unselfish and less acquisitive lines.

Given the existence of inequalities of wealth and income, some of the important sociological problems that arise include:

1   the deprivation suffered by a large proportion of the population in terms of educational opportunity and good health
2   the temptation for crime to increase as the have-nots attempt illegally to bring about a more equitable society
3   the environmental problems of poor housing and undernourishment and the fact that inertia tends to continue the inequality rather than correct it.

Although sociologists had hoped that the extension of the social security services, combined with progressive taxation, would have brought about a far more equal distribution of income and wealth, investigations have suggested that great inequalities still remain.

There is more than a hint from a number of studies that income inequality has been increasing since 1949 whilst the ownership of wealth, which is far more highly concentrated in the United Kingdom than in the United States, has probably become more unequal and, in terms of family ownership, possibly strikingly more unequal, in recent years. (Richard M. Titmuss, *Income Distribution and Social Change*, Unwin University Books, 1962)

Unit 29   The Organisation of Work

29.1   The division of labour

In a very primitive society where needs were simple it would have been possible for a man to be self-sufficient. Robinson Crusoe was able to survive on his lonely island before Man Friday arrived. Crusoe was able to grow his own corn, milk goats, and make clothes from skins, while his shelter was a rough wooden hut surrounded by a defensive stockade. However, his life was made easier because he had tools, rescued from the ship, and which had been made by a specialist craftsman. If Robinson Crusoe had been shipwrecked with his family it is likely that he would have divided up the labour: a wife could have prepared the meals, made or mended clothes or cleaned the house. Man and wife would have divided the work between them each according to their several abilities. If there had been any children they would have been allotted tasks depending upon their ages, abilities and aptitudes. In primitive societies it was customary for the very young to be given the job of ensuring that the fire was kept alight, whilst elder children might have looked after a flock just as David looked after the sheep in Biblical times. The more numerous the group, the more specialised the tasks of the members. A commune in China or a kibbutz in Israel may be almost self-sufficient, although goods from outside the community will be required if living standards are to be comparable with other societies, eg they would need new seeds, fertilisers, farm implements and more complex machinery. The *division of labour* is concerned with workers concentrating upon one task or perhaps a few tasks. In medieval times a village community would have its own blacksmith, carpenter, tailor and wheelwright.

It was in eighteenth-century Britain that the division of labour was employed for the first time in an industrial setting with workers specialising in some small part of the productive process. Division of labour of an industrial nature began in workshops that used some means of mechanical power: 300 workmen were employed in a silk mill at Derby in 1719. The credit for organising factory production based upon the division of labour is usually given to Richard Arkwright and Jedediah Strutt, who established the first cotton spinning factory at Cromford in 1771. These workers were assisted by water power and the factory on the river Derwent still remains as a fine example of industrial archaeology. In *The Wealth of Nations*, Adam Smith described an eighteenth-century pin factory where ten persons manufactured 48 000 pins a day, whereas if the workers had 'all wrought separately and independently, and without any of them being educated to this peculiar business, they certainly could not each of them have made twenty, perhaps not one pin a day'. Mass production by the conveyor belt system has resulted in the division of labour being operated so intensively that a worker's task may take only a matter of seconds. Production of the famous Ford Model T motor-car was divided into 7882 different pieces of work so that the simplicity of each job was such that '670 jobs could be filled by legless men, 2638 by one-legged men, two by armless men, 715 by one-armed men and ten by blind men'. (Henry Ford, *My Life and Work*, Heinemann)

It has been said that most of the advantages of the division of labour are economic, whereas most of the disadvantages are social. It is true that the division of labour has the great economic advantage of enabling output to be increased while piece-work rates of pay can be used to

Division of labour allows production to be increased. Girls making boxes at Rowntree Mackintosh Ltd, York.

encourage workers to speed up their production, but some of the advantages are also social. Some of the social advantages are listed below:

1 Jobs can be found for people who would otherwise not find employment because of limited mental or physical ability.

2 Although the tasks performed may be automatic, workers quickly acquire skill at a particular task and can even take pride in mastering a job which would seem uninteresting to the majority of people.

3 Working with others on a conveyor belt system or an assembly line may bring a worthwhile feeling of co-operation at work.

4 Some workers regard long periods of training as tedious and unremunerative, so they are pleased to learn their task quickly and get on with the job of production.

5 Employers can use aptitude and vocational tests to see that each worker finds a job that suits his particular talents.

6 Some firms, on the other hand, move workers from one task to another so that they do not become too bored.

7 Apart from not having to learn to use different tools, workers are saved the bother of setting aside one tool whilst they select another tool for the next task.

8 There are some people who do not want to exercise responsibility or take on work which requires mental effort, so they are quite happy to perform very simple tasks and be able to chat or listen to music while they work.

9 Workers are able to purchase goods which would be beyond their means were it not for the decreased costs made possible by division of labour.

10 The woman's role has been changed greatly by mass production because she has gadgets that could not be cheaply produced without the division of labour, and these time-saving devices decrease her household chores so that she can find work, money and companionship at the local factory.

However, there are serious social disadvantages of the division of labour.

1 There is a loss of job-satisfaction because the worker is not involved with all processes that lead to the finished product.

2 The work is so repetitive that it is difficult to take much pride in the task itself, and the worker may rarely see the finished article.

3 Boring work may destroy creative abilities, so that even non-work time is spent passively and the employee is unable or unwilling to express any individuality in his leisure activities.

4 Monotonous work leads to fatigue.

5 There has been a decline in individual craftsmanship and many unskilled factory hands have no opportunities of displaying any artistic talents or merit at work.

6 Standardisation leads to dull uniformity both of products and producers.

7 The class gap between employer and employee widens as the old personal relationship between master and man is whittled away.

8 The large-scale employment of married women may lead to the neglect of children and increases in juvenile delinquency.

9 Workers may have a high risk of unemployment, because they may be replaced by modern machinery, or a large work-force may have to be stood off if a few key workers come out on strike.

10 Although 'economic sociologists are currently at loggerheads over the relative merit of the basic causes of strikes' (N. J. Smelser, *The Sociology of Economic Life*, Prentice-Hall) strikes are apparently more frequent when a large number of workers are employed under one roof, eg in a motor car factory.

Emile Durkheim was the first to draw attention to the sociological importance of the division of labour. Durkheim linked the use of this specialised industrial process with social differentiation and social evolution. He stressed that the division of labour enhanced the significance of social relationships in occupational groups and thus influenced the moral ideas of an industrialised society.

29.2   Technology and automation

Changes in technology such as the use of automation or computers have
an important impact on social relations. Technical changes in methods of
production have made possible what Dr James Burnham has referred to
as the managerial revolution, whereby paid managers are able to control
vast business enterprises and those who work for these enterprises.
Burnham predicted that the main holders of power in future societies
would not be communists, socialists or capitalists, but rather people who
possessed expert technological skills.

   Some of the classical sociologists of the nineteenth century realised
that the change to industrialised production played a vital part in the
evolution of society. 'The mode of production of material life conditions
the social, political and intellectual life process in general.' (K. Marx and
F. Engels, *Selected Works*.) A modern French sociologist distinguishes
three stages in the development of technology:

1   the disintegration of a worker's skill, eg by division of labour
2   the mechanisation of productive techniques and the development of an
integrated system of production
3   the advent of automation whereby the worker merely controls and
superintends
(A. Touraine, *An Historical Theory in the Evolution of Industrial Skills*,
McGraw Hill).

   The economist J. K. Galbraith has taken up the theme that power has
passed to the *technostructure* and that technological planning by-passes
the market (J. K. Galbraith, *The New Industrial State*, Hamish Hamilton). It is almost as if advanced technology has brought some realism to
the once discredited Say's Law that supply creates its own demand. The
ultimate in productive technological changes is a robot-controlled
automatic factory with articles produced without human participation:
raw materials would be fed automatically in at one end of the factory and
the finished products would emerge at the other end. The ultimate in
automation is rarely reached and there are so many stages in automation
that one may include many technical developments that make production
simpler. The ultimate state of a completely automatic factory or office is
described as *full automation* (*Automation*, HMSO).

   Automation may be considered as the reversal of the division of labour
because whereas the latter divides up work into many parts to be performed by a large work-force, automation involves the use of complex
machinery which performs many tasks with the minimum work-force.
The social consequences of automation will depend on the extent of the

Automation involves the use of complex machinery which performs many tasks with a minimum work-force. The main control room of a CEGB power station.

automatic processes but certain general social gains and losses are inevitable.

The social advantages of automation may include:

1 the lessening of the soulless nature of work that is so much a part of the division of labour

2 more time available for leisure pursuits (this will be more advantageous to those who are capable of using their leisure in a worthwhile way: in ancient Greece menial chores were performed by slaves, leaving the élite to pursue artistic and intellectual activities)

3 more opportunities for full-time education in a technological age demanding greater expertise and high qualifications

4 more economic goods available so that the standard of living can be raised

5 an expansion of service industries (such as catering, holiday agencies, entertainment and sport) especially as less work-time will be spent in manufacturing and people will look for new ways in which to spend their increased leisure-time

6 a shorter working week and longer holidays in which to relax

7   more resources available to keep the sick and the aged: 'within twenty-five years automation will have made the old concept of charity obsolete' (Sir Leon Bagrit, *Automation*)

8   the expansion of the do-it-yourself (DIY) movement as people seek satisfaction from using their hands.

Some of the unfortunate social consequences of automation are likely to be:

1   an even greater gap between the rich and the poor because the means of production will be controlled by the wealthy technocrats   ·

2   a large increase in the number of unemployed in the short run, especially amongst less qualified workers who will be faced with redundancy

3   a shortage of purchasing power for those who cannot find work

4   an inability by trade unions to protect members who are unskilled

5   the extension of synthetic and artificial entertainments (we have already had boxing matches by computer)

6   over-production of goods, consequent upon under-consumption by the unemployed

7   social revolutionary tendencies brought about by a lack of a purposeful life for those unable to adapt or find a place in a technological society

8   *white-collar workers* gaining at the expense of the rest of society with subsequent trade union quarrels.

So technological advances are bringing radical changes to our society. There is a continual trend towards increased industrialisation and urban living, together with a decline in rural activities. The work-force is becoming more skilled and mobile; occupational structure is inevitably altering. Changes are far more rapid than they have ever been before; it is best to make the most of the technological advances that generally appear advantageous to society, but to attempt to control the pace of these changes. In what ways can man establish a more enlightened morality in keeping with rapid technological advances so that the social problems which accompanied earlier industrial revolutions are avoided?

29.3   Relationships between employer and employee

Relations between employer and employee generally become more strained in an industrial society. When firms are large, and labour relationships impersonal, a 'them' and 'us' atmosphere develops. However the interests of employers and employees are not necessarily fundamentally opposed: if the firm is a going-concern and productivity is increased, then it is more likely that employees will enjoy security of employment and improved earnings. Good employers are concerned that their workers should be well-paid, happy people. In societies where slavery was permitted, many slave-owners appreciated that they would get more work if their slaves were well fed rather than emaciated. In a capitalist society, a philosophy of high wages may be conducive to more work and greater output. In any society it is preferable that there should be mutual respect between bosses and workers. The interests of employers and employees may sometimes be divided in a capitalist society, when the employer class is preoccupied with the maximisation of profit without regard for the welfare of their workers. Even in a *mixed economy* such as that found in Britain, strikes and other forms of unrest still occur in the public-sector industries that are controlled by the state and where profit is not the main motivating influence. Some of the reasons for industrial strife include:

1 employers attempting to secure labour on the cheap

2 workers believing that they are not securing their fair share either of the industrial organisation's initial profit or of extra profit brought by increased productivity

3 some workers believing that they are a special case and not receiving a just award for their labour

4 day-to-day frictions which arise when communications break down and one side of industry does not give full consideration to the other side's point of view

5 quarrels between workers' organisations such as:

a craft unions versus industrial unions

b manual workers versus white-collar workers

c demarcation disputes over who should do a particular job

6 a lack of effective *negotiating machinery* so that causes of dissatisfaction cannot be adequately discussed and eradicated.

Effective negotiating machinery between employers and employees in a modern society pre-supposes the existence and acceptance of trade unions. Where trade unions and employers are able to arrange a system of successful co-operation then industrial disputes will be minimised. The main functions of trade unions are:

1 to improve the standard of living and increase the *real earnings* of their members (real earnings are not just monetary earnings, but rather the goods and services that can be bought with money earned)

2 to work for better peripheral money benefits such as higher overtime rates, piecework rates and bonuses

3 to strive for subsidiary *socio-economic benefits* such as shorter working hours, longer holidays and workers' amenities

4 to attempt to safeguard the jobs of their members especially where redundancies can be avoided

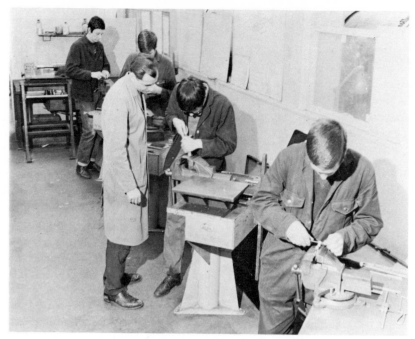

Apprentices at work in the Engineering Department, Rowntree Mackintosh Ltd, York

5   to be concerned with industrial education and especially with the adequate training of apprentices

6   to provide occasional benefits similar to the old friendly society benefits when trade union members experience industrial accidents, sickness, strikes, temporary unemployment or retirement

7   to work for the reform of industrial legislation possibly by participating indirectly in political matters (eg by contributing to the finances of the Labour Party)

8   to co-operate with employers and the Government in the establishment of effective bargaining machinery.

Bargaining machinery in Britain may be considered in three stages; each stage is of a slightly more serious nature although strikes may occur at any stage, if bargaining procedures break down. The stage at which bargaining between employer and employee may cease to operate depends upon the industrial climate and the amount of goodwill, or lack of goodwill, that exists between the two parties. The three stages are:

1   negotiations by employers and unions to secure a settlement to a dispute without calling upon outside help

2   conciliation by Department of Employment officers in an effort to draw the parties closer together

3   arbitration by a third party that gives an independent decision although often employers and unions will not agree to be bound by the findings of an arbitration board.

Strike action is usually the last resort by a trade union: even in a society that provides reasonable social security benefits, workers are likely to suffer most from a strike; employers may lose business, goodwill and profit while shareholders may suffer from a loss of dividends, but it is unlikely that they will have to cut down on foodstuffs or have a rental firm reclaim the TV set. Before strike action takes place trade unions are likely to use other bargaining weapons. Workers may deliberately *go slow*, or *work to rule* by rigidly adhering to an employer's rule-book. Relationships between employer and employee depend to a considerable extent upon the type of trade union to which employees belong. There are five main types of trade unions in Britain today:

1   *General unions* are the largest unions representing workers in a number of jobs. These include the three largest unions, ie the Transport and General Workers' Union (1 700 000 members), the Amalgamated Union of Engineers and Foundry Workers (1 400 000 members) and the National Union of General and Municipal Workers (800 000 members). The general unions have great financial strength but their power is often not so great as their membership would suggest because their members are engaged in different occupations.

2   *Industrial unions* represent workers in one industry and their power derives from the common interest of their members. The National Union of Mineworkers and the National Union of Railwaymen have displayed their unity by national stoppages during the 1970s.

3   *White-collar unions* are becoming more important as the service industries expand and more people work in the spheres of administration, finance, government, science and the professions. Nearly forty per cent of all trade unionists could be classified as white-collar workers by 1975.

4   *Craft unions* are the oldest and most numerous unions, but their membership figures are decreasing. About 450 craft unions represent less than 5000 members each.

5   *Confederations of unions* are organisations of unions that join in a loose way to give workers the strength that comes with unity. Their main importance, so far as the relationships between employers and employees are concerned, is that they enable workers to face the large confederations of employers with something approaching equal strength. An example of such a confederation of trade unions is the Confederation of Shipbuilding and Engineering Unions.

Industrial relations in Britain have been in a somewhat unhappy state in recent years. The Royal Commission on Trade Unions and Employers'

Associations (the Donovan Report) drew attention to the fact that, although Britain's number of days lost through breakdowns in relationships between employers and employees was not excessive up to 1968 (compared with countries such as Australia, Canada, Italy and the USA, which had far worse records), about ninety-five per cent of strikes in Britain were unofficial strikes. These *wildcat strikes* were to some extent caused by a double system of industrial bargaining: the informal system of negotiations between individual employers and shop stewards often clashed with the formal system of official associations of employers and workers.

The Industrial Relations Act of 1971 attempted to eliminate the double system of bargaining, but the Act was comparatively unsuccessful because of friction between the Government and the unions, culminating in the Trades Union Congress advising unions affiliated to the TUC not to register under the Act. Unregistered unions lost their legal protection, but the Conservative Government, elected in 1970, was forced to negotiate with these unregistered unions in an attempt to establish harmonious industrial relations. In 1972 the Government was accused of preventing the operation of its own 1971 Act when an almost unknown official called the Official Solicitor secured the release, against their will, of five dockers imprisoned by order of the National Industrial Relations Court set up under the 1971 Act. Their continued imprisonment could have brought a national dock strike and probably a complete breakdown of industrial relations in Britain. So a stalemate arose and the singular lack of success of the Industrial Relations Act of 1971 was indicated by the 1972 strike record of about 24 million workdays lost. The 1971 Act was replaced in 1974 by the Labour Government's Trade Union and Labour Relations Act which restored the privileges of the unions. It would seem that the most successful industrial relationships are found where employers and employees are left to negotiate freely without the Government attempting to force industrial co-operation by legislation.

Unit 30 Work and Leisure

30.1 Occupations

We have seen in Chapter 2 how important someone's occupation is in telling us something about him, and how the Registrar General divides occupations into five classes (see Figure 2.1). If you were conversing with a stranger it would probably not be long before you asked him about his occupation. If you found out what job he did, then you would be likely to make some pretty shrewd assessments about his life, interests and position in society.

The five classes used are necessarily arbitrary and it is sometimes very difficult to decide into which class, according to his job, a person belongs. As occupations change so classifications must be modified, eg the *Classification of Occupations*, 1970, omitted some groups previously included: boiler scalers; chimney sweeps; coopers, hoopmakers and benders!

Some examples of the groups in which various occupations are placed are given in Table 9.4 below.

Social class		
1	Professional	architects, chemists, surveyors
2	Intermediate	farmers, social welfare workers, physiotherapists
3	Skilled	plumbers, turners, woodworkers
4	Partially skilled	fishermen, counterhands, waiters
5	Unskilled	charwomen, office cleaners, window cleaners

Table 9.5 Examples of occupations according to social classes
(Source: *Classification of Occupations*, 1970, HMSO, Appendix D)

A postman clearing a pillar box. In which group would he be placed in the classification of occupations, and why?

As our society becomes better qualified there is a tendency for the percentage of workers in classes 1 and 2 to increase, and the class 5 percentage to decrease (see Table 9.5). The two main reasons for these percentage changes are the improved educational opportunities available, and the greater demand for higher-grade workers in an affluent modern society.

	1951		*1961*	
Social Class	*Number (Thousands)*	*Percentage*	*Percentage*	*Number (Thousands)*
1	494	3	4	591
2	2146	14	15	2368
3	8041	52	51	7933
4	2433	16	21	3237
5	2258	15	9	1422

Table 9.6 Changes in the social class-distribution of males (occupied and retired)
(Source: D. Marsh, *The Changing Social Structure of England and Wales 1871–1961*, Routledge & Kegan Paul, 1965)

There are close relationships between occupations and the way in which non-work time is spent. There is a double-pull involved because a person's occupation will influence his attitudes, but the opposite may also be true because specific occupations attract people with certain attitudes. Although less time is spent at work than was the case fifty years ago (largely because of shorter hours and longer holidays) nevertheless the average person is more involved with his occupation than people were centuries ago. Before 1761 there were forty-seven recognised holy days (often holidays) in England, and in the thirteenth century the skilled artisan worked only '194 days a year'. (H. L. Wilensky, *The Uneven Distribution of Leisure: The Impact of Growth on Free Time*) The average person is in many ways more occupationally-orientated nowadays. Greater involvement in one's occupation means that it is increasingly difficult to distinguish between work and non-work activities. This is especially true of the professions and higher grades of work. A doctor may get great satisfaction from delivering a baby, even though it may be late at night. At home a teacher may study background material related to his subject, mark school exercises and prepare lessons for the next day. A professional footballer might be very willing to enjoy a game and display his skills even if no remuneration were involved. Where does work stop and non-work begin in these occupations and in the case of architects, farmers, nurses and scores of other jobs? Indeed, for many people the time spent outside their main occupational role may be considered subconsciously as the hardest work of all. The university professor might be asked by his wife to spend an evening putting up a shelf, but to a non-technical, academically-minded man this might be one of the most difficult occupations of all. In an economic society based upon mechanisation and division of labour, there are millions who work merely because they get paid for it, but the most satisfying occupations are those that people would be willing to do even if they were not paid. Work is any productive activity whether one is paid or not. The housewife who is proud of her home and the mother who looks after her baby with loving care, are both fulfilling worthwhile unpaid occupations. But in the economic world we are concerned with occupations in market situations. A man's place in society is governed not merely by his type of occupation but by the amount of goods and services he can command because of the money he receives for carrying out his occupation.

Some of the occupations that have been the subject of special studies by sociologists have been jobs which have a great socialising influence upon those engaged in the occupation: these workers are employed as a team and their very lives may depend upon each other. Thus Jeremy Tunstall's study *The Fishermen* (MacGibbon & Kee, 1969) shows how a trawlerman sees himself as a member of a class drawn together by occupation so that 'he has indelibly printed on him certain habits, reflexes, patterns of spending, attitudes to life . . .' Similarly, the coal miner faces a life of occupational hazards; he could not work alone and he spends his free time in the pub with his mates (Dennis, Henriques and Slaughter, *Coal is Our Life*, Tavistock Publications, 1969). But the schoolteacher spends much time in a classroom and a research scientist in a laboratory, often separated from colleagues doing similar work, so that in these occupations there is little socialisation. In the latter cases it is less likely that people with similar occupations will spend their leisure time together: they work separately and they play separately. 'A knowledge of the ways in which work and leisure are inter-related helps us to understand that the problems of leisure are not likely to be successfully tackled without some consideration of the quality and meaning of working life.' (S. R. Parker, *The Sociology of Industry*, Allen and Unwin)

30.2 Leisure

We have seen that there is a close connection between work and leisure. If two men are watching a cricket match they may be at work, at leisure or participating in both work and leisure. One man might be paid for writing an account of the match for the press, or for scoring or umpiring. Another man might write and describe the match to an absent friend, or he might be very happy to score or umpire if he were asked, and he might be quite willing to do these things voluntarily for pleasure. The difference between work and leisure in these cases is very difficult to distinguish. If the first man, who was being paid as a journalist, scorer or umpire, would rather have been doing something else such as sailing or gardening, then work becomes more clearly discernible from leisure. But is gardening work? It can be work or leisure depending upon the person, place and time.

Yet having established this close relationship between leisure and work, it is clear that there are many cases where the two pursuits can be separated with greater clarity. The *Concise Oxford Dictionary* defines leisure as 'opportunity *to do, for*, afforded by free time, time at one's own disposal, . . . not occupied, without hurry.' It is this opportunity to do what one wants to do, indulging in one's chosen pursuits, having free time at one's own disposal, that is the real substance of leisure. In the past it was common for people to spend their spare time in an unhurried way, but modern leisure pursuits may include flying, motor racing, running 10 000 metres in the fastest possible time or playing twenty simultaneous games of chess against the clock. Dr Parker has pointed out that we cannot comprehend the problems of leisure without considering a man's working life, but the contrary also applies because a man's work may affect his leisure in different ways. A man who enjoys his work will want it to carry over into his spare time, whereas another man may wish to have a complete change of activity.

It should be clear why we are considering leisure in this chapter entitled The Economy and Employment. Firstly, a man must have leisure time if the economy is to be efficient and work is to be done well. Secondly, there are a whole series of leisure activities upon which a large number of people in the tertiary or service industries are employed; the provision of leisure by the organisation of bingo halls, professional football matches, package holidays etc. is an industry in itself. In the broadest sense, those engaged in providing library or museum services are part of the leisure industry, although their primary purpose may not be to provide pleasure pursuits. Need leisure coincide with enjoyment? Can leisure be spent upon activities that a person would rather not do?

If a person is engaged in mass production at work then he may well seek mass pleasures of a synthetic nature because his work has left him so dried-up that his creative abilities are nullified. The affluent society has provided the possibility of greater indulgence in leisure pursuits. The Duke of Wellington was worried that poor people might move about too much and get ideas beyond their station, but the growth of railways and other means of travel has popularised holidays away from home with the provision of many facilities for enjoyment. Transport has had a great influence upon leisure. Today there are about 16 million motor-cars in Britain and apart from providing a facility for pleasure, the motor calls for so many other ways of spending one's spare time: the car has to be cleaned and maintained. Other methods of travel such as aircraft and boats have extended leisure opportunities.

The sociologist, Dr Mark Abrams, has classified five ages of leisure, and the first of these is the teenage period which is considered in Youth Culture (Topic 13.3). The young are the most concerned with out-going pursuits and with people of their own age. The young and the old (ie retired people) have more free time to spend than other members of society, but the young have more money and energy than the old. The normal teenager is less inclined to spend time in passive or home-based pursuits such as watching television. Table 9.7 sets out the five main stages of leisure. What other typical activities would you think might be added to each group?

Table 9.7 is over-simplified, but gives a generalised picture of leisure pursuits such as watching television. The table gives some of the main compensations and limitations: the teenager should be full of life and energy but may be easily bored; newly-weds often find it difficult to manage financially but they are wrapped up in each other, and young children give much pleasure; the thirty-five to forty-five year olds have time and money to spend outside the home, although they are probably still struggling to get 'established'; the forty-five to sixty-five year olds have most to spend and fewer financial worries but it is often a time of frustration and cynicism; the over sixty-fives have more time for leisure after retirement but usually have not the money to get the best from their spare time. All the various ages of leisure are influenced by a search for *status* as Thorstein Veblen argued in *Theory of the Leisure Class*: the young man wants a high-powered motor bike; the young marrieds are proud of their home and children; the middle-aged show their home

1st Age *Teenager/Youth Culture*	2nd Age *Young Marrieds*	3rd Age *35 to 45 years*	4th Age *45 to 64 years*	5th Age *Over 65 years*
Much time spent outside the home in company with peer group; working-classes have more spending money than middle-classes in many cases.	Set up home and have children; 70% women and 55% men married before they reach 25; essentially home-centred.	Home ties decrease as children are less demanding; more time spent outside the home.	Most affluent age; very few have responsibilities of children; less physical energy; status seeking.	Retirement of women at 60 and men at 65; physical and mental decline; little spare cash.
Mass sports; sexual freedom; luxury spending on non-essentials; search for danger to ease boredom.	Purchase of home and car; child caring; TV, reading; DIY and hobbies; home and car maintenance.	Public houses; visiting friends; dinners and dances; church and small group activities; camping and caravanning.	Eating and drinking more expensively; golf and bridge; colour TV; continental holidays.	Inexpensive pursuits such as reading; gardening; knitting; whist; bingo; walking (often cannot afford pubs and cinemas).

Table 9.7   The Five Ages of Leisure

movies or their car of the latest model; the old still have their pride and resist charity, but as Ronald Fletcher maintains, 'If old people could be made materially secure, there is no reason why the period should not be regarded in a positive, constructive way.' (*The Family and Marriage*, Penguin Books, 1962)

Terms used in this chapter

factors of production
entrepreneur
capitalist economy
working population
labour mobility

full employment
white-collar workers
wildcat strikes
mixed economy
tertiary workers

Questions

1 Name five goods which you regard as necessities and five that you regard as luxuries.

2 Since 1972, the 450 head-office staff of the London and Manchester Assurance Company have worked when they liked so long as they put in thirty-five hours per week. What are the advantages and disadvantages of such a scheme?

3 Why did Lord Beveridge consider that full employment should be regarded as a situation where not more than three per cent of the working population are unemployed?

4 How do you think the National Income could be more fairly distributed?

5 According to Community Industry (Britain's first public works agency for lower-qualified school-leavers) teenage unemployment will be a major factor in the British job market until at least 1976. Why is this and what steps can you suggest to avoid teenage unemployment?

6 By using newspapers and periodicals find examples of three recent cases of the use of automation.

7 If you were Secretary of State for Employment how would you seek to get unions and bosses to come together so that industrial unrest can be lessened?

8 Michael Argyle has written about 'the formation of personality as a result of socialisation for work' (*New Society*, 16 November 1972). Now the nature of work is being changed by technology, in what ways will a worker's personality have to change?

9 What educational and housing factors work for and against the mobility of labour?

10 If you were a member of the Countryside Commission, responsible for recreational planning in Britain, what measures would you take to improve outdoor leisure facilities?

Questions from GCE 'O' Level Sociology Examination Papers

1   In what ways does a person's work influence his non-work behaviour? (AEB, November 1969)

2   Some areas have high unemployment rates whilst jobs are available in other parts of the country. What factors tend to prevent unemployed workers moving into other areas where there are jobs? (AEB, Specimen Paper for New Syllabus, 1972)

3   What are the major social problems of unemployment? (Oxford Local Examinations, 1972)

4   Why in recent years have some young people been able to command relatively high wages? (AEB 1968)

5   Distribution of wealth by groups of owners

Percentage of wealth owned by:	1961	1970
Most wealthy 1%	28.4	20.7
5%	50.6	40.7
10%	62.5	51.9
25%	79.2	72.5
50%	92.5	90.2

(Adapted from *Social Trends* 1972)

Discuss the argument that Britain is now a classless society, making some use in your answer of the above figures.

6   What is the difference between automation and industrialisation? What effect is automation likely to have on the lives of employees? (AEB, November 1974)

7   Would you prefer a white-collar or a manual job? Why? (Oxford Local Examinations, 1972)

8   What do you understand by the term 'division of labour'? Illustrate your answer with reference to any *one* industry or occupation. (Oxford Local Examinations, 1974)

9   What are the major sources of 'alienation' in industry? (Oxford Local Examinations, 1974)

10   What are the most important social consequences of automation? (Oxford Local Examinations, 1973)

11   Young people entering employment 1967

Ages 15, 16, 17	Total numbers	Apprenticeships	Clerical work	Other work
Boys	253 000	43%	9%	48%
Girls	234 000	7%	39%	54%
Total	487 000			

a   Explain why there should be more boys than girls entering employment in 1967.

b   Account for the sex differences in the figures for apprenticeships and clerical work. (AEB, November 1969)

12 What do you understand by the term 'automation'? What effects does automation have on job satisfaction? (Oxford Local Examinations, 1975)

13 What are the causes and consequences of the increased employment of married women? (AEB, November 1969)

14 What are the major causes of industrial disputes? (Oxford Local Examinations, 1972)

15 What is a 'shop steward'? What part does he or she play in the British system of industrial relations? (Oxford Local Examinations, 1975)

16 Outline the major changes which have taken place in the distribution of trade union membership since 1945. (Oxford Local Examinations, 1974)

17 Occupation has a marked influence on leisure. Discuss. (AEB, 1968)

18 Two men are watching a cricket match: one of them is working, the other is enjoying his leisure time. Explain how this might be true and say exactly what you mean by work and leisure. (AEB, June 1971)

19 'There is a growing literature tracing the ways in which the kind of work men do influences their pattern of life. Studies of leisure which have hitherto focused on social class differences are now developing the theme that there are occupational differences within class and status groupings which play a large part in determining the style of leisure, family behaviour, political orientations, as well as more general values.' (S. R. Parker)

a   Explain this passage in non-technical language.

b   Give some examples of the class differences referred to. (AEB, June 1972)

20 What do you understand by leisure? Describe some of the different ways in which various groups spend their leisure time. How could you account for these differences? (AEB, Specimen Paper for New Syllabus, 1972)

21 'The kind of work a man does influences his whole way of life.' Discuss this statement giving examples wherever appropriate. (AEB, November 1972)

22 Describe and account for the changing pattern of leisure activities during the last fifty years. (AEB, June 1969)

10 Social Control
Unit 31 Social Order and Social Control

31.1 Social Order

To begin thinking about the term *social order*, we will start by looking at a school, which is something close to everyone's experience. In a school there are a great many pupils and staff, each with different backgrounds and interests. Despite this variety, we can think of individuals grouped together in clusters because they share the same interests and identify with one another. For example, pupils and staff who share a primary interest in sport make up one group in the school; those interested in sociology, another; a third group could be those students whose main interest is in leaving school at the earliest opportunity. Of course, a pupil could be thought of as belonging to all three of these groups at the same or different times in his school career.

In society there is a wide variety of people, with different backgrounds, involved in different activities but clustered together in groups because of their shared interests and goals. For example, there are many people in our society, from widely differing backgrounds, who are parents. However, when they get together and share their common experience as parents we may consider them as a group. The men and women who are teachers in a school or a college are another example of a group. These groups, parents and teachers, share a concern with bringing up children, so we can think of the groups as being broadly interested in the same activity.

Not all groups in society have interests in common and this can lead to disagreements. For example, one of the most pressing jobs of town planners is to think of ways of coping with the increased number of private cars brought into city centres. One scheme has been to build multi-storey car parks in or near town centres. The goals and schemes of town planners, however, are not always thought of as such good ideas by other groups in the town who wish to preserve old buildings or scenic views in preference to providing multi-storey car parks.

These are small, local issues, but there is also conflict on a much wider

The goals and schemes of town planners are not always considered good ideas by groups who wish to preserve old buildings

scale in society between large and powerful social groups. One of the most conspicuous examples of this in Britain today is the basic differences of interest which exist between workers and management in industry.

Our society, then, is made up of many different social groups some of which co-operate with one another while others compete or conflict with one another. Why is it that groups do not merely seize what they want? Of course, force is used in society and groups do succeed, by fair means and foul, in furthering their own interests. The feudal barons of England furthered their schemes for getting more land by driving out neighbouring barons and force, though usually of a more subtle sort, is just as much a part of the society we live in today. The surprising point is not that force is sometimes used, but that we so often employ more peaceful means, such as discussion, to settle differences of interest.

Despite these varied interests, society does not collapse under the strain of their conflicting pressures. We know this because, generation after generation, society changes but endures. Sociologists therefore speak of there being an underlying unity and order in social life. It is this order that makes it possible for everyday life to carry on. For example, we go to school or to work and know that there will be someone to drive the bus, heat the building, help us with our work and cook lunch. We assume that the bus driver will stick to the route, the caretaker will not burn down the building, the schoolteacher or the boss will not scream at us and throw our work out of the window. In fact, we never think about these things because we take responsible behaviour for granted. Because other people act in customary ways, life is, to a considerable degree, predictable, and we are able to plan and organise what we do to achieve our objectives. For example, hire purchase companies assume that their customers will continue to pay for their goods and the customers themselves use hire purchase arrangements because they are confident that they will be able to continue paying.

Social life is carried on according to rules, rather like a game of chess. For instance, the player himself decides how he will move his chess pieces but every move will obey the rules for the game of chess. The match can be played because each player knows and understands these rules; this allows both of them to plan their game and reach their objective of winning the match. If a player should suddenly invent his own rules his opponent would be confused and the game could not go on.

In the same way there are rules which control how we act in social groups and in society; if the rules are broken the situation becomes confusing, no one can be sure what anyone else is going to do, and social order is threatened. Imagine what driving a car would be like if there were no rules of the road.

31.2   Formal social control

There is a wide range of rules in society: rules about where to park the car; how to claim a tax refund; what to do if you are late to school; and how to treat other people. Some rules are considered to be more important than others. The sociologist distinguishes several different types of social rules. The most evident rules in society are those which constitute the law.

Over the centuries, laws have been decided upon by powerful social groups, written down, reviewed, altered and added to, so that now there is a vast body of material which is called the law and which applies to almost every aspect of social life. In order to ensure that everyone abides by these laws there are specific penalties, such as fines or imprisonment, for anyone found guilty of breaking the law. Breaches of the law are of two sorts: civil offences, which are offences against only the wronged individual, and crime, in which an offence has been committed against social order. A civil offence would be letting your dog bite the postman; a criminal offence would be stealing the postman's registered letters. The authority of the law in society is backed up by a complex system of agencies such as the police, the courts, the legal profession and the prisons, which ensure that the law is enforced and that those who break the law are punished.

The law is a means of social control: by the threat of punishments it affects what people do. However, the law also controls our actions in a less obvious way: there is widespread belief that the law is morally right and therefore should be obeyed. This respect for the justice of the law is one other way in which the law acts as a means of social control.

The sociologist refers to the law as a *formal social control*. This is because the law, unlike other types of social control, has special authority in society, and a complex system exists to ensure that the law is enforced. Laws are set out in writing and specific penalties have been drawn up to punish people who break the law. The police and courts are dependent on the law being set out clearly, otherwise it would not be possible to enforce it. In Britain, laws have been formally drawn up and administered since Roman times, but in England the law is not rigidly defined as it is in the USA (Codified Law and the Constitution). It is open to very flexible interpretation based upon Common Law, ie the accepted interpretation of the law arrived at by High Court Judges, whose decisions have become part of the Common Law.

31.3   Informal social control

Norms

Not all social rules are written down and there are many types of unwritten rules which exist in society. For example, one of these is that parents spend time playing with their children. An unwritten rule such as this is called a *norm* (it should be noted that 'norm' in this sense is entirely different from a *statistical norm*). A norm is a standard or pattern for the way we expect people to act and behave. Such a standard must be generally accepted by two or more people in society before it can be called a norm. It is not written down, and the individual who breaks the rule is not subject to specific constraints and penalties enforced by police or courts, although, as we shall see later, some norms are bound up with the law; the sociologist therefore refers to norms as *informal social controls*.

A norm, like a law, is part of the culture of a society and is passed on from one generation to the next through socialisation. An individual, as he grows up will learn the norms of his particular society. For example, in our society we think it is right that children should grow up living at home with their parents, at least in the first few years of life. By contrast, until quite recently, it was a norm that children growing up in the kibbutzim of Israel should live, from the first months of life, almost entirely in the company of other children and in the care of specialised nurses and teachers.

We are so familiar with the norms of the society we grow up in that they are almost second nature to us; we take them for granted, seldom reflecting on them, questioning their importance or considering whether there may be better alternatives.

Mores

Some norms are particularly important in society; for example, those that refer to the way we should behave towards one another, treating each other justly and honestly. These are norms which have embedded in them the idea that it is morally wrong to treat people unjustly or to be dishonest. The sociologist calls such norms *mores*. Some of the most widely-held mores in our society are concerned with respecting the lives and the property of other people. Although there is variation between the mores of different societies, western industrialised societies have many fundamental mores in common.

Mores are important in society because of the *moral values* they maintain. For example, men and women think it is morally important not to steal, to kill or to deliberately injure. Values are part of the culture of society and there are sometimes differences between the values of one society and another. This must be taken into account when considering the mores of societies different from our own and should make us wary of judging the merits of the mores of other societies. On the other hand, values such as the right of human beings to life and dignity are widely accepted in many different cultures and the violation of these values, as happened, for example, in Nazi Germany, elicits moral condemnation.

Mores play an important part in maintaining social order and many have been written down and incorporated into our laws. We can now understand why the law is usually thought of as being morally right. This does not mean to say that the law always reflects the social mores. Sometimes the law is at variance with popular social mores and it becomes regarded as more moral to break the law than to observe it. For example, in the USA, many young people thought that it was wrong for the country to be involved in the war in Vietnam and they therefore illegally evaded the draft by which young men were sent to fight there.

How Norms Affect Behaviour

Even though people cannot be made to obey norms in the same way that the threat of punishments may make us obey the law, norms do succeed in controlling what we do. How is it that they are effective? The reason is, we control each other. This can be seen if we think of someone learning a new role, for example as a student, a secretary, a wife or a laboratory assistant. In every case we are socialised into the role through the reactions of other people: a waitress who pours soup into the lap of the customer learns from the annoyance of the customer and the restaurant manager that this is not expected of her in her role as a waitress. Of course, most people will know this already, because, besides being influenced by other people directly we are also influenced indirectly by the views expressed through films, magazines and television.

We control one another's actions in other ways besides showing annoyance: for instance, praise and reward encourage us to go on behaving as we are. Showing surprise, disappointment, disgust or completely ignoring someone are some of the other ways in which we bring people's actions in line with perceived social norms.

Folkways

The norm that people should form a queue when waiting for the bus is not usually one that is taken so seriously that there are heavy penalties for ignoring it. This is for two reasons: first, standing in line when waiting for a bus has little to do with being a morally right thing to do, although we often feel it is the fairest way to cope with this problem; secondly, there is no widespread agreement that forming a queue is so important that people should be made to conform. This, then, is an example of a type of norm which the sociologist calls a *folkway*. Other examples include: eating with a knife and fork; celebrating birthdays; and exchanging greeting cards at Christmas. Folkways are norms which are generally observed in society or by social groups but breaking them is not considered to be morally wrong.

Customs are folkways which have existed for a long time in society. The use of holly and mistletoe at Christmas is a custom. Fashion is also a folkway and differs from custom because it is less permanent. Fashions in dress, such as mini or maxi skirts and studded leather jackets, are examples of this type of folkway. How important do you think these are? Do we control each other in any way so that we will conform to styles of dressing?

Folkways are part of the culture of a society and therefore we must remember to view them in the context of the society in which they arise. Often, folkways which at first sight seem better or worse than our own, are in reality different simply because of the cultural differences between the societies. Take, for example, customs about the way we greet one another. In this country we shake hands; in Italy or Greece it is not at all unusual for good friends to embrace one another.

Norms and values are part of the culture of society and like any other aspect of culture, they change. For example, in Britain in the mid-nineteenth century, it was considered right that middle-class married women should remain at home and devote themselves to being good wives, mothers and mistresses of the house. Today, there is little objection to married women going out to work. Of course, technological inventions such as the washing machine and the fridge have helped to change the woman's role, but these by themselves would have made little difference if there had not also been changes in such norms and values as the one to the effect that 'woman's place is in the home'.

Norms and values are not always the same for everyone in society. Different social groups have different norms and values. We can see this if we think of the different ways in which people spend their leisure time. For example, it is a middle-class rather than a working-class norm to spend time off at the theatre, the ballet, the opera, at evening classes or taking part in amateur dramatics.

Unit 32 Religion: Another Type of Social Control

32.1 Beliefs and belief systems

What an individual does, makes sense to him. This is because there are reasons behind what we do; we usually know what these are and they seem sensible to us.

Suppose that a man puts money in a charity collecting-tin; he may do this for any number of reasons: he knows the person who is making the collection and cannot refuse; he has a relative who works for the charity or who benefits from its care; his wife or children want him to make a donation; his neighbour is looking on; he cannot get into the shop unless the collector comes out of the doorway; he thinks it is his Christian duty; he thinks it will keep away the Evil Eye. The list is incomplete, but the point is that there are factors controlling his actions. In every case his reason for putting money in the tin is the result of informal social controls affecting what he does. We can never know for certain which of these reasons made him act in this way.

We hold *beliefs* and these affect what we do. For example, if a man believes that there is an evil power in the world called the Evil Eye and that putting money in charity collecting tins will help to keep this away then this belief is the reason behind his putting money in charity collecting tins. Beliefs affect our actions and are another important type of social control.

What are beliefs?

A belief is an idea that we hold about what is true or factual. For example, some people think it is true that walking under ladders will bring them bad luck and a person believing this will deliberately avoid walking under ladders.

The beliefs that people hold vary from ideas about 'the fish that got away' to very serious and complicated ideas about such things as life after death. Some we can test to see if they are true or not: for example, men found out by walking on the moon that it is not made of green cheese. Some we cannot test to see if they are true or not. For example, beliefs about the Evil Eye, the existence of God and the purpose of life cannot be tested using any of the methods used by scientists to see whether they are true are not. This is because these beliefs are of a different sort from those concerning the physical world around us.

Belief Systems

At any moment in the day we usually have several beliefs in our minds. Some of these will be about ordinary everyday things, such as whether there is sponge syrup pudding for lunch, whether school will close early because of the bad weather, whether the Channel Tunnel will ever be built. These ideas are not so important to us that they affect us over a long period of time. More important and deeply-held beliefs, however, may affect us for most of our lives. These are beliefs about such things as our spiritual nature, our relationship with a god, or with other human beings.

Religious beliefs, such as Christianity and other world religions, come into this category of deeply-held beliefs and have a great deal of influence on the actions of the people holding them. Religious beliefs are reinforced by symbolic actions, and participation in these rituals has the effect of binding together the believers into a moral community.

The sociologist looks on religious beliefs as examples of *belief systems* rather than as isolated beliefs. This is because a religion is made up of a number of related ideas and it is impossible to hold just one belief without also believing in several others.

Religious belief systems serve to relate the worldly affairs of life with a sacred sphere. The sociologist is not interested in the philosophical problems of whether the particular beliefs are valid or not: what he wants to find out is how people holding these beliefs are affected by them in their day-to-day lives. If he can understand more about the reasons for a person's actions by looking more closely at the particular doctrines of a religion, the sociologist will study the content of a religion. For example, doctrines that hold out the hope of a heaven or a better existence in a future life, affect the way people live out their daily lives in this life. In the same way, the threat of punishment for ignoring religious doctrines can also affect how people act in their day-to-day lives.

Belief systems are not confined to religious beliefs. There are other ways of thinking about man's place and purpose in the world. For example, a Marxist holds certain beliefs, about what is happening in the world, which depend on ideas about history and economics. His beliefs include no reference to any 'god'.

Belief systems are part of the culture of a society. Children learn the religion of their society. For example, many of us have grown up learning little or nothing about Buddhism, Hinduism or Islam. Children growing up in Asia are more likely to learn about one of these major religions. Asian families coming to live in this country continue to hold their religious beliefs even though they are many miles from home. This is because Hinduism or Islam is an important and familiar part of their daily lives and continues to have a meaning for them in this country. A Christian living in India or Pakistan would continue to practice his religion because, in the same way, it remains an important part of his way of life.

32.2   What part does religion play in society?

Sociologists have suggested that religion serves functions which are broadly similar in most societies.

1   Religious beliefs give an explanation of uncertainties like failing crops, human life and death: these are problems which would otherwise be difficult to explain. In modern western industrialised society we have many scientific explanations which help us to understand the causes of such things, but these explanations cannot help people in the same way as religion in explaining for example, why there are such things as life and death.

2   Religions are carried on in ways which can be seen and understood: for instance, by rites and rituals. Religious rites, such as the Christian Communion service, help people to express their religious beliefs and reinforce their social

behaviour. Religious ritual helps to bring the believers together to participate in some common activity. In this way, religious rites help to strengthen the believers, uniting them into a moral community.

3 Taking part in religious rites gives the believers a feeling of well-being and comfort.

4 The ceremonies which are carried out by different religions carry on generation after generation. To the people who take part in religious rites such as Holy Communion, this event affects their actions and serves to link them with the past, present and future actions of members of society.

We can see that, where everyone in society holds the same religious beliefs, as in many traditional societies, religion plays an important part in unifying society and maintaining the existing social order.

32.3 Religion in Britain

In many towns in Britain today, sights similar to the one in the photograph can be seen. Does this mean that religion is no longer important in Britain today? This is a tricky question because it is really several questions wrapped up in one and each needs to be looked at very carefully before we can set about giving an answer.

It is not uncommon to see churches for sale these days

1   Was there a time when religion was important in Britain?

2   How are we going to find out how much religious belief there is in Britain today?

3   Has religious belief declined?

4   Does religion play any part in the life of Britain today?

These questions will be looked at in turn. In each case only the Christian religion will be considered, although it is recognised that other religions such as Judaism and, more recently, Hinduism and Islam are part of British culture.

Was there a time when religion was important in Britain?

Television programmes, films and, perhaps, even Christmas cards seem to have conspired to present a picture of nineteenth-century Britain as a time when everyone attended church regularly. Although nineteenth-century statistical material is not always reliable, the results of a mid-nineteenth-century survey are useful and would seem to disagree with this picture. In 1851, the results of the only English Census of Religion ever taken showed that only thirty-nine per cent of the total population had gone to church or chapel on a particular Sunday in the year. Of this percentage, the majority were undoubtedly from the middle classes.

In his *Notes on England*, published in 1861, the Frenchman, Taine, describes a typical middle-class English family at Sunday prayers:

On Sunday evening he (the head of the household) is their spiritual guide, their chaplain: they may be seen entering in a row, the women in front, the men behind, with seriousness, gravity, and taking their places in the drawing room . . . The master reads aloud a short sermon—next a prayer; . . . lastly, he repeats the Lord's Prayer and, clause by clause the worshippers respond.

By the first decades of the twentieth century, religious activity had reached a peak in this country. Even then, however, it was still a predominantly middle-class activity, the efforts of organised religious groups such as the Church of England, the Methodists and, after 1878, the Salvation Army, to bring the poorer working classes into the church, having generally failed to make any widespread impact on this social group.

How are we going to find out how much religious belief there is in Britain today?

So far, we have used statistics giving the percentage of persons attending church as a means of finding out how much religious belief there is in society. The 1851 survey can be used as a rough guide to the extent of religious belief in nineteenth-century England, but, in general, statistics of religious activities like going to church, must be used with care as a source of information on religious beliefs in society. What, then, are the limitations of such statistics?

First, most of us have heard people say: 'I don't need to go to church to be a Christian'. Whether this is true or not is not important to the sociologist, but these people go unrecorded in statistics of religious behaviour, such as going to church, and he can never be sure of the numbers of people in society who think of themselves as Christians and yet who never take part in church activities. The sociologist D. A. Martin in *The Religious and the Secular* (Routledge & Kegan Paul, 1969), notes the difficulty of really finding out what religious beliefs are held in Britain, by giving the example of research conducted during the period 1964-5, which showed that eighty-five to ninety per cent of people believe in God and call themselves Christians, while only fifty per cent believe in the related idea of the life to come. There are many sociologists who are doubtful if the figure for the numbers of people calling themselves Christian and believing in God are really as high as this research suggests. David Martin himself points out that many people think of being a Christian as the same as being respectable.

Secondly, the people who go to church and take part in other religious activities, like prayer meetings, may be doing this for a number of reasons, none of which have anything directly to do with religious belief. For example, going to church may be a habit, a way of passing time, or the result of family pressures.

Sociologists suggest that the statistics of the number of christenings, weddings and burials performed, for example in the Church of England, are not reliable guides to religious belief. We will return to this point later.

Thirdly, the biggest limitation of religious statistics is that in each religious group, such as the Church of England or the Baptists, the statistics are really recording different things. For example, to look at membership figures for the Roman Catholic Church and to compare these with figures from the Church of England or the Methodists is misleading. In the Roman Catholic Church membership means everyone baptised as a baby into the Roman Catholic Church, and some of them will have drifted away from the church as they got older. To look at membership in the Church of England gives us a choice between figures for Baptism, Confirmation, the Electoral Roll and Easter Day communicants. The sociologist is wary of using the first three. This is because being

I think it's a lovely name for a boy. But I still can't see why they have to christen it on the day of our last match of the season. (Going to church may be the result of family pressures.)

baptised or confirmed does not necessarily mean that a person has continued to join in church activities in his adult life. The Electoral Roll is a list of lay persons, over seventeen years old, who are eligible to take part in committees to do with some of the parish's affairs. This often has a lot to do with the personal ambitions of people rather than religious beliefs. Sociologists, therefore, make use of the figures of Easter communicants. A person who does not usually go to church but continues to think of himself as a member of the Church of England will almost certainly try to get to the most important event in the Church's year, the Easter Day Communion. The numbers of people attending this service can therefore give us the best idea of the practising membership of the Church of England. In the Methodist Church, membership figures refer to the men and women who, as adults, have joined the Methodists by attendance at a membership service.

From this account of what membership means in three different churches, it is possible to see how misleading it would be to make comparisons without first finding out the most appropriate statistics by which to look at church membership. Also, in trying to discover the extent of religious belief we must select only statistics about activities relevant to providing a reliable guide to belief.

Has religion declined?

Now we know something about the problem of using statistics of religious behaviour as a guide to religious belief in Britain, we can look at Figure 10.1 knowing that it must be interpreted carefully. In the figure, selected categories of statistics have been used which are appropriate indices of religious belief in each group.

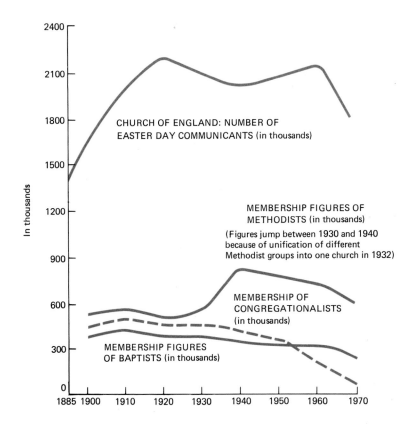

Figure 10.1 *Changes in 'membership' of some British religious groups, 1885–1970* *(Sources: Church Information Office;* Church of England Year Book; Baptist Handbook; *Minutes of the Methodist Conference;* Congregational Year Book)

From Figure 10.1 it can be seen that in the Church of England there has been some falling-away in the numbers of people attending Easter Day Communion. In other religious groups, the Methodists, the Congregationalists and the Baptists, there has been a gradual falling-away in membership, from the first decades of the twentieth century to the present.

The decline in the numbers of people interested in religious activities can also be seen in such things as the decline in the numbers going to Sunday service and Sunday school and in the numbers of magazines published by religious groups. The decline in attendance at Sunday services in groups such as the Methodists is a useful statistical trend to look at in terms of estimating the extent of real religious belief in these churches. This is because if someone belongs to such a group then they are usually expected to attend services regularly and a falling-away in attendance means a falling-away in belief.

Some of the smaller religious groups such as the Plymouth Brethren, are called *sects* by the sociologist. These have managed to keep about the same level, or, in some cases, have increased the level of membership during the course of the twentieth century.

In addition to looking at the national figures for different religious activities, sociologists also look at the records of religious activities in different communities. The overall decline on a national scale covers up regional differences such as the continuing importance of religion in parts of Wales, Scotland and Northern Ireland. In his book *The Religious and the Secular* David Martin calls these places 'the last bastions of majority religious practice in the United Kingdom'.

Does religion play any part in the life of Britain today?

In order to answer this question we can look at two things. First, we must consider the importance of religion in the personal lives of men and women. Secondly, we must assess the importance of organised religious groups, such as the Church of England, in influencing what other groups, such as the Government, do in society.

We have seen that it is not necessarily possible to find out how people feel about Christianity by looking at the statistics of organised religious groups. Many people think of themselves as Christian without ever going near a church or chapel. However, there are occasions in the life-cycle of the individual when he or she may well attend a church service. These are times such as baptisms, weddings and funerals. For example, in 1967, over fifty per cent of all infants born in that year were baptised, about sixty-six per cent of all marriages were celebrated in churches or chapels

Nuns are a less common sight in Britain today

and over ninety per cent of burials were conducted with religious rites. In many cases, these events may be a reflection of religious belief, but sociologists are inclined to think that they have a different significance for most people. With the exception of burials, for which very few people make prior arrangements, these religious events have taken on an importance in marking stages and changes in the role of the individual in the course of his life-cycle. For example, the change from being single to being married is a significant one for the individual and in the eyes of society. The event is well-marked by a solemn ceremony in a church. Because of the importance of these religious rituals in marking stages in the individual's life-cycle, the sociologist calls services such as baptisms, weddings and burials *rites de passage*. Bryan Wilson, in his book *Religion in Secular Society* (Watts, 1966) suggests that the churches are thought of today almost as an additional department of the Welfare State, to be used as, and when required.

Looking at the part played by religion in society in terms of the influence which groups, such as the Church of England, can have on the course of events in society, we can see that these bodies continue to have much power and influence. This can be seen especially in matters which are to do with the family or education. For example, the Church of England, as the Established Church of this country, voices the Church's concern over issues such as divorce and abortion when it seems that changes in the law may affect Christian marriage and the family. However, the church is increasingly losing its position of authority on such matters and being replaced in many cases by spokesmen of the social sciences.

In terms of education, some background to the Christian religion is taught in schools, although this is not such a central part of school curricula today as it was a century ago. The Church of England, the Roman Catholic Church, the Methodists and several other religious groups were among the first social groups to set up schools and colleges in the nineteenth century. There are fewer of these today and they are no longer so free from government control. It is a sign of the decline in the importance of religion in modern society that religious knowledge is not so highly valued in society as other types of knowledge, scientific, for instance.

Unit 33 The Law

33.1 Law and morality

We have already seen some of the points which are common to formal laws and informal social rules, such as norms. Both are types of social control. We know also that important mores, such as those about deliberately injuring or killing someone, or stealing property, are written down and become laws, which can be enforced by the threat of punishment. However, morality and the law do not always go hand in hand.

People's opinions about what is right and wrong change. The problem is that the law, because it is written down, involves all sorts of procedures and so is not always quick to change and reflect the ideas current in society. For example, ideas have changed about how right or wrong it is for married couples to be able to divorce (see Chapter 3). By the 1930s ideas about the morality of getting a divorce had changed more quickly than the law. A. P. Herbert, in trying to introduce a Bill to change the divorce laws of the time gave many accounts of how couples were forced to contrive ridiculous situations because adultery was the only grounds on which they could get a divorce. Men and women were having to plan something that either looked like, or was, adultery, in order to get a divorce. This made a mockery of the existing laws, which were changed in 1937 to include other grounds for divorce. There is only one ground for divorce in England now, ie that the marriage has irretrievably broken down (Divorce Reform Act 1969).

The law can also sometimes pave the way for changing popular opinion about what is right and wrong. Acts of Parliament are sometimes designed to bring about a change in public opinion. For example, the use of the death penalty as punishment for murder has been a very controversial issue for a long time. In December 1969 the death penalty for murder was finally abolished in the Murder (Abolition of Death Penalty) Act, despite a widely publicised result of a public opinion poll which showed that eighty-four per cent of the population wished to bring back hanging. One MP gave this view of the difference between public opinion and the role of Parliament: '. . . one must pay regard to public opinion but that does not mean that we must be bound by public opinion . . . Parliament has the duty to make up its own mind . . .' (Hansard, December 1964— S. C. Silkin, MP for Dulwich).

We have seen that norms are not always the same for everyone in society, but whose views do laws reflect? Many sociologists would agree that the law reflects the views of those people who have enough power in society to make sure that their ideas are put into effect. For example, laws which punished by death anyone found guilty of stealing cattle were in existence in this country until 1832. We may be sure that it was the people who owned cattle and not the poor people who stole them who introduced that law.

33.2   The police

There are forty-seven police forces in England and Wales and each of these has two basic departments, the uniformed branch and the CID. In some forces, such as the Metropolitan, these incorporate such different branches as the mounted and river police; but each is concerned with the same job, making sure that the laws are enforced.

The strength of each police force varies from district to district, but most forces are at present very understaffed for the work they have to do: in 1971, the ratio of police to the general public was one police officer to every 500 in Britain. The ratio has not altered appreciably in recent years.

In the course of their training, policemen learn that it is the primary duty of the police to prevent crime. Police duties also include the preservation of life and the maintenance of public tranquillity.

Actual or suspected offences may be reported to the police, or the

The police are concerned with making sure that laws are enforced

police themselves may discover that an offence has been committed. All criminal acts which come to the attention of the police are called 'crimes known to the police' and this is an important category used in the collection of criminal statistics. These statistics are sometimes used as a measure of the success or failure of the police. However, it is important to remember that the statistics cannot record the absence of those crimes which the police may have prevented.

The success of the police in enforcing law and order is affected by the type of contact that there is between the police and the public. In recent years this relationship has been influenced by several factors. The police force increasingly looks on itself as a profession: that is, skilled in the prevention of crime. However, at the same time, the police force is understaffed. For the individual police officer this often means that he is under pressure to provide his superiors with suspects in the hope that this will lead to the solution of crimes and swell the total number of crimes known to the police which are cleared up annually. The police officer today usually works in an area which he does not live in: this presents problems because he does not know the people of the area, their way of life or their difficulties. Under these circumstances, he is forced to fall back on any means he knows by which to identify suspects and these tend to involve the ideas formed by his upbringing, his family and, most influential of all, his fellow officers. The typical suspect is often seen as an individual who has been in trouble or who comes from a problem locality,

Watcha, Bertie—considering there is only one policeman for every 500 people in Britain you're a very lucky man. I am about to give you my undivided attention.

known to have produced offenders in the past. Young working-class lads in noisy groups are more likely suspects than well-mannered, respectful middle-class youths; boys and men are more likely suspects than girls.

In a study called *Crime, Police and Race Relations* (Oxford University Press, 1970), John Lambert describes police relationships with immigrants, with particular reference to the situation in Birmingham. He makes the point that Irish immigrants are not confronted with the same problems as Asians or West Indians in their relationships with the police. The difficulties appear to arise from the fixed ideas that each group has about the other. For instance, Lambert describes how a police officer talking to a mainly West Indian class at a London girls' school found that most of the children thought that everyone who went inside a police station was beaten up, this idea coming largely from the culture of the West Indies. This belief, however, was not found everywhere: children in Birmingham had a much more favourable impression of the police. Lambert suggests that in the case of Asian immigrants the problem arises because they see the police as corrupt and corruptible, an image which does not go down too well with the police. In the case of West Indians, the police's ideas about the excitability of West Indians does not help to improve relations between the two groups.

The relationship between the police and the public has been affected by the problem of motoring offences, which are not always seen by the general public as offences. According to the report of the 1962 Willinck Commission of Police, this problem has strained relations between members of the middle classes and the police.

The ideas of the police about some groups in society being more likely offenders than others influence the way in which law and order is enforced in this country. For example, the police make decisions about whether or not an offence has been committed, whether to caution an individual or to issue a summons, whether or not to prosecute and, in all these instances, the judgement and views of the individual police officer about who are the guilty will affect the way in which these matters are decided.

33.3   The judicial system

The judicial system is the system of courts that exists in Britain to deal with civil and criminal offences.

What do we hope to do by punishing people who break the law?

There are four main ways of thinking about this:

1   We want to get our own back: that is, 'an eye for an eye'. This explanation is called the *retributive* reason for punishment. Today this seems a rather barbaric way of going about things and the other reasons for punishment are usually seen as being more appropriate.

2   By carrying out the threat to punish persons who break the law we hope to deter other people and make the offender think twice before committing any offences in the future. This is called the *deterrent* explanation of punishment.

3   By removing the offender from society and putting him in prison, or by limiting his actions by some other means such as a fine, we are restricting his opportunities to commit more offences and also protecting the public at the same time. This is called the *preventive* explanation of punishment.

4   By punishment we make the offender repent what he has done in the past. If the punishment takes time, such as a period of imprisonment, the prisoner is given a chance to reform. By this we mean that through some form of treatment the offender can be helped to think in a new way about himself and society, so that he will not want to commit any more offences. This type of explanation is called the *reformative* theory of punishment.

Of these four main explanations, the last three are now usually considered to best justify why we punish people who break the law. However, there is no reason to suppose that the first explanation has disappeared from modern society: for example, many people think that, for retributive reasons, it would be a good idea to bring back the death penalty for convicted murderers. Also, some sociologists suggest that by reforming a person through treatment we are really doing no more than disguising the old retributive reasons for punishment.

Breaking the Law

Actions which break the law are called offences and are of two sorts: *indictable* and *non-indictable*.

Indictable offences are those which at one time were triable before a jury, but most may now, by consent of the accused, be tried by magistrates. Ninety per cent of indictable offences in Britain are tried by magistrates but some, for example, murder, must still be tried by jury.

A non-indictable offence is one which is heard in a court such as a magistrates' court, which does not make use of a jury. In deciding the guilt or innocence of the person involved and in passing sentence, such courts are carrying out what is called *summary jurisdiction*. Most criminal offences are decided in the courts of summary jurisdiction. Trial by jury, then, is the exception rather than the rule.

The Judge and the Jury

Criminal cases which are not settled in the courts of summary jurisdiction are brought to trial in other types of courts where there is a judge and a jury. The jury is responsible for deciding whether a person is innocent or guilty of the crime of which he has been accused; it is up to the judge, within certain guidelines, to decide on the sentence which should be given to the convicted offender. The bench is the term usually used for people such as magistrates and judges who have the responsibility for making the decision on behalf of society as to the sentence which should be passed on a convicted offender.

The Courts

In considering the court systems of England and Wales it is important to bear in mind the statement of the 1969 (Beeching) Report of the Royal Commission on Assizes and Quarter Sessions that in giving a brief account, 'there is virtually nothing which can be presented as a common feature (in the court system) without . . . reference to exceptions.' The two systems of courts which exist in England and Wales for dealing with civil and criminal cases are summarised in Tables 10.1 and 10.2.

Table 10.1   Courts which are concerned with civil offences

Many civil cases never reach the courts and are settled 'out of court' through the solicitors of the persons concerned. The Courts Act, 1971 centralised the resources of the higher courts of the two systems.

A *County courts*	These are courts which deal with smaller civil offences. There are nearly 400 of them in the counties. Cases of libel, slander and defended divorce cases are not dealt with at this level but go to the next higher courts.

B *High Courts*
   Queen's Bench
   Chancery
   Family Division
   High Court of Bankruptcy
	The Administration of Justice Act, 1970 altered the organisation of the High Court, so that there is now a separate new division of the High Court called the Family Division which deals with cases involving family and marriage. The Act also made provision for a Commercial Court to be set up within the Queen's Bench Division of the High Court.

Table 10.2   Courts which are primarily concerned with criminal offences

Part 1

A   *Magistrates' Courts**
These are of two types: those presided over by stipendiary magistrates, sitting alone or with lay magistrates; and those presided over only by lay magistrates. Stipendiary magistrates sit mainly in the Greater London area, but may also be found in larger cities. Lay magistrates predominate in more than 900 magistrates' courts in England and Wales. Magistrates' courts are able to send a case on to be tried at a higher court (see Part 2 in the Table).

B   *Juvenile Courts*
Juvenile courts can deal with any criminal offences (except homicide) committed by young persons aged from fourteen to sixteen. They also deal with all children and young persons of up to sixteen years who are brought to the courts as in need of care, protection and control.

Most crimes are 'petty offences' such as driving offences. Nearly one million motoring offences and over half-a-million other non-indictable offences are dealt with in magistrates' courts each year. About 98 per cent of criminal cases are dealt with in the courts so far described in the Table.

Some of the cases brought before the courts will be dismissed, for example for lack of evidence, and no sentence will be passed.

Part 2

C *Crown Court*
Under the 1971 Courts Act, the Crown Court replaces the old system which consisted of courts called quarter sessions and courts called assize courts. Crown courts have a number of full-time and some part-time judges who preside at the courts. More serious cases are passed from the magistrates' courts to these courts; the maximum sentences which can be passed in these courts are longer than those that can be passed in the magistrates' courts.

D *The Central Criminal Court*
This is now a crown court; it is the special criminal court of London which is held at 'The Old Bailey'.

* These courts also deal with some civil cases.

The Individual and the Judicial System

There are ways in which we hope to look after the rights of the individual and to make sure that in the eyes of the judicial system he remains innocent until proved guilty. For example, in both the civil court system and the criminal court system the individual has a chance to appeal against the verdict of the court. Some of the courts outlined in Table 10.2, such as crown courts, hear appeals, but these may also be taken to specialised higher courts such as the Court of Appeal and the House of Lords.

Although there are such safeguards built into the court system, the time and money involved in taking a case through the courts of appeal deters many people from appealing against the decision of a lower court. Also, the individual does not always know enough about the ways in which his rights are safeguarded to make use of them. For example, many people do not know or make use of their right to apply for legal aid although the availability of legal aid is publicised in all police stations and Citizens' Advice Bureaux. Since the Legal Aid and Advice Act of 1949, people who cannot afford to pay the costs of a solicitor and counsel to defend them in court may apply to the individual court for legal aid to help them with these costs. The Legal Advice and Assistance Act, 1972 (which came into effect from April 1973) makes it possible for a person whose means are below a certain amount to receive up to £25 worth of assistance from a solicitor. This depends of course on the individual knowing how to get in touch with the solicitor in his office. The decision to give legal aid rests with the individual court and the Home Office points out that over eighty per cent of applications for legal aid for summary trial in magistrates' courts are granted. However, this figure does not take into account regional differences in the granting of legal aid or the fact that this percentage represents only a few of the people who come before the courts. For example, in only about three per cent of all cases tried summarily by the magistrates is the accused represented by a lawyer under the legal aid scheme.

There are other problems facing the person who attends a court. Even when his case has been dismissed or he has been shown to be innocent, public opinion is such that, very often, the fact that he has been to court is enough to make him seem guilty in the eyes of the general public.

Sentencing

In determining the guilt of individuals and in passing sentence, some of the following information may be used by the bench:

1   police reports on the accused
2   reports of the Probation Service
3   reports of the prison authorities
4   medical reports
5   the case of the prosecution
6   the case of the defence.

These reports often reflect the ideas which each group holds about the background of an offender. We have seen already that the judgement of the police is sometimes biased against some groups in society and this affects the material which the police present to the bench. The bench itself is influenced in its decision by police reports.

The people who sit on the bench themselves, like anyone else, have views which influence their judgement. The bench is sometimes criticised for ignoring new schemes and ideas that develop about the treatment of offenders, for example, in prisons, and sentencing people to punishments which are no longer thought suitable for offenders. In Holland, part of the compulsory training of judges at all levels in the system is in penal reform.

In 1967, the Criminal Justice Act provided for a new type of sentence, the suspended sentence. Under this scheme a person does not go to prison: his sentence is suspended, but, if he commits another offence before his suspended sentence is up, he will have the length of this sentence taken into account in any subsequent sentence which is passed on him as a result of his second offence. The effects of this Act have now had some time in which to show. In 1972 the Criminal Justice Act made some alterations in the system of suspended sentences. The old provision that, in certain cases, courts *must* give suspended sentences, has been removed. Under the 1972 Act, the maximum period of suspension has been lowered from 'from one to three years' to 'from one to two years with a period of supervision'. Another important part of the Act affects the sentencing of offenders by stating that, in most cases, the court shall not pass a sentence of imprisonment on a person aged twenty-one years old and over who has not been sentenced to prison before, unless it states its reason for doing so and has ensured that the offender is legally represented or has refused to be represented. Courts are required to obtain and consider information about an offender before reaching any decision to pass a sentence of imprisonment. This Act reflects the hope of most people concerned with penal reform today that, as far as possible, persons convicted of having committed petty offences will be kept out of our over-crowded prisons.

33.4   The penal system

The penal system is made up of the many different types of institutions which exist to carry out sentences requiring an individual to be kept in detention or under supervision. Despite this *custodial function*, not all institutions are prisons. Young offenders cannot be sentenced to prison and there are other types of institution which are designed for the young offender.

The organisation of these institutions has been changing recently as a result of two Acts, the Children and Young Persons Act (1969) and the Criminal Justice Act (1972). Under the Children and Young Persons Act young persons under the age of fourteen cannot be prosecuted, except in the case of homicide. Children under fourteen years old can be taken into the care of local authorities, and children between the ages of fourteen and sixteen also can be placed in the care of local authorities, although this does not rule out the possibility of criminal prosecution of the young person in some circumstances. This Act also required local authorities to establish Community Homes for young people in care. These are to replace the old system of various institutions such as approved schools and remand homes.

The treatment of young offenders is also affected by the Criminal Justice Act, 1972 which installed a system of community service for offenders. Anyone aged seventeen or over found guilty of an offence which is normally punishable by imprisonment may receive a community service order in place of a sentence. This means working in the community for between forty and 240 hours, in some activity that is designed to help people in the community. At present, this is an experimental scheme.

Borstals continue to be part of the system of institutions for young people. These are for persons between fifteen and twenty-one years old who have committed a serious offence. In borstals young persons receive education and training in skills for various trades.

Adult Offenders

An adult who is sentenced to a period of imprisonment will be sent to one or more of the sixty or so prisons in England and Wales. These are of two main types, local prisons and central prisons, both categories including some open prisons where prisoners are not confined to cell blocks behind prison walls.

There are several different types of local prisons, but the largest group consists of general local prisons. These receive prisoners from court, most of whom will remain there for the length of their sentence. Central prisons are for prisoners serving longer sentences and some of these have special security blocks. At present almost all prisons are overcrowded, the general local prisons having taken the brunt of the recent increase in prison population. In addition to sentenced prisoners, general local prisons house prisoners who are on remand and awaiting trial or sentence and this adds to the overcrowding and confusion. At present, some ten per cent of the prison population consists of unsentenced persons on remand.

As a result of the Government White Paper *People in Prisons* (1969) money is being spent on a programme of new prison building and renovation of existing structures. The effect of the provisions of the 1972 Criminal Justice Act will probably also help to improve prison conditions by reducing the numbers of people sentenced to a term of imprisonment.

What is it like in prison?

'Prisons are becoming more like rest homes.' So said Mr Duncan Sandys, MP, on 26 September 1967. We have seen that prisons are overcrowded; how does this affect the lives of the prisoners? Are prisons 'more like rest homes?'

Many of the prisons in use today were built in the nineteenth century. Pentonville prison in London was a model prison of its day, and many of the older prisons are modelled on it. Cells in Pentonville are thirteen feet by ten feet by seven feet and, today, house three people. An ex-prisoner from Chelmsford prison describes what it is like to be in a cell:

'...when you first go in you're in this sort of dog kennel, because it's no bigger than that, with one bunk on top of the other, and the third bed on the floor. You get three chamber pots, three wash bowls, three tables, three chairs, three washstands, and you're normally there from four in the evening to seven o'clock the next morning. You've got to be very easy going, very passive—it's easy to get into fights.' (Frank Norman, *Lock 'Em Up and Count 'Em*, Charles Knight & Co, 1970)

Under conditions of old buildings, overcrowding and understaffing it is hard for prisons to carry out any programme of treatment by which the prisoner is helped to reform.

There are, however, two new prisons in England which have enough staff and resources to come closer to the idea of a treatment-centred prison. These are Grendon Underwood, a small psychiatric prison hospital in Buckinghamshire, and Coldingley, a prison in Surrey, which sets out to carry on industrial work under the same conditions as the outside world.

How effective is the penal system?

People who habitually break the criminal law are referred to as *recidivists*. The number of recidivists is usually taken as a guide to the success of the penal system in reducing the level of criminal activity in society. At the present time, these figures show no sign of reducing. However, the figures must be looked at with caution, for they cannot be taken too literally as an indication of the success or failure of the penal system. For example, of the people who are not reconvicted we can never know whether this is because the penal system has been successful in reforming them, or because they may have died, or may still be involved in breaking the law but because of their time spent in prison now know how not to get caught. It is not yet possible to assess how the 1972 Criminal Justice Act will affect the numbers of recidivists. It may be that by keeping some offenders out of prison, and therefore free from exposure to a criminal subculture, recidivism will be lowered.

The problem of recidivism is also affected by the way the public thinks about prisoners. There is a stigma attached to a person who has been to prison, which sometimes makes it hard for him to get a job and to set up a life for himself outside. Better after-care might help the prisoner in his move from prison life to the outside world, but funds are just as short in this area of the prison service as in others. Some hostels are provided for long-term prisoners reaching the end of their sentence, and prisoners' organisations, such as PROP, are in the process of setting up hostels for ex-prisoners.

In 1967, the Criminal Justice Act introduced the parole system so that a prisoner can now be released on licence after serving one-third of his sentence or one year, whichever is longer. Although the parole system takes the prisoner out of the prison environment it is not yet certain whether parole has any direct advantages for the reform of the prisoner. However, it does help to lower the number of people who are in prison and this, as we have seen, could have an effect on the success of prisons as reforming institutions.

In estimating the success of the penal system, the present state of affairs could be summarised in this reflective graffiti written on the wall in Pentonville and noticed by the criminologists Terence and Pauline Morris (in *Pentonville*, Routledge and Kegan Paul, 1963): 'As long as there are prisons men will exist to fill them. It is regrettable.'

Terms used in this chapter

social order	beliefs
social control	belief systems
norm	rites de passage
mores	sect
folkways	summary jurisdiction

Questions

1   Find two examples of social groups in your locality working in co-operation with one another. Can you find two that are not in agreement with one another?

2   List ten folkways of our society. Can you think of ten fashions that were popular a few years ago, but are no longer fashionable?

3   How much religious activity is there in your school or college? Find out how many people, for example, go to church or Sunday school and, if you can, find out whether there has been any decline in these activities in the local churches in the last twenty years. List five publications of any religious body in Britain today. Find out what the contents of these publications are mainly concerned with. Have the numbers of such publications increased or decreased in the course of this century?

4   Find out what are the beliefs of any religious sect in your area. Why do

you think these groups have managed to keep their members and, in some cases, increased their membership?

5   What is the work of the priest today? Find out what are the jobs that your local vicar has to do. What do people think about the occupation of priest today? Draw up a list of ten occupations, including priest, and ask your class-mates to list them in order of their interest in the job and what they think is the importance of the occupation in society. Summarise your results. You might try the same thing with older relatives and friends and contrast your findings with those for your peer group.

6   What is the work of the women members of the police force?

7   What is bail? Can a person always have bail?

8   Find out where your local magistrates' court meets and what type of cases are brought before it.

9   If we did not have prisons, what would you put in their place?

10   Find out where your nearest local prison is. How many prisoners does it usually have? How old is the prison and how many staff work there? What is the work of prison officers?

Questions from GCE 'O' Level Sociology Examination Papers

1   What do you understand by 'poverty'? To what extent has poverty been reduced in the UK since 1945? (AEB, November 1974)

2   What are the social functions of religion? (AEB, June 1973)

3

Church of England

Persons enrolled per 1000 population of appropriate age in England

Date	No. on roll in thousands	Enrolment rate per 1000 population
1930	3693	147
1940	3423	120
1950	2959	96
1960	2862	89
1964	2692	81

Do the figures in the above table tell us anything about

a   a decline in religious belief?

b   a decline in religious influence in England over the last forty years?
(AEB, June 1971)

4   Why are sociologists interested in religion? What kinds of studies of religion do sociologists make? (AEB, June 1972)

5   What influence does religion have on social behaviour? Is there any evidence to suggest that the influence of religion is declining? (AEB, June 1969)

6   What means exist in this country for the enforcement of law? (AEB, June 1968)

7   What factors within society help to maintain law and order? Discuss some of the proposals which have been made in recent years to promote law and order in this country. (AEB, June 1968)

8   What forces, other than law, influence social behaviour? (AEB, June 1968)

9   'Innocent until proved guilty.' This is generally regarded as one of the ways in which the individual is safeguarded by the English legal system. Describe some of the ways in which an individual's rights are protected. How satisfactory are the safeguards

a   from the point of view of the general public?

b   from the point of view of the police? (AEB, November 1970)

10   'We all know something about criminal law: the law forbidding theft, fraud, murder . . .' Why do most people obey these laws? What machinery exists to ensure that these laws are upheld? (AEB, June 1969)

11   Outline the major reasons which have been suggested for the continuing rise in juvenile delinquency in Britain. (Oxford Local Examinations, 1974)

12   What, if any, is the connection between social class position and criminal behaviour? (Oxford Local Examinations, 1975)

13   Church attendance figures are sometimes used as indicators of the strength of religious belief. Do you consider it acceptable to use the figures in this way? (AEB, November 1974)

14   'All crime is deviant but all deviance is not necessarily criminal.'

a   What is deviance?

b   Explain what is meant by the above statement giving examples where appropriate. (AEB, November 1974)

11 Social Problems
Unit 34 Deviancy and Crime

A social problem is a condition in society which is judged to be undesirable and in need of reform or elimination by influential groups in society. Conditions such as poverty, unemployment, crime, delinquency and drug-taking are referred to as social problems although not everyone necessarily agrees that all these conditions should be viewed in this way. For example, the person who smokes marijuana may not agree that his behaviour constitutes a social problem; still less would other drug-takers, such as cigarette smokers or beer drinkers see their behaviour in this light or expect to be categorised in this way.

In society, some voices are heard louder than others; groups who are powerful and influential make decisions about which conditions in society are social problems and should be remedied, and we usually become accustomed to looking at these conditions in this way.

34.1 Deviancy

Abnormality has always interested and fascinated people. Behaviour which is out-of-the-ordinary arouses the curiosity of people far more readily than normal, everyday behaviour. The mass media have recognised this fascination very profitably for years.

The person who ignores or breaks the rules of a social group or of society is called a *deviant* by others in society. If the social rules are not considered to be very important, as in the case of fashions, then the people who break the rules are merely eccentrics. If the rule is a more important norm or a law, then the people who persistently break these rules are likely to be penalised and their behaviour may be seen as a social problem by many in society.

There are several important points to be remembered when we think about deviancy and deviants.

1 There is nothing about an action that, in itself, makes it deviant. What is thought of as deviancy is a result of the ideas we have in society, about what

actions are right and appropriate. For example, a pupil who shouts and cheers may be considered a model of perfection at the school football match but the same behaviour will be considered inappropriate at prayers in school assembly. The action, however, is the same in both cases.

2   Behaviour which is looked on as being deviant in one society may not be seen in that way in another. For example, in our society, drinking alcohol is considered to be a pleasant way to pass the time with friends. In Moslem society, this is strictly forbidden. The deviant, in fact, would be the drinker rather than the tee-totaller.

3   Ideas about what is deviant change over the years as the norms and values of society change. For example, in the early twentieth century a woman who smoked in public was looked upon as being something of a 'tramp'. Smoking was not considered appropriate for a woman.

4   When we label some people in our society deviant we ought also to look at how they have come to be put in this position. In other words, whose rules have they broken? For example, are these rules drawn up and enforced mainly by powerful middle-class groups in society? If so, these may not be the norms with which every group in society agrees.

5   Having called some actions deviant and the people who commit them deviants, we react to these people as being different from ourselves. We set the deviant apart from us, and get fixed ideas into our head about how he thinks, what he does or how he dresses. The mass media help to keep these impressions

No daughter of mine is going to be seen with a shambles like you, mate . . . !

alive and we build up a kind of fixed picture of, for example, what an alcoholic is like. These fixed pictures are called *stereotypes* and they mould our ideas about deviants in society. We also have stereotypes with which to view every type of behaviour in society from that of policemen to that of publishers. The attitudes that people hold about the deviant do not go unnoticed by the deviant himself. When this labelling process has the effect of preventing the ex-prisoner, the homosexual, or the unmarried mother from getting a job and somewhere to live, these individuals begin to think of themselves as being fundamentally different from other people. The results can be far-reaching, forcing the person into the stereotyped role society has given him.

6   To try and remedy social problems, we often try to find explanations for why a person has wandered away from what we call normal behaviour. For example, we may say an alcoholic can't cope with the problems of his life and therefore he turns to drink. But the alcoholic himself may explain his behaviour in a very different way. We often forget that people do things for reasons which seem sensible to them, although other people would not always see the sense in what they do.

7   Not all forms of deviancy are equally condemned. For example, it is usually considered wrong for a person to steal money from a friend; however, where a person steals from his workplace or avoids paying income tax, this deviant behaviour may be tolerated and encouraged. The latter are examples of illegal deviant behaviour which many people in society today do not regard with disapproval.

'Tell me about those tax loopholes you keep dreaming about.'

34.2   Crime and juvenile delinquency

Crime is behaviour which breaks the criminal law. Delinquency is a term which describes law-breaking whether this is committed by an adult or a young person. Juvenile delinquency in Britain is considered as any violation of the law by someone less than seventeen years old.

We hear a lot about crime and delinquency nowadays and the press ensure that these problems are kept alive in the public's mind. It is said that crime is increasing at present. What are the facts? The information that we have about crime comes from the statistics published by the Home Office in their *Criminal Statistics for England and Wales*. These are a record of crimes known to the police and of convictions.

Non-Indictable Offences

Out of the total number of non-indictable offences, traffic offences are by far the largest single group. In 1970, there were a little under one million persons found guilty of traffic offences, which represented about sixty-six per cent of the total of all non-indictable offences.

Indictable Offences

Figure 11.1 shows the numbers of persons found guilty of indictable offences, in thousands, from 1945–70. The graphs show a steady increase in the numbers of persons found guilty of indictable offences, and in particular a sharp increase in the numbers of convictions for theft in recent years.

Criminal Statistics

Criminal statistics are notoriously misleading and it is a good idea to see why this is so before jumping to the conclusion that we have an enormous crime wave. Undoubtedly crime has increased, but the statistics need interpretation.

For example, the statistics only record crimes known to the police and the numbers of persons found guilty. The police may not be equally interested in all groups of the population as suspects: on the whole middle-class law-breakers are less likely to be detected and therefore do not appear so often in criminal statistics as they ought. Also changes in methods of detection can affect the numbers of cases known to and cleared up by the police.

Criminal statistics therefore present only a partial picture of the extent of crime in society and their fluctuations over a short period are not necessarily a good guide as to whether crime is increasing or decreasing.

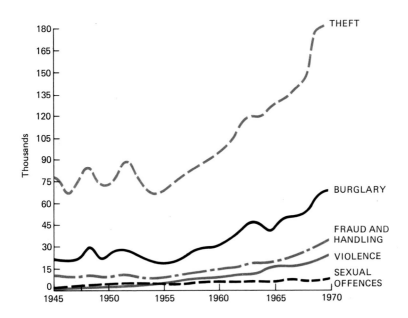

Figure 11.1   *Persons found guilty of indictable offences in England and Wales,*
1945–1970

In the same way, we have only a little information about some people who break the law, and it would be misleading to think that this holds good for all law-breakers.

What do we know about juvenile delinquency?

In 1970, about thirty-eight per cent of persons convicted of burglary and twenty-two per cent of persons convicted of theft were juveniles (persons under seventeen years old). The most common juvenile offence is theft. The overwhelming majority of offenders are working-class boys, although every year some girls (and women) are found guilty of offences such as shop-lifting. In the late 1960s the peak age for juvenile crime was in the fourteen-to-fifteen age group. It has been suggested that this may be because working-class adolescents experience a great deal of frustration in being at school rather than out in the world and feel this most keenly in the year before they are due to leave.

Explanations of Crime and Delinquency

The recorded crime rate for adolescents and young people is much higher than for other age groups in the population. If we are going to explain crime, then, we have to account for its being more prevalent among young working-class males than other groups in society. However, it must be remembered that in trying to explain crime by reference to the pattern of criminal behaviour recorded in our criminal statistics, we can only put forward an explanation which applies to people who are recorded in those statistics. These explanations will not hold good for the offender who is crafty enough to avoid getting caught or to those wrongfully convicted.

Over the years, many theories have been suggested to explain why people become criminals. These have ranged from the idea that criminals have certain characteristic features to the suggestion that family background accounts for criminal behaviour. It is likely that there is no one clear and simple explanation of criminal behaviour, particularly when we bear in mind the only reason these people are categorised together is due to the fact that they have broken the law. The criminologist D. M. Downes, in his book *The Delinquent Solution* (Routledge and Kegan Paul, 1966) suggests that, from his study of delinquents in Poplar and Stepney, working-class areas in the East End of London, there are social factors which account for the high rate of delinquency in working-class areas. The boy from a working-class home is rejected by the middle-class school system early on in his school career; he is no good at school work and therefore he is termed a failure. This is a humiliating experience and leaves him uninterested in school. Because of his lack of success at school he is bound to take an unskilled or semi-skilled job when he leaves school and this is equally boring and monotonous. (With changing technology, such as automation, these jobs may become scarcer.) Also he has failed in the eyes of society to get a good job and he is, once again, a failure. Under these circumstances his leisure time becomes his opportunity to find satisfaction and success. But youth clubs and other youth organisations are run according to middle-class norms and values and do not hold any attraction for him. Downes says that working-class youths' 'aversion to the present Youth Service sends them on the town.' In this situation, the youths, out for excitement and something to give them a sense of satisfaction and success, are likely to end up committing delinquent acts. After marriage, at an early age, the working-class youth will 'settle down'. This is reflected in a lowering rate of convictions for groups from the early twenties. Downes is not optimistic about the future of working-class youths and adolescents: 'The streets of our urban slums are slowly filling with young men who have no prospect of finding manhood through work: who are coming of age in a society which neither wants them nor needs them.'

Some sociologists have suggested that traditional theories overlook one or two things. For example, in society we react in certain ways to someone who has been convicted of an offence. It is often difficult for the ex-convict, or the boy who has been in trouble, to get a job. By setting people apart in this way, we contribute to their problems and put them into situations where they are more likely to continue committing criminal offences. Also, the fact that crime is seen as largely confined to working-class youth may tell us that the laws in society are made and enforced by middle-class groups rather than anything specifically about the criminal.

Unit 35 Drug-taking

35.1   What are drugs?

If we wanted to stop the pain of toothache we might go to a chemist's shop and buy some aspirin. If we were suffering from a more severe pain it is likely that we would go to the doctor and he would give us a prescription to take to the dispensing department of the chemist's shop. Here the pharmacist would give us the drug which the doctor had prescribed for our condition. Drugs are substances usually used in medicine, for example to reduce the level of pain. However, some substances which are also called drugs, such as cannabis, are not usually used in medicine. When we think of drugs as a social problem we are not concerned with their use, under careful supervision, for healing the sick. The social problem is the compulsive use of drugs by people, not because they are ill but because they want to experience the effects which the drug can produce, such as a sense of happiness and well-being. There are basic terms which are used when looking at drug-taking and before going any further we should look at these.

Drug Addiction

Some drugs, after prolonged use, can have the effect of causing a person's body to become dependent on the drug. At this point the person has become addicted. For example, the prolonged use of heroin results in a person becoming physically addicted and developing a compulsive need to take the drug.

Drug Habituation

There are other drugs which do not cause physical addiction. Instead, a person may become dependent on the drug because he develops a state of mind where he wants to continue using the drug, because it gives some satisfaction and pleasure. This is called drug habituation. Cannabis is usually associated with this.

Drug Dependency

The terms addiction and habituation have often proved to be difficult to apply. This is because there are so many ways in which individual people are affected by various drugs that there is not always a hard and fast division between drug addiction and drug habituation. In 1965, a World Health Organisation Expert Committee on Addiction-Producing Drugs decided that it was better to use the term drug dependency as this would include all the variations in the effects of drug-taking. This term is generally used today, but drug addiction and drug habituation continue to crop up.

Table 11.1 shows the main types of drugs, with examples of each kind, their broadest effects and the type of dependence which may develop amongst people using the drug. The information in the table must not be taken as being a hard and fast rule that anybody taking a particular drug will end up addicted. Jock Young in *The Drugtakers* (MacGibbon and Kee, 1971) has pointed out that people come to take drugs and learn about them in all manner of circumstances. These personal backgrounds and the ideas that people in society have about drug-taking will make a lot of difference to the way a particular drug affects an individual.

35.2 Drug-taking in Britain

Drug-taking in Britain is no new thing: alcohol has been drunk in large quantities and enjoyed for many generations and it has been estimated that seventy-five per cent of men and fifty-eight per cent of women regularly smoke tobacco. In 1969, it was estimated that we spent about £1500 million a year on tobacco, that is about the same as the total amount spent annually on new cars, furniture, televisions and refrigerators, combined (N. Tomalin: 'Cigarettes; the Secrets of the Trade', *Sunday Times*,

8 June 1969). Also, it has been pointed out that there are about 90 000–100 000 deaths per year attributable to tobacco.

We hear a lot about the drug scene from newspapers, magazines and television and this usually concerns the use of drugs such as heroin and cannabis. It is often overlooked that in Britain there are large numbers of people who are dependent on other drugs such as barbiturates, and these are not the depraved young people that the press tells us about. For example, about seven per cent of all National Health Prescriptions are for barbiturates and many of the people who depend on them are women in the forty-five to sixty-four age group. Table 11.1 summarises some kinds of drug-taking; we will concentrate on the two drugs which receive so much attention, cannabis and heroin, while bearing in mind that this is not the entire picture of drug-taking in Britain today.

Cannabis

People using cannabis usually smoke it in a form of cigarette mixed with tobacco known as a joint. Smoking marijuana normally takes place when people are in groups: it is a habit which gives more satisfaction to the individual when he uses the drug in the company of other people. Sometimes the joint will be passed around between members of the group so that it can be shared by everyone. Jock Young considered the way of life of groups of young people, living in Notting Hill, London, who smoked marijuana regularly. ('The Role of the Police as Amplifiers of Deviancy, Negotiators of Reality and Translators of Fantasy' in *Images of Deviance* ed. Stanley Cohen, Penguin Books, 1971.) He noticed that smoking marijuana is not usually the sole purpose of the group meeting together. Pleasure from many other sources, such as listening to music, painting, talking, is heightened by the use of marijuana, and therefore the drug is part of the whole way of life of groups of people who are more interested in these things than in joining the rat race to compete for a good job.

According to the research carried out by the Government Advisory Committee on Drug Dependence, 1968 (The Wootton Committee Report) an estimated 30 000 to 300 000 people in Britain have used marijuana. However, this figure, which at the most represents only 0.52 per cent of the population, has been criticised as being far too conservative an estimate. The report said that as far as we know at present cannabis is not a drug which leads to addiction, but the Committee was concerned that smoking marijuana might lead the drug-user on to taking more harmful drugs, such as heroin. Jock Young thinks that this happens in some cases not because of the drug itself but because of the way people

Some important categories	Example	Nickname	Effects	Dependence
sedatives	barbiturates	'downers' 'sleepers' 'mandies'	Relaxes the individual; removes inhibitions	Can be 'state of mind' type, although sometimes also physical
stimulants	amphetamines	'spansules' 'bombers' 'B' 'dubes' 'dex'	Excites the individual; he gets very 'worked up' and full of nervous energy	Can be 'state of mind' type
analgesics (pain killers)	heroin	'H' 'smack'	A state of sleepy well-being immediately after a dose (a 'fix')	After a while severe physical type. Compulsive need to take the drug
drugs which heighten the awareness	cannabis (marijuana; hashish; hash)	'grass' 'pot' 'dope' 'weed'	Increases the individual's 'sensitivity' and 'awareness', for example, to music	It is thought dependence does not arise in taking the drug. The individual merely prefers to continue to use it

Table 11.1 A summary of drug-taking

react to deviants in our society. For instance, selling or being in possession of marijuana is illegal and this means the groups who smoke marijuana run the risk of arrest. This results in the marijuana smoker thinking of himself as different and in an atmosphere where people see themselves as deviants the use of stronger drugs may creep in. On the whole, though, the pleasure-seeking way of life of the cannabis user is so different from the obsessive world of the junkie that the cannabis user is not automatically attracted to trying something stronger.

Heroin

Heroin can be taken into the body in a number of ways, such as by tablet, or by injecting under the skin ('skin popping'), or into a main vein ('main lining'). The slang term for a person who becomes addicted to heroin is a junkie. In March 1970 there were just over 2000 known heroin addicts in Britain. A person using heroin does not become addicted immediately, but gradually he needs more doses to achieve the same effect and his body eventually becomes addicted to the drug. When this happens, the individual will be totally preoccupied with where his next dose ('fix') is coming from. As soon as the effects of one dose have worn off he must start thinking about the next one. If he cannot get another dose, very severe pains and complications set up in his body. Severe addiction can lead to death. This may not result directly from his addiction but be caused by the addict's neglect of himself, for instance through lack of hygiene while giving himself an injection.

Since 1968 the heroin addict has been able to get his supplies through government-organised treatment centres. Not all addicts obtain their supplies in this way and illegal supplies are still available. It is thought that the legal prescription of heroin to addicts through treatment centres has helped to prevent the development of widespread organised crime in this country. In the USA, by contrast, there is no parallel system and the heroin addict steals and robs to get money to buy heroin supplied through the channels of organised crime. Today, addicts are mainly young people who have become 'hooked' on the drug as a result of drug-abuse rather than, as was once the case, as a result of medical treatment with the drug. There are members of the medical profession who are addicts; however, not much is known about these people, perhaps because this matter can be hushed up or dealt with within the medical profession itself.

It is often suggested that one of the best reasons for making the selling and possession of cannabis illegal is that this prevents people taking cannabis and beginning a career of drug-taking, possibly ending up as

Young drug addicts discussing some of their problems at a special clinic

heroin addicts. However, although many heroin addicts have taken cannabis, not all cannabis smokers automatically go on to try heroin.

Explanation of Drug-taking in Britain and the Control of its Use

Drug-taking is often very broadly explained by reference to the strains and stresses of a modern industrialised society. However since not everyone turns to illegal drug-taking this is not a very good explanation. But there are other ways in which people legally relieve their frustrations, for example by taking alcohol and smoking tobacco. The people who drink in moderation or smoke tobacco are not looked on by society in the same way as the people who use illegal drugs. Some portions of the mass media paint a picture of the illegal drug-taker as a depraved or weak individual unable to stand up to the realities of life. Some sociologists think that this picture and the public's response to the drug-taker contribute to changing him into the person the public thinks he is. The control of drug-taking presents many problems. Cannabis is illegal at present although many people think that there is no reason why its use should not be legalised. In 1971 the Government passed the Misuse of Drugs Act. This Act has introduced penalties which are different for the illegal possession and for the illegal selling of drugs. Illegal possession

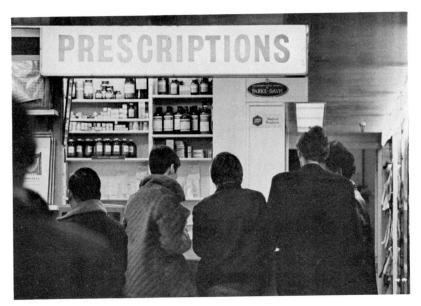

Young people at a drugs counter

now merits a lower penalty than the selling of drugs. It is too early to know if this will substantially affect the abuse of drugs in our society; it might have the effect of making the illegal selling of drugs become the concern of big well-run organisations that are successful in avoiding detection.

Even if the supplies of drugs are successfully controlled, it is difficult to see how the underlying tensions and anxieties which people experience and which make the use of drugs attractive, can be removed.

35.3 Alcoholism

Alcohol

It is no accident that, after looking at particular examples of drug-taking in society, we have turned to consider alcoholism because alcohol, too, is a drug. It is a sedative type of drug and therefore in the same category as barbiturates (see Table 11.1).

Alcohol relaxes people and relieves their tensions and anxieties. In 1954 and 1955 the World Health Organisation Expert Committee on Addiction-Producing Drugs concluded that alcohol was a drug which is somewhere between those drugs, such as heroin, which, in time, almost always lead to addiction, and drugs, such as cannabis, where there is a desire to

The fact that alcohol and tobacco are drugs is often overlooked.

carry on using the drug, but nothing more. In other words, alcohol can sometimes lead to physical addiction but it need not always have this effect. Jock Young in *The Drugtakers* says that the way to understand the varying effects which a drug produces is to look at the circumstances in which the drug is taken. For example, in drinking alcohol a person might *want* to reach the point where he had lost control over his drinking and this could be the difference between one person becoming an alcoholic while another does not.

'Have a drink?'

According to one inquiry, forty-seven per cent of British people over sixteen years old drink regularly at least once a week, and 11.5 per cent drink every day (Hulton Readership Survey). Drinking alcohol is a social habit which, in moderation, is encouraged in our society; it is also a very lucrative and time-honoured business.

In our society there are norms about drinking. For example, we have unwritten rules to the effect that a person should know when to stop drinking. It is acceptable to drink in moderation, but to drink regularly to the point of being completely drunk is not acceptable. Amongst men, drinking is often taken as a sign of being manly.

Who are alcoholics?

Because alcoholism is very often seen as being a sign of weakness and inability to stand up to life, people go to some lengths to try to conceal their dependence on alcohol. The social stigma attached to alcoholism affects the life of the individual in many ways, isolating him from other people in society. At work, if a man is discovered to be an alcoholic he may be sacked immediately. The information that we have about alcoholics is therefore very limited. According to the Office of Health Economics, there are in the region of 200 000 to 400 000 alcoholics in Britain (*Alcohol Abuse*, Office of Health Economics, 1970).

We know something about a proportion of these alcoholics, because some of them are treated through charitable organisations and others may receive treatment in National Health hospitals. For example, in 1971 there were about 8000 alcoholics in National Health hospitals.

It has been estimated that there is one woman dependent on alcohol to every three men who are so dependent (M. M. Glatt, 'Alcoholism and Drug Dependence under One Umbrella?' *World Dialogue on Drug Dependence* ed. E. D. Whitney, Beacon Press, 1970). The person who is dependent on alcohol is often middle-aged and male, but Alcoholics Anonymous have recently reported an increase in the number of young people requiring treatment and they have opened eight new centres specifically for these young alcoholics (reported in *The Economist*, 31 July 1971). There are some alcoholics amongst publicans; this may be because they have more opportunity to drink to excess.

Alcoholism as a Social Problem

One of the reasons why alcoholism is considered to be a social problem is that it costs the country money. For example, the Medical Council on Alcoholism estimates that alcoholism costs industry as much as £250 million a year as a result of employees who are dependent on alcohol absenting themselves from work. There are other reasons which cause alcoholism to be considered as a social, rather than an individual, problem: for example, prisons would be less overcrowded if it were possible to eliminate the problem of the drunkard who is arrested and ends up in gaol because he is unable to pay a fine. Drunken driving threatens the life not only of the person who has been drinking but also the lives of other people on the road at the same time, so this too is a cause of concern to society. People are also concerned about alcoholism as a social problem because it affects the lives and happiness of individuals and their families, often because of the social stigma which is attached to alcoholism in our society.

Despite the fact that alcoholism is a serious problem, it does not receive as much attention, for example from the media, as other forms of drug-abuse. The fact that drinking is a time-honoured social custom tends to overshadow the social problem of alcoholism.

Explanations

It is misleading to try and look for one way of explaining alcohol dependency. The range of backgrounds of people who are known to be alcohol dependents and the number of different circumstances in which they come to be dependent make it impossible even to talk of alcoholism as a single problem. It would be better, in fact, to talk of alcoholisms.

Some sociologists suggest that a person who does not know the norms which surround restrained drinking in the company of other people is more likely to become a compulsive drinker than someone who knows the rules of drinking socially.

However, we have at present no very satisfactory ideas explaining alcoholism. The only thing we do know about it is the way in which people tend to react to someone who has passed beyond the level of drinking which we look on as being acceptable. The stigma attached to someone in this condition is likely to have the effect of pushing the excessive drinker still further into the state of being dependent on alcohol.

How can we prevent alcoholism?

Not knowing very much about the real sources of the problem we can only attempt to deal with the symptoms; that is, try to get a person off his dependence on alcohol. The work of organisations such as Alcoholics Anonymous helps in this way, and, as a result of the two Criminal Justice Acts (1967 and 1972), the Government is taking steps to deal with the problem of the habitual drunken offender and to remove him from the prison to specially-staffed treatment centres. Also, the Government recently allocated £2 million for the general development of treatment centres for alcoholics.

Of course, one of the most important ways in which the problem can be tackled is by trying to change people's ideas about the alcoholic and to reduce the social stigma which surrounds alcoholism.

Unit 36 Some Other Social Problems

36.1 Illegitimacy

Illegitimacy is a term which is used to describe the conception and birth of children to couples who are not married to one another. This is often seen as deviant behaviour because sexual intercourse outside marriage appears to threaten the place of marriage, which in our society is seen as providing a firm relationship within which children can be cared for on a long-term basis. Were sexual intercourse entirely unregulated, the child-rearing functions of the family would be difficult to carry out.

In the period 1870–2 recorded illegitimate births were 5.6 per cent of all live births in England and Wales. It must be remembered, however, that a large number of illegitimate births were not recorded in the nineteenth century, because of the social stigma associated to illegitimacy. The proportion of illegitimate to all live births had declined to 3.9 per cent in the period 1900–02 and since that time there has been an increase in the proportion of illegitimate births, until by 1970 this proportion was 8.3 per cent.

Illegitimacy and the Permissive Society

The recent steep increase in illegitimate births is seen by many people as confirming their suspicions that an increasingly permissive society has brought about a detached and cynical attitude towards sex amongst young people and that promiscuity is widespread. However, illegitimacy is not primarily a teenage problem. Although births to unmarried mothers under twenty years old represent nearly a third of the total number of illegitimate births, the majority of such births occur to mothers aged between twenty-five and twenty-nine years old. Statistics on the numbers of illegitimate births do not necessarily give us a clear-cut guide as to whether people are observing the sexual mores of society. For instance, many children conceived outside marriage may have been legitimised because the parents later got married. However, there has been a decline in the number of births legitimised in this way. This may tell us something about the way people are thinking about illegitimacy today; perhaps we are more prepared to accept the fact that a couple or a mother on her own can bring up her child without being married. The majority of unmarried mothers today want to keep their baby. This has been made possible by the change which has taken place since the nineteenth century in the woman's role, making her able to be independent of men and to earn her own living. Nevertheless the problems facing unmarried mothers are still great, as is shown in the extract from a letter sent to the National Council for the Unmarried Mother and Her Child:

Dear Sir or Madam,
   . . . I'm an unmarried mother with a child of three who is getting on for four. I'm in my mother's house which is overcrowded. It's a council house and I'm to get out . . . I just don't want to be chucked out into the street as I have nowhere to stay so could you help me? What do other girls do when they are in a position like me?
(From *Case Histories*, a selection of letters, etc. from the National Council for the Unmarried Mother and Her Child, 225 Kentish Town Road, London NW5 2LX).

The unmarried father, has, of course, also broken one of the norms of society, but there is a dual standard which exists with regard to sexual relationships, and the same social stigma is not attached to an unmarried father as to an unmarried mother.

36.2   Abortion

Abortion is the ending of a woman's pregnancy by preventing the further development of the foetus. This is achieved by many different techniques and the practice itself is very old. It has been used in many parts of the world for centuries and at the present time Hungary, Poland, Czechoslovakia and Japan are among the countries where legal abortion is widely performed.

Abortion in Britain

Before the Abortion Act of 1967 legal abortion was not possible in this country. It has always been possible to obtain abortion illegally, however. The 1967 Act made it possible for people in particular circumstances to obtain an abortion legally. These are where continuing pregnancy

1   risks the life of the pregnant woman, or
   2   might cause her injury, physically or mentally, or
   3   might injure the physical or mental health of any of the children already in her family.

The National Health Service is under no obligation to carry out abortions and doctors and nurses are free to refuse to perform abortions if they think that such an act is morally wrong. It seems that many doctors working in National Health Service hospitals have exercised this right, judging by the fact that, of the 103 000 lawful recorded abortions performed in Britain, only 60 000 were performed by NHS hospitals. The remainder were performed through low-cost charitable groups or the more expensive, private clinics. The difficulties of obtaining an abortion are not always appreciated:

. . . (I am now) three-and-a-half months pregnant. My doctor did all he could for me and tried to get my pregnancy terminated at our local hospital but without success. I have been up to London to see if I could get an abortion but that was unsuccessful . . .
(Taken from a letter sent to the National Council for the Unmarried Mother and Her Child. The writer was separated from her husband and had two children.)

Many cases do not come within the terms of the Act and, even when they do, it is not certain that the local hospital will be able to help. Under these circumstances, illegal abortions continue to be performed. It has been estimated by François Lafitte in his article 'Abortion in Britain Today' (*New Society*, 14 December 1972) that there are probably 'several thousands' of cases of successful illegal abortions per year in Britain at present.

Abortion, whether legal or illegal, is often pointed to as evidence that young single people are increasingly promiscuous in their relationships with one another. In this sense, abortion is seen as a social problem because it appears to be the result of behaviour which breaks the sexual mores of society and takes parenthood irresponsibly. Newspaper reports which describe hundreds of young people flocking to clinics and hospitals to have abortions, help to keep this picture alive.

Who has an abortion and why?

It has been estimated by François Lafitte that the total number of recorded and unrecorded abortions in Britain each year is in the range of 115 000 or 120 000. This figure shows no appreciable change from the numbers of abortions that, it is estimated, were performed before the Abortion Act of 1967.

The women who have these abortions are not all single, promiscuous young women as the newspapers would have us believe. About 1.25 per cent of all fifteen-year-old girls become pregnant, of whom about two out of three have an abortion; amongst pregnant girls between sixteen and nineteen years old, some of whom are married, a lower proportion get abortions, and amongst women between twenty and forty years old, most of whom are married, about ten per cent of pregnancies are terminated by abortion. According to one study, far from being cynical and callous individuals as newspaper reports suggest, the young unmarried women who have abortions have them as a 'result of sexual inexperience, ignorance, an idealistic set of sexual morals, and a romantic vision of sex and human relationships'. (*Abortion and Contraception—A Study of Patients' Attitudes*, T. M. Williams and K. Hindell, PEP Report No. 536, 1972)

36.3 Suicide

Suicide is death resulting from a deliberate act of self-destruction. In 1972, there were 4238 recorded suicides in Britain. This figure represents about 0.6 per cent of all deaths. The number of recorded suicides has dropped since the early 1960s when the figures were well above 5000 suicides per year. However, as with any statistics, these figures should be viewed with caution.

Attempted Suicide

Sometimes a person does not succeed in taking his own life. When this happens it is called attempted suicide. Often there are circumstances which make the person's act appear a little different from a suicide attempt which has been successful. For example, a woman may turn on the gas at a time when she knows her husband normally returns from work. It would seem as though she had intended her husband to find her before the gas had its effect. Attempted suicide is often seen as being a way in which people draw attention to their conflicts and problems, without any real intention of committing suicide.

The Official Record of Suicides

Before the 1961 Suicide Act, suicide was considered a criminal offence and people who had survived a suicide attempt could be prosecuted. This is not the case today. Before a death can be categorised as a suicide it has to be considered by a coroner and an inquest held. It is up to the coroner to establish that a person *intended* to take his own life as this is the official difference between suicide and other categories of death, such as accidental death.

Explanations of Suicide

There are many problems which surround attempts to explain the conditions which give rise to suicide in society. For example, we have only a very limited amount of information to go on: a person only becomes part of our information when he has committed suicide and, of course, at that point it is too late to ask him any questions about the circumstances that led him to take his own life.

The statistics which we have give us information about the suicide rate in society, but as with all statistics, they must be used with caution. There may be circumstances where a death which is a suicide goes unrecorded. For instance, suicide may be covered up by a family for insurance purposes: or, because many Christians see committing suicide as a sin, a family may go to some lengths to ensure that the suicide of a member is officially recorded in some other way, for example, as accidental death. Also, in areas where deaths often happen through accidents, suicides may be mistakenly recorded as accidental death. For example, a person may drown in a dangerous river or canal, or fall from a mountain side and this may be usual enough locally for a suicide to go undetected.

Sociologists do not try to explain suicide in terms of the individual's personality. Instead they look for an explanation in the ways in which we live our lives in society. A sociologist might ask: 'Are there particular pressures that some people have to face in society today that lead them to take their own life?'

Using statistics on suicide, sociologists have put forward theories which show how suicide can be associated with social factors. One of the most significant early studies to approach suicide in this way is that of Emile Durkheim, a French sociologist. He claimed to have shown that the suicide rates were associated with the quality and degree of integration of the individual in social groups. For example, in some cases, the individual's sense of personal responsibility for his actions is so intense that, where there is a corresponding lack of support from the social group, the individual may feel the burden of responsibility so keenly that suicide results. Durkheim called suicide associated with such social circumstances, *egoistic suicide*. By contrast, *altruistic suicide* results from a high level of individual integration and commitment to the social group so that, under some circumstances, the individual will take his own life because of his close identification with the needs and demands of the group. Durkheim distinguished a third set of conditions associated with suicide, in this case termed *anomic suicide*. Anomic suicide occurs when the individual experiences a period of social or personal disorganisation. This may occur, for example, when a period of economic crisis disturbs the pattern of the individual's life; the pressures and uncertainties accompanying such circumstances may lead the individual to commit suicide.

Some of the factors which, it has been suggested, are associated with suicide are:

1   being male
2   increasing age
3   having a history of a broken home in childhood
4   being widowed, single or divorced
5   being childless
6   living in big towns
7   having a high standard of living
8   having a history of mental disorder or physical illness.
9   economic crisis
10 high density of population.

Heavy drinking of alcohol is also frequently associated with suicide, although it would be difficult to determine whether this is in any way a cause of suicide, since both actions may derive from a third factor such as loss of job.

Although one or more of these factors may be likely to appear in the background of a person who has committed suicide, it is important to remember that, despite this, we cannot say with certainty that a broken home or any other specific factor was the *cause* of a person committing suicide.

Research results of this sort very often seem to do no more than confirm the impression of the man in the street that a person who is isolated and therefore unhappy is more likely to commit suicide than a person who is totally wrapped up in a full and happy life. The voice of the expert gives a little more authority to these ideas and they are readily taken up and used by the mass media and so become part of everyday ideas about suicide.

Mr S was a thirty-year-old married man with two children; he gambled, ran into financial trouble, and couldn't sleep. Instead of finding out why, his doctor gave him a prescription for sleeping tablets.

In this newspaper account, the doctor who is describing what happened in this case is quite certain that a background of gambling leading to financial trouble will, given the opportunity of a bottle of pills, make the man commit suicide.

Some sociologists have suggested that, in trying to explain suicide, we should look into some of the ideas that we have about suicide in our society, rather than concentrate on using official statistics. After all, suicide cannot be precisely recognised in the same way as, for example, a birth; the coroner has to decide if a suicide has occurred. The way in which he reaches his decision will tell us something about the ideas that are commonly held in society about the circumstances under which suicide occurs. For example, he will be more likely to suspect a suicide has taken place where a person has died from gas poisoning in front of a gas oven than if she had died in a road accident, because we do not usually think of suicide taking place in the latter way. Coroners often look for evidence of suicide in the circumstances of a death. If, for instance, a person went to a great deal of trouble to make sure that his attempt would succeed, then the coroner is likely to decide that the death was a suicide. In other words, the coroner adds to the ideas in society about what are the circumstances which make a death into a suicide.

The ideas we have about what pressures drive a person to suicide will also cause some people to be more likely to commit suicide than others. For example, a young man who is a student knows that many students commit suicide. If he finds that there are pressures which are making life unbearable he may see suicide as an appropriate way to solve his personal

	1964	1965	1966	1967	1968	1969	1970
Population in millions	47.40	47.76	48.08	48.39	48.67	48.83	48.94
No. of suicides	5566	5161	4994	4711	4584	4370	3939
Suicide rate per 100 000	11.70	10.80	10·40	9.70	9.40	8.90	8.00
Samaritan branches	56	68	75	86	92	95	115
No. of new clients	12 355	16 422	20 875	31 780	42 241	51 412	68 531
No. of volunteers	nr	6537	7116	7688	11 204	8910	12 832

nr   not recorded
Table 11.2   The Samaritans and suicides in England and Wales
(Source: *New Society*, 15 March 1973, table compiled by Richard Fox)

problems. It is not possible to ascertain the effect that the Samaritan movement has had upon the recorded rate, but Table 11.2 indicates that the rate fell from nearly twelve per 100 000 people in 1964 to only eight in 1970.

Unit 37 Minority Groups and Social Integration

37.1 Minority groups

A minority group is any group in society which, by virtue of some particular characteristics, such as having a different culture or religion, or being racially separate, is sometimes placed at a disadvantage in society. This is often because the group is treated as different by other people in society and, because of this, denied the opportunities which are open to others. Minority groups in Britain include Jews, Irish, Indians, Pakistanis, West Indians and Chinese. Many minority groups came to Britain in search of work, a home or freedom from persecution. In the nineteenth and twentieth centuries, many Jews, fleeing from persecution in Europe, were amongst the immigrant groups who came to live in this country. In the 1940s Britain was host to about 30 000 Poles who came to this country as a result of events in their own country during World War II and many of these later settled and remained in Britain. In 1956, Britain absorbed 30 000 Hungarians in the wake of the Russian invasion of Hungary, about the same number as the British Asians who came to live in Britain as a result of the Africanisation policy in Uganda in 1972. Many of the groups and individuals who have come to this country in the past from other countries, for all manner of reasons, now pass unnoticed in the population of Britain. Other groups preserve their special way of life because this is important to them and maintains a long tradition. This is true, for instance, of Orthodox Jews, for whom their distinctive life-style serves to link members of this ethnic group across the world.

Immigrants

As we have seen, in the past many people have come from different parts of the world to live in Britain. Today, also, many people come from other parts of the world, such as Europe and countries in the Commonwealth

to make Britain their home. The terms New Commonwealth, and Old
Commonwealth are sometimes used about Commonwealth countries.
New Commonwealth countries are those which were formerly part of the
British Empire but have achieved independence and joined the Common-
wealth since 1945; Old Commonwealth countries are countries such as
Australia, Canada and New Zealand, which have been self-governing
Dominions for many years. Among the people from both the Old and the
New Commonwealth countries who have come to Britain in recent years
are groups from Asia and the West Indies. We hear a lot about coloured
Commonwealth immigrants in our society but we do not often realise
how many people there are from other places also living in Britain.

Asian Immigrants

Asian immigrants first began coming to this country in significant
numbers in the 1950s. Some Commonwealth Asian immigrants come
from India and Pakistan, but others come from Kenya and Uganda. For
example, in 1967–8 Kenya began a policy of Africanisation and many
Asians living in Kenya, holding British passports (and therefore freely
entitled to enter this country) left Kenya and came to live in Britain. In
the middle of this crisis, the Government passed the Commonwealth
Immigrants Act (1968) which limited the numbers who could enter to
those possessing employment vouchers and their dependents. After that
date 1500 vouchers per year were issued. Events in Uganda in 1972 forced
several thousand British and other Asians to make Britain their home.
The Ugandan and Kenyan Asians came to this country under emergency
circumstances and had to leave behind skilled and professional jobs and
high standards of living.

West Indian Immigrants

West Indians first began to come to this country in the 1950s and, together
with Asian immigrants, have helped to meet Britain's demand for labour.
Both groups stood to improve their standard of living. For example in
1969 the average income per head for people in Jamaica was £223, and
for people living in India it was £37 in 1970, whereas the figure was £833
for England in 1970. The majority of West Indian immigrants are from
Jamaica. It is often not realised how different the West Indian islands are
from one another and what great distances separate the islands; for
example, Jamaica is about the same distance away from Trinidad and
Tobago as London is from Gibraltar.

Immigration and Legislation

Immigration has become a controversial issue in recent years and there is a wealth of information, some reliable and some not so reliable, which has been put out by various official bodies and individuals on the subject.

Immigrants from the new Commonwealth have added to our skilled and professional labour force. This Asian lady is teaching a withdrawal group.

The controversy hinges around the number of immigrants who come to this country from the New Commonwealth. For instance, many people see Asian and West Indian immigrants taking up jobs that, they say, white people need. Arguments of this sort overlook the fact that the areas with the highest unemployment rate, such as Scotland and Wales, are areas where there are very few coloured Commonwealth immigrants. Also, immigrants from the New Commonwealth countries have increasingly been adding to our skilled and professional labour force. In the case of medicine, for instance, many Asians are included amongst the overseas doctors who make up twenty-five per cent of the total employed by the National Health Service. On the whole though, immigrants from the New Commonwealth are taking jobs, such as driving buses and working in factories, that many other people would prefer not to do.

It has been suggested that if too many people were admitted from New Commonwealth countries our social services and educational facilities would come under strain, particularly as immigrants from these countries have a higher birth rate than native Britons. Asians and West Indians come to this country from areas where it is customary to have larger families and they are usually young and therefore produce children; as they become older, three generations will be represented and therefore there will be fewer children born per thousand of the New Commonwealth immigrants, in addition to which they may well have adopted the idea of having smaller families. In Britain we have a population of about 56 million people and this includes (January 1969) about 1.2 million immigrants from the New Commonwealth countries. According to the Institute of Race Relations (1969), on the basis of the numbers of babies born to coloured Commonwealth immigrant parents at the present time, there will be about 2.4 million people in 1986.

The Commonwealth Immigrants Act of 1962 set up a system of work vouchers for immigrants coming to this country, which had the effect of lowering the numbers of people, particularly unskilled people, coming into Britain. Since that time there has been a Government White Paper (1965) and a Commonwealth Immigrants Act (1968), which also imposed various standards for controlling and limiting the number of immigrants per year entering the country from the New Commonwealth. The result of this legislation has been that almost the only people who now enter Britain from these countries (apart from emergency groups such as the Ugandan Asians) are the wives and families of immigrants already in Britain. Figure 11.2 shows the changes which have taken place in the case of immigrants from Pakistan. The latest legislation is the Immigration Act, 1971 the provisions of which now replace almost all the provisions

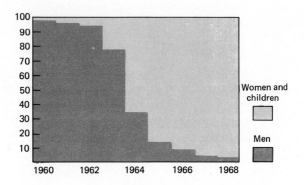

Figure 11.2   *Pakistani immigration figures—percentage of working men to women and children*
(*Source : Compiled from Home Office statistics for immigration by Clifford Hill in his book* Immigration and Integration, *Pergamon Press, 1970)*

of earlier legislation. The Act introduced the terms *patrial* and *non-patrial* which, in future, will be used to find out a person's right of entry into this country. Broadly, patrials have recent ancestors who were closely associated by birth with Britain.

Non-patrials do not have this background and therefore will be admitted to this country only if they are allowed a work permit. This will be for a particular job and normally given at first for a fixed period of twelve months. Some dependents will also be admitted. Under this Act non-patrials may apply for citizenship under certain conditions, and provision is made for deportation in some circumstances. Non-patrials already in Britain are not included under the terms of the Act. The main effects of this Act will be to make it even more difficult for members of the New Commonwealth to enter this country, because they are mostly non-patrials, and to cause some anxiety to existing residents who feel that, as non-patrials, their position is insecure.

37.2   Race relations

Race

We hear a lot at present about *race relations* in society. What is it all about? First, we must look at the term *race*. Race is a classification for grouping together people in society who have the same characteristic physical features, such as shape of eyes, head, skin colour or eye colour.

If people have a certain set of characteristics, then we say they belong to a certain race. Any other ideas that we might have about the characteristics of racial groups, for example that all black people have a good sense of rhythm, derive from the stereotypes of racial groups that we build up in society. Tensions between racial groups spring up where these stereotypes affect human relationships. *Race* and *nationality* are not to be confused: race depends on physical characteristics, nationality on the person being a citizen of a certain nation, such as France or the USA. The nation itself exists because of political boundaries which separate one area of land, or nation from another.

Prejudice

Prejudice is a favourable or unfavourable attitude directed towards members of a social group to which one generally does not belong. These attitudes rest on oversimplified and overgeneralised beliefs about the social characteristics of members of certain groups. For example, prejudice may be directed towards an individual because he is a member of a particular religious, ethnic or racial group. This is because ideas about the individual derive from preconceived beliefs about the social characteristics of all members of this group. In other words, prejudiced attitudes depend on the use of social stereotypes. We can see then that prejudice, whether favourable or unfavourable has no reliable basis and is a misleading way in which to view individuals and groups in society.

Racial Prejudice

Racial prejudice is where these unreflective attitudes are adopted towards members of a group who possess particular racial characteristics. Where there is intolerance between members of different racial groups, the basis of this conflict often lies with the prejudices which each group holds about the other.

The question of the extent of racial prejudice in Britain was the subject of a sample survey carried out in 1966–7 in five London boroughs having a high proportion of New Commonwealth residents. Some broad results of the survey are summarised in Figure 11.3.

From the chart we can see that a majority of people were recorded as tolerant or tolerant-inclined in their attitudes towards members of other racial groups. The results of this and other research by the Institute of Race Relations led the social scientists involved to be optimistic about the future of race relations in Britain, although others have been critical of these conclusions.

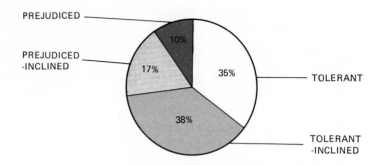

Figure 11.3   *Incidence of prejudice among respondents in the survey*
(Source: Colour and Citizenship, A Report on British Race Relations, *E. J. B.*
Rose et al for the Institute of Race Relations, Oxford University Press, 1969)

Discrimination

Discrimination is where one group of individuals is treated differently
from others, the root of this action lying with the prejudiced attitudes of
one group towards another. Discrimination may be to the advantage of
the group treated differently, of course, but usually we think of the term
being applied to a group in society which is treated less favourably than
the rest of the population because of mode of life, sex, or racial characteristics.

Racial Discrimination

If there is widespread injustice towards people in society because of their
race, and in particular because of the colour of their skin, we should all be
concerned because there are no reasonable grounds for behaving in this
way: a man has no control over his skin colour any more than he has
control over how tall he is. Several surveys have set out to find out the
nature and extent of racial discrimination in Britain and almost all of
them point to housing as being one of the ways in which coloured
Commonwealth immigrants experience discrimination. For example, a
PEP Report in 1967 found that where owners of private accommodation
were, separately, approached about renting, by a white Hungarian, a
white Englishman and a West Indian, the West Indian was rarely offered
the accommodation on the same terms as the others. Afterwards, the
landlords gave their reasons in these terms: 'Nobody wants this to become
a little Jamaica, do they?' and 'My wife doesn't go for them much and

anyway it would look bad with the neighbours' (PEP *Racial Discrimination in Britain, 1967*). There have also been reports of discrimination towards coloured Commonwealth immigrants wishing to rent council houses. The situation has altered with legislation, but as Dilip Hiro points out in his book *Black British, White British* (Eyre and Spotiswoode, 1971): 'Awareness, and acceptance, of widespread discrimination makes (the immigrants) generally reluctant to apply for a council house.' Problems such as these, combined with the general housing shortage, confine the Commonwealth immigrant to living in certain areas in the towns and cities where he can get accommodation. This is usually old, decaying property and, mistakenly, this is often taken to show that Asian and West Indian families do not know how to look after a home. The PEP report and subsequent reports have also described the problems facing the West Indian or Asian in getting a job or in such things as car insurance.

Difference in Culture

People are inclined to forget that most New Commonwealth immigrants come from countries with a very different way of life, often having a different language and religion from ourselves and from other immigrant groups. The majority of Pakistanis are Muslim whereas most Indian immigrants are either Hindu or are members of the Sikh religion, and often West Indian immigrants were regular Christian churchgoers before coming to Britain.

Problems may arise from the fact that families in New Commonwealth countries are often larger than in our own society and their members are used to having relatives living close at hand. This customary dependence on the extended family can raise problems for the married woman living over here, as is shown in this extract, where John Rex and Robert Moore in *Race, Community and Conflict* (Oxford University Press, 1967) describe the life of 'Mrs K' (from Pakistan):

(Mr K) kept his wife in strict Purdah and she has not been out of the house for two-and-a-half years. Having no female kin to help her with the housework and the children she found her pregnancy very difficult and she always misses her own family. She has no visitors, no women to chat with. Mrs K. would prefer to be back in Pakistan.

Legislation

Since 1965, there have been attempts to outlaw discrimination against anyone, whatever his skin colour, nationality or cultural background.

These have gradually been extended by various legislation (The Race Relations Act of 1965 and the Extension of the 1968 Race Relations Act in 1972) to cover almost every aspect of life. For example, it is now illegal for an employer to refuse to employ a person on the ground of 'colour, race or ethnic or national origins'.

There are many differences of opinion as to how far it is possible to legislate for harmonious race relations; many think that these will develop only when all English people come to accept New Commonwealth immigrants on the same terms as everyone else in society.

Terms used in this chapter

social problem	drug dependency
delinquency	minority groups
juvenile delinquency	race
deviance	race relations
stereotype	racial discrimination

Questions

1   List ten conditions in society which, in your opinion, are social problems. What are your reasons for calling these conditions social problems?

2   Give examples of the following:

a   behaviour which is deviant and illegal

b   behaviour which is deviant but not in itself illegal

c   behaviour which is considered deviant by some sections of society but not by others

d   behaviour which was once considered deviant but is not seen this way today.

3   What stereotyped ideas do we have about criminals and juvenile delinquents? Look through recent editions of some of our daily newspapers and see if you can pick out any stereotypes used by the press in reporting criminal cases.

4   Alcohol and tobacco are used by many people in society.

a   Make up a brief questionnaire that will help you find out:

i   How many people in the class (include students and their families) smoke tobacco in some form, for example as cigarettes?

ii   How much, on average, each person spends per week on tobacco.

b   From the results of your survey find out the total average weekly expenditure on tobacco for the whole class, including their families.

c   Do the same thing for alcohol.

d   What is the grand total for alcohol and tobacco expenditure?

5 Who are Alcoholics Anonymous?
a What are the aims of the organisation?
b Who can belong?
c How is it organised?
6 What is the work of the National Council for the Unmarried Mother and Her Child?

Fatherless families have a far greater chance of becoming homeless than complete families . . . In the year ending 31 March 1968, 3157 illegitimate children were received into care because their mothers were unable to provide a home for them.
(Director, National Council for the Unmarried Mother and Her Child, at Health Congress, Royal Society of Health, 1969.)
What problems are likely to confront the unmarried mother and her child?

7 a What is the Family Planning Association?
b Is it part of the National Health Service?
c Where can you get reliable contraceptive advice?
d Is this a free service or do you have to pay?
8 Who are the Samaritans?
a What do they do?
b Is this a voluntary or state-run organisation?
c Have you a local branch of the Samaritans?
d How is it organised?
9 Find out about Hinduism, or Islam or the Sikh religion. In what ways does the religion you have found out about affect the daily lives of the people who believe in it? What problems are the people who observe the rules of these religions likely to come across when they live in Britain?
10 The Race Relations Board was set up under the Race Relations Act of 1965. What other organisations are concerned with promoting good race relations in Britain today?

Questions from GCE 'O' Level Sociology Examination Papers

1 What do you understand by deviance? Give some examples of deviant behaviour, including at least one example of behaviour which is deviant and illegal, and at least one example of behaviour which is deviant but not in itself illegal. (AEB, November 1971)
2 Why is the crime rate for adolescents much higher than for any other age group? (Oxford Local Examinations, 1970)
3 Why is juvenile delinquency more common amongst the working class than amongst the middle class? (Oxford Local Examinations, 1972)
4 Account for the difference between male and female rates of juvenile delinquency. (Oxford Local Examinations, 1973)

5   Is there a race problem in Britain? (Oxford Local Examinations, 1972)
6   What are the most important problems facing immigrant groups in Britain? (Oxford Local Examinations, 1973)
7   What are the causes and consequences of colour prejudice? Reference should be made to the United Kingdom and at least one other country. (AEB, June 1969)
8   Give an account of some of the problems arising from immigration into this country during the last twenty years. (AEB, June 1968)
9   Outline the major changes which have taken place in the pattern of migration into and out of Britain since 1945. (Oxford Local Examinations, 1974)
10   What sociological evidence is there that racial prejudice and racial discrimination exist in Britain? (Oxford Local Examinations, 1975)

12 The Individual and Society
Unit 38 What Makes the Individual?

38.1 Intelligence and personality

We have seen how society is shaped on the small scale and the large scale: the way in which our lives may be influenced by economic forces, by government decisions, or by changes in population; how the individual is moulded by the family, peer group, school and work. A human being undergoes a multitude of experiences which cause attitudes and opinions to be formed. Class position in society has a strong influence in determining behaviour and performance. Physical characteristics and environmental surroundings together play their part in making the individual what he or she is as a person. But how far is our personality predetermined by inherited characteristics, and how far do our experiences in life influence character and achievement?

There is some argument among geneticists and psychologists about the degree to which *inherited characteristics* cause an individual's behaviour, and how far *environmental experience* makes us behave in a certain way. In Victorian times it was believed almost all behaviour patterns were inherited; humans could be classified and stereotyped. An imperial myth was that Britons possessed innate (or inborn) qualities of leadership and determination, and that the coloured peoples of the British Empire needed British leadership and rule as they were incapable of governing themselves. Among the lower strata of society criminal behaviour was thought to be inherent and criminal types could be recognised by their facial features. One Victorian criminologist thought that he could obtain a picture of the typical criminal by superimposing all the photographs from the police 'Rogues' Gallery' upon one another: the end result was a rather benign elderly gentleman. If intelligence is used as a guide (and there is much controversy as to what intelligence actually is) in determining how much of our personality is inherited, and how much is gained from environmental factors, the proportion of sixty per cent inheritance to forty per cent experience is most widely accepted by geneticists and psychologists. One method of calculating this proportion is to look at the case histories of identical twins, usually orphaned, who have been brought up in different family circumstances from an early age. The comparative results of IQ tests and the kinds of occupation that they enter provide the measure that social scientists will require; a twin that has been brought up in a middle-class situation is more likely to do better in a verbal intelligence test than a brother or sister brought up in a working-class environment.

Just as we cannot choose our genetic make-up, we have no choice of the family circumstances that we are born into. The different rates of social mobility and *attainment* indicate how important the family is as a determining factor of the individual's eventual position in society. Not only is class background important, but even family size has an effect: verbal intelligence tests have shown that children from large families perform less well than those from smaller families (John Nisbet, 'Family Environment and Intelligence', *Eugenics Review XLV* 1953). Of course, working-class families tend to be larger than middle-class families and this is likely to be a decisive factor in determining a lower verbal ability among working-class children. The youngest son may marry the princess in the fairy stories, but sociological evidence shows that the eldest child is more likely than the youngest to perform well in school and likely to obtain better employment after school. The contact between parent and child is of considerable importance and it may be argued that in large families the parents' attention has to be divided between too many children, or that most attention is given to the first-born child. Studies of very bright children in Britain and the USA have destroyed the myth of the 'weedy intellectual'; the exceptionally gifted in intelligence are usually found to be healthier, taller and stronger than average, while the least intelligent are often weaker and smaller than average. Once again, class differences may account for middle-class physical superiority (due to better feeding and environmental factors) being linked to higher intelligence performance.

38.2   Class, education and the individual

Half of what we learn for life is learnt before the age of five years. Children who were fortunate enough to go to nursery school usually do better in the primary and secondary school than those who did not receive any *pre-schooling*. Pre-schooling and the kind of education that a child experiences have a significant impact upon behaviour and attainment. Class underlies almost everything that we experience, and different class situations during our earliest and school years affect the social structure of Britain. The average working-class child comes from a larger family than the average middle-class child; more middle-class than working-class children attend nursery and pre-school playgroups. We have seen in Chapter 4 how linguistic ability is related to class, and how this provides middle-class children with an advantage over working-class children. The middle-class advantage is continued at school until the statutory leaving age is reached, when more middle-class pupils stay on past the age of sixteen years. Middle class parents tend to take more interest in their children's education: for example, they are likely to provide them with better facilities for homework; and maybe they are more prepared and able to help with the homework. Children from the Registrar General's Class 5 have been found six times more likely to be poor readers at the age of seven than children from Social Class 1 backgrounds. A child from Social Class 5 is fifteen times more likely to be a non-reader at the age of seven years than a child from Social Class 1, according to a study made of 17,000 babies born in March 1958 who have had their development traced regularly every four years (Butler, Davie and Goldstein, *From Birth to Seven*, Longman, 1972). The class gap is hard to close after children have entered school despite the structural changes in education designed to compensate for the disadvantages, such as more money for schools in deprived areas, and possibly the introduction of comprehensive education. Social mobility in a society where there was complete equality of opportunity would rest largely upon educational attainment. Theoretically our educational system does provide an equality of opportunity, but the middle-class head-start is maintained throughout the school years.

Ralph Turner, an American sociologist, was the first to define two kinds of social mobility, which he termed *contest* and *sponsored mobility*. Contest mobility is the form of mobility where the top positions in society are dependent principally upon ability and effort by the individual, and where such groups as the Establishment have little control over mobility. Sponsored mobility is the form of mobility where recruits to the top or élite positions in society are chosen, not so much on individual merit, but by selection from their own class by the upper strata. In Britain both types of mobility exist, but the greater educational advantage enjoyed by the middle class ensures that the contest factors of ability and effort become sponsored by the extra impetus given to middle-class children from their earliest years. It is not surprising, therefore, that a middle-class student is more than six times as likely to receive the benefits of a higher education than the working-class student.

38.3   Work, welfare and the individual

Having established that middle-class school-leavers are more likely to
enter middle-class occupations, what are the effects of work upon the life
and welfare of the individual? After all, the greatest proportion of our
lives is not spent at school or in retirement, but at work of some kind.

The average working week in Britain, including overtime, is forty-five
hours, which means that the working day is divided between one-third
sleeping, one-third working, and one-third travelling, eating and relaxing.
Because so many of our waking hours are spent at work, the work situation
must affect the individual significantly. In 1847, Marx wrote in *The
Communist Manifesto*:

Owing to the extensive use of machinery and to the division of labour, the work
of the proletarian has lost all individual character, and, consequently, all
charm for the workman. He becomes an appendage of the machine, and it is
only the most simple, most monotonous, and most easily acquired knack that
is required of him.

There are few really oppressive work situations now to be found in
Britain; nevertheless most work performed is of a routine kind, and the
number of people engaged in creative work or decision-making is comparatively small. We are an industrialised nation, and many people do
work in manual, routine jobs on the production line in factories. Because
this work is often boring it is necessary for them to have sufficient time for
leisure and recreation. It has been argued that industrial unrest is not so
much due to an economic need for higher wages, which may be the pretext
for strike action, but rather a deeper dissatisfaction with the work
situation. Routine clerical work too can be stultifying, and work studies
have shown that greater efficiency can be achieved by varying the tasks
performed in offices. For example, if, instead of being assigned a particular aspect of the clerical process with limited responsibility, people
are allowed to see a matter through thus having more variation of occupation and accepting greater responsibility, productivity increases. The kind
of job that we do may well indicate the kind of person that we are, but also
our attitudes and opinions may be modified and reinforced by our
experience in the work situation and our contact with others at work.

To have allowed a national holiday on the Queen's Silver Wedding in
November 1972 to all, instead of to school children only, would have
meant a greater number of working hours lost than the total number of
hours lost through strike action in the same year. Our Common Market
partners have more paid public holidays than we enjoy in Britain, yet

economic growth is higher in Europe than in Britain. This does not necessarily mean that there is a direct connection between the holidays enjoyed and economic production—there are too many other variables, but arguments may be advanced for more public holidays in Britain. Few would deny that Members of Parliament are extremely hard-working, but the Parliamentary session lasts for only 160 or so days a year.

This century has seen the development and expansion of welfare services. A welfare state is one which attempts to ensure reasonably high material living standards for all. The basis of our Welfare State was laid down in the Beveridge Report of 1942. It was conceived in a spirit of war-time political consensus but in recent years many aspects of the Welfare State have received severe criticism from both the political Left and the Right. The Left argue that welfare provisions do not go far enough or that they benefit the wrong groups; the Right consider that there are too many parasites living off the benefits of the State. Theoretically Social Security acts as a safety net which catches those who are unfortunate enough to be without the minimum of economic resources; but though the majority of those who take advantage of social security provisions are legally and morally entitled to their benefits, a small minority undoubtedly abuse the system, and equally a minority miss the net altogether, such as the elderly lady who died of cold and hunger in January 1973 after eating cardboard. A measure of protection is afforded to the individual through the Welfare State, but it will be a good measure of our social progress when the Welfare State becomes unnecessary: we have not yet reached that time by a long way.

Unit 39 Society Today

39.1 How society is shaped

We have seen some of the conditions and constraints that will limit the individual's freedom of choice and action and how behaviour may be conditioned in many ways. As a condition, freedom is hard to define; it is much easier to see the things which limit freedom of action than to list the things that we are free to do. The forces which shape society are those which limit choice and freedom of behaviour. Economic forces may affect the choice of occupation open to someone, the amount of money that may be earned, what they may buy and what they may sell. Political forces may control economic forces to some degree; at the same time

economic forces may condition political forces. The question is, how
important are these invisible forces in shaping society, or how far can the
individual change or re-direct those forces?

A political leader may be able to directly change the course of history
by profoundly altering matters of state which would have taken a different
course had it not been for his direct intervention: the more powerful the
leader is, the less responsible he is to other members of his government
and the more dramatic can be the effect of such intervention upon events.
Examples of individuals who shaped society are Stalin and Hitler who
were able to impose their will upon whole nations: their personal feelings
and prejudices led to dramatic political, social and economic upheaval in
Europe. Fortunately there are few men such as Hitler or Stalin to wield
such enormous power. Yet if Hitler or Stalin had not been born, would
matters have been very much different? Were the invisible forces of
history such in Germany in the 1930s that an extreme right-wing dictator
would have emerged anyway, offering a solution to the social and
economic problems of the Weimar republic?

Some social theorists maintain that events in history are cyclical, that
history tends to repeat itself (of course not exactly) over a period of time.
An example of this theory would be to say that war inevitably breaks out
in Europe every generation. Two opposing theories of history are: that

Hitler addresses the Hitler Youth at a rally in Nuremberg

history, or the conditions in society, are largely *predetermined*; or alternatively that *chance* really governs what will happen. Between these views is a middle view that to a greater or lesser degree the invisible forces of history and social conditions do exist, but certain people or events are able to alter the pattern of things to a greater or lesser degree.

Revolutions and wars are times of great social change. Technological progress has been one of the few benefits of war (eg the development of aviation during the First and Second World Wars) and this has been accompanied by social change. Are revolutions and wars made by individuals, or by the populations that participate in them and who act together (in T. S. Eliot's words) as 'vast impersonal forces'? If we accept the view that history is a mixture of predetermination and chance, we must look a little more closely at these vast impersonal forces for they are composed of individuals who possess a common cause born out of a common experience which the leadership must recognise if it is to direct them with any degree of success. Carlyle may have been responsible for the statement that 'history is the biography of great men', but in his *History of the French Revolution* he wrote:

Hunger and nakedness and righteous oppression lying heavy on twenty-five million hearts: this, not the wounded vanities or contradicted philosophies of philosophical advocates, rich shopkeepers, rural noblesse, was the prime mover of the French Revolution; as the like will be in all such revolutions in all countries.

A 'which comes first, the chicken or the egg?' type of question confronts us: does the individual make society, or society make the individual? The answer, like that of the chicken and the egg, is that really they are inseparable. Society shapes the individual, but the individual helps change society. When a dictator or small group of people significantly alter the shape of society they still require thousands of others to execute their wishes. Very few historians or social scientists would be bold enough to ascribe a relative importance to such factors as social, economic or political forces in shaping historical events; yet any serious attempt to understand what happened in history, or what is happening in society, must require the apportioning of some weight to both the invisible forces and individual factors that are at work.

39.2 The future of society

We all have different visions of what will happen in the future, but no one can be certain about his predictions, least of all a social scientist. Certain

trends are discernible and it is upon these that we may base our conclusions.

Before considering the future of society, we must consider the pro-
position that mankind *will have* a future. Various prophets of doom
maintain that there is a high risk of international thermo-nuclear war,
either by accident or design, and that few would survive. It is argued that
we have already been close to nuclear war on several occasions, such as the
Cuban Missile Crisis of 1962, and because of our political and geographical
position in Europe Britain would be directly involved in any war between
East and West. No matter how optimistic some might be about our
chances of survival in a nuclear war, there is already the equivalent
explosive power of a ton of TNT for every man, woman and child on this
planet in the stockpiles of nuclear weapons held by the great powers. A
dozen hydrogen bombs on Britain would be more than sufficient to
exterminate our entire population.

Some economists estimate that the world's natural resources are
diminishing so rapidly that even if all national populations were to
stabilise themselves (and there is little chance of this in many of the
underdeveloped countries) there would not be enough resources to provide an adequate standard of living for everyone within the next two
centuries. Linked to the problem of diminishing resources are the
problems of *ecology* and the environment. Man's exploitation of the earth
has meant that many parts of the world are faced with pollution problems.
On his journey across the Atlantic on the raft *Ra*, Thor Heyerdahl found
a disturbing amount of oil pollution and other evidence of indestructible
garbage floating on the high seas. The problem of *pollution* in our cities
is a familiar one, but recently scientists have found high levels of the
poison DDT in the bodies of penguins in the Antarctic, thousands of
miles from continents where the DDT could have been sprayed. Fortunately there is a growing consciousness of the problems of pollution,
together with a recognition of diminishing resources, but international
action can be the only solution and this is as yet in its earliest stage, since
the first international conference on these problems was held in Stock-
holm in 1972.

Not all scientists and social scientists agree upon the extent of the
world's resources, or the future size of population and its needs. How far
mankind will be able to overcome these problems is likewise a matter of
dispute. The projections range from the optimistic to the pessimistic, yet
there is a measure of agreement that something has to be done in the field
of conservation. Such things as scientific and technological discovery, the
use of different materials, the re-use and *re-cycling* of resources and the

education of people to these problems may mean that we shall obtain a cleaner planet and preserve our resources in the future.

In previous chapters we have examined some of the changes that are taking place in the institutions of society: for example how the family is no longer so dependent upon the extended family system; how education has expanded; or how the population of Britain appears to be stabilising. Although we have not found complete solutions to the various problems of society such as poverty, homelessness or the growth of crime, at least it can be said that in most respects Britain is a better place to live in for the average citizen than it was a generation or more ago.

Social change is occurring more rapidly than ever before. Possibly we are sacrificing such things as *community spirit* and the better aspects of traditional life-styles in exchange for material progress, and the modern concentration upon economic growth of all kinds may well have contributed to many of the social problems and difficulties that have been described. The study of sociology should make us aware of the many changes that are taking place within society, and perhaps able to point out some of the least desirable aspects of change. The growing recognition of sociology as a subject and the validity of the findings of sociological research have meant that governments, politicians and planners do not embark upon schemes (although there have been some highly-publicised exceptions) without weighing up the cost in human terms.

We have seen how sociology is linked to the other disciplines of social science from our study of the subject. Changes in sociology are linked to changes in the other disciplines: economic change must mean social change; political change may cause both economic and social changes. At the same time it would be impossible to calculate how much freedom of choice is open to those who exercise the greatest immediate power in society, the politicians, since there are so many variables of human behaviour found within the individuals who collectively make up society. We can only say that in the last quarter of the twentieth century society will probably undergo its greatest transformation, greater even than the change that occurred at the end of World War I in the first quarter of the century. As sociologists and students of sociology we should seek not only to understand these changes but also to ensure that they are what is best for society and mankind.

Terms used in this chapter

genetic factors   invisible forces
attainment   predetermination
contest and sponsored mobility   ecology
routine   re-cycling
pre-schooling   pollution

Questions from GCE 'O' Level Sociology Examination Papers

1   What forces other than school and family control the social behaviour of the individual? (AEB, November 1969)

2   In what ways has your study of sociology affected the way you see the world? (AEB, Specimen Paper for New Syllabus, 1972)

3   Some of the rules and customs which we regard as important in this country are also accepted elsewhere; others are not. Explain this. (AEB, June 1970)

4   'The content of moral prohibitions varies wildly not only as between one society and another but even within the same society as between one social class and another or between one historical period and another.' Discuss.

Explain the difficulties that an individual might face in going to live in a society very different from his own. (AEB, November 1970)

5   Select any two of the following groups a to d and by giving examples or by any other method show clearly that you understand the difference between the pair of terms in each of the selected groups.
a   deviant and delinquent
b   an extended family and a nuclear family
c   ability and achievement
d   comprehensive school and secondary modern school.
(AEB, November 1972)

6   Choose two of the following terms, state briefly what they mean, and show how they helped you to understand some aspect of society:
norm   socialisation
social class   attitude
stereotype   peer group
(AEB, Specimen Paper for New Syllabus, 1972)

7   Take any two technical terms you have encountered in your study of sociology (eg social class, stereotype, bureaucracy, social institutions, socialisation, role, status etc.) and show how they have helped you to understand your own society. (AEB, June 1971)

8 Can you suggest any sociological reasons why today our society is faced with the problems of:
a juvenile delinquency
b the care of the aged?
(AEB, November 1969)

9 Select two of the following groups *a* to *d* and show clearly that you understand the difference between the pair of terms within each of the selected groups.
a nuclear family and extended family
b class and caste
c social group and a collection of people
d education and socialisation.
(AEB, November 1970)

10 Select two of the following groups *a* to *d* and by giving examples or by any other method show clearly that you understand the difference between the pair of terms within each of the selected groups.
a automation and industrialisation
b an urban area and urbanisation
c migration and mobility
d a pressure group and a political party.
(AEB, June 1972)

11 Explain clearly but briefly what you understand by three of the following terms:

bureaucracy	stratification
social control	deviance
socialisation	attitude
segregation	stereotype

(AEB, June 1970)

12 Show clearly, in any way you choose, that you understand the difference between three of the following *pairs* of words:
a ascribed role and achieved role
b race and nationality
c culture and society
d laws and norms
e mores and folkways
f class and status
g sociology and anthropology.
(AEB, June 1970)

13 Describe
a what sociology is
b the kind of research sociologists do
c what more you now understand about your own society as a result of studying sociology.
(AEB, June 1972)

14 In what ways has studying sociology helped you to understand the family in Britain today? (AEB, November 1974)

15 Select *two* of the following groups *a* to *e* and show clearly that you understand the difference between the pair of terms in each of the selected groups.

a   role and status
b   socialisation and education
c   capitalism and communism
d   proletariat and bourgeoisie
e   control group and experimental group.

(AEB, November 1974)

16 The following statement is a comment on the roles of men and women in society: 'How else could matters be arranged? As a matter of fact, matters can be, and are, arranged very differently in other parts of the world. Our concept of what is "natural" to men and "natural" to women ... is culture bound. What we think of as "natural" is simply what we are used to.'

(*Understanding Society*, Open University)

What is the value of the term 'socialisation' in explaining the above passage? (AEB, November 1974)

17 Briefly explain what is meant by *three* of the following terms:

a   peer group
b   automation
c   social mobility
d   urbanisation
e   bureaucracy

Index